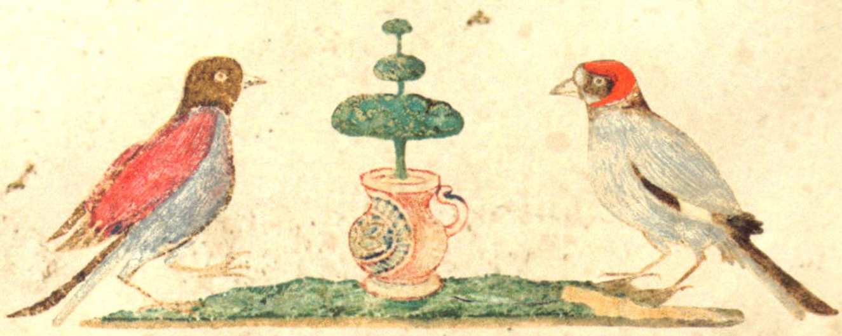

THE WASHINGTON HAGGADAH

THE BELKNAP PRESS OF
HARVARD UNIVERSITY PRESS
Cambridge, Massachusetts
London, England

THE LIBRARY OF CONGRESS
Washington, D.C.

2011

THE WASHINGTON HAGGADAH

COPIED AND ILLUSTRATED BY

JOEL BEN SIMEON

Introduction and Translation by

DAVID STERN

Introduction by

KATRIN KOGMAN-APPEL

Printed in the United States of America

Designed by Annamarie McMahon Why

Library of Congress Cataloging-in-Publication Data

Haggadah (Ms. Washington Haggadah). English & Hebrew.
The Washington Haggadah / Joel ben Simeon ; introduction and translation by
David Stern ; introduction by Katrin Kogman-Appel.
p. cm.
Includes bibliographical references.
ISBN 978-0-674-05117-1 (alk. paper)
1. Haggadot—Texts. 2. Seder—Liturgy—Texts. 3. Judaism—Liturgy—
Texts. 4. Washington Haggadah. 5. Manuscripts, Hebrew—Facsimiles.
6. Jewish illumination of books and manuscripts. I. Joel ben Simeon, 15th cent.
II. Stern, David, 1949– III. Kogman-Appel, Katrin. IV. Title.
BM674.63.W3713 2011
296.4′5371—dc22 2010045838

Contents

THE WASHINGTON HAGGADAH

The Washington Haggadah: The Life of a Book

David Stern

The remarkable book you are now holding in your hands—this facsimile edition of the Washington Haggadah—takes its name from its final home, the Hebraic Section in the Library of Congress of the United States of America, in Washington, D.C. This title is a recent one. It marks the final destination in a lengthy journey that this volume has taken in the course of its life as a book. Completed "on the twenty-fifth day of the month of Shevat in the year 238 according to the short enumeration" (January 29, 1478)—as the book's colophon (fol. 34v) states—by one of the most important and prolific scribes and illustrators in the history of the Jewish book, Joel ben Simeon, this unusually well preserved and beautifully illustrated haggadah marks an important moment in the history of Jewish culture. It provides a rare window into the world of its producers and readers, the Jews of late fifteenth-century Europe.[1]

In its life as a book, the Washington Haggadah also exemplifies the lives of Jewish books more generally. After being written in Germany, the Washington Haggadah traveled to Italy. Then, after passing through the hands of a series of owners, it was finally brought to America in circumstances that themselves bear remembering.[2] In these circuitous journeys, the Washington Haggadah is like many Jewish books that similarly have wandered across continents and through the lands of the Diaspora with their Jewish owners.

Finally, as a Passover haggadah, the Washington Haggadah bears within itself the religious and literary history of its genre. The life of any haggadah begins much earlier than the moment of its own production. It begins with the formulation of its text, a process that took at least ten centuries; and that text itself derives from a ceremony, a ritual, that goes back to the earliest beginnings of the Israelite nation. In tracing its history, then, we traverse nearly the entirety of Jewish history.

After the Bible, the Passover haggadah is probably the most widely circulated classic Jewish book. The Passover seder, the festive banquet that it accompanies, is arguably the single most popular Jewish observance, celebrated by Jews throughout the world in remarkably similar ways since the early Middle Ages, and one of the few classic Jewish religious rituals to have maintained its centrality to Jewish culture despite all the upheavals of modernity and secularization, albeit often in a radically transfigured and reinvented form. Since the beginning of Jewish printing in the late fifteenth century, more than four thousand separate editions of the haggadah have been published, and these editions, especially during the last century, chart the many transformations and changes experienced by modern Judaism.[3] Yet before print—and the inevitable standardization that went along with the printing revolution—there existed a variety of haggadot in manuscript form, that is, written by hand. These distinct traditions vividly reflect the vicissitudes of Jewish history and the diasporic cultures in which they were produced.

The Passover haggadah also holds a special place among Jewish books because it is the classic Jewish text devoted to the idea of redemption. In the classical period, this idea was closely associated with the traditional messianic hope; in more modern times, it has become a cipher for every conceivable type of religious, ideological, political, and sexual liberation. In either case, the most striking feature of the haggadah—perhaps its most distinctively *Jewish* feature—is the way it intertwines the dream of future redemption with the memory of the past (specifically of Israel's enslavement in Egypt and miraculous liberation) and collapses past and future into a present that invariably has been colored by the diasporic culture in which the specific haggadah has been produced. The history of the haggadah, as a text and as a book, can be charted, virtually step-by-step, as its Jewish producers have moved deeper and deeper, as it were, into their various Diasporas and places of geographical and historical exile—from Roman Palestine to Parthian Babylonia, from Babylonia to the European centers of Ashkenaz and Sepharad, and from those centers to all the later homes of Jews in North Africa, Arabia, Eastern Europe, the Americas, and, finally, to the State of Israel. As we follow these journeys, we see how closely linked in the Jewish experience are exile and redemption; the imagining of the latter is inevitably shaped by the experience of the former. It is this linkage that most profoundly informs the haggadah's history. The Washington Haggadah captures one specific moment in that history, which is also the story of the Jewish imagination.

A Short History of the Seder

The haggadah—literally, a "telling" or "recitation"—is the script of the seder, the traditional name for the festive ritual banquet held on the first night of the festival of Passover (and in the Diaspora, on the second night as well). The word *seder* literally means a "sequence" or "order" and refers to the series of ritual acts and recitations that constitutes the celebration. Without the seder, there would be no haggadah. And while today the seder is virtually unimaginable without the presence of a haggadah—the book, that is—at the seder table, in historical fact the ritual banquet long pre-dated the book and itself went through a lengthy process of development. To understand the history of the haggadah as a book, then, we must begin with the seder.[4]

Like much else in Judaism, the roots of the seder lie in the Bible, specifically in the Book of Exodus (Chaps. 12–14) and its account of the departure of the Israelites from Egypt. As the Bible tells us, God commands the Israelites to sacrifice a lamb, one per family, on the fourteenth of the month of Nisan; He then tells them to smear the blood of the lamb on the doorposts of their houses as a sign, so that He will spare their first-born children from the plague that He will visit upon the Egyptians that same night; finally, He instructs the Israelites to eat the sacrifice that night, "with your loins girded, your sandals on your feet, and your staff in your hand . . . hurriedly," before embarking on the Exodus (Exod. 12:11). And yet, even before they have left Egypt and offered and eaten this sacrifice for the first time, God commands the Israelites to observe the sacrifice "for all time" (Exod. 12:24) in order to *remember* the Exodus from Egypt—a paradoxical command given that the event they are ordered to remember has not even occurred yet! With this verse begins the dramatic collapsing of time—past, present, and future—that, as we shall see, marks much of the inner dynamics of both the seder and the haggadah as they subsequently develop.

After commanding the Israelites to offer the Passover sacrifice, God also enjoins them to observe a seven-day *Hag ha-Matsot*, a festival of unleavened bread, in which the Israelites are required to remove all leaven from their property and are prohibited from eating leavened food for the duration of the holiday (Exod. 12:14–20). Within the biblical corpus, these two separate observances—the Passover sacrifice and the *Hag ha-Matsot*—are enjoined upon the Israelites several more times. Curiously, while the two observances are repeatedly juxtaposed to each other, they are never fused in the Bible into a single holiday, a fact that has led some scholars to speculate that the two observances were originally separate spring rituals, one observed by farmers for the seasonal wheat harvest (namely, the festival of unleavened bread), the other by shepherds to mark the first birthing of their flocks (the Passover sacrifice).[5] By the time of the Bible's final composition, the two separate rituals had been fused into a single holiday, but the holiday's agricultural, seasonal rationale was never entirely lost in Passover's subsequent development. In the beginning of the twentieth century, when the Passover seder was "reinvented" by pioneer *halutzim*, those avowedly secular and nonreligious settlers of kibbutzim in British Mandate Palestine, the seder became the pioneers' occasion for celebrating the spring harvest in their new Zionist calendar.

Whatever may have been the prebiblical origins of the two rituals, the sacrifice and the feast of unleavened bread are both "historicized" in the biblical narrative, that is, turned into watershed moments in the sacred history of Israel, the one commemorating the divine salvation of the first-born sons from death, the other the miraculous Exodus of the Israelites from Egyptian servitude. Furthermore, this very act of historicizing the rituals is represented in the Bible as an occasion for pedagogy, for teaching the *meaning* of these rites. In the cases of both the unleavened bread and the sacrifice, the Bible records a variant of the following text in which a child asks his father, "What do you mean by this rite?" to which the father responds, again in one variant or another, "It is the Passover sacrifice to the Lord, because He passed over the houses of the Israelites in Egypt when He smote the Egyptians, but saved our houses" (Exod. 12:26–28; cf. Exod. 13:8). (In 13:14–15, the same pedagogical scenario is repeated in connection with the consecration of the first-born child to God, another commandment connected to the sparing of the first-born sons; and in Deut. 6:20–25, it is recorded for a fourth time, but now in connection with all of God's commands.)

These passages are among the few instances in the Bible where the observance of a ritual is explicitly connected with the act of explaining its meaning. While these verses hardly lead in a direct line to the Passover haggadah as we know it, it is clear that the pedagogical element in the seder—using the ritual as an occasion for parents to teach their children about the meaning of the festival (and, by extension, about Judaism)—has its roots in the Bible.

The three features I have mentioned—the sacrifice, the unleavened bread, and the pedagogical use of the ritual foods—are virtually everything we know about the early observance of Passover. The Bible itself records few other details. Nor do the many literary works surviving from the early postbiblical, later Hellenistic, and early Late Antique period (that is, works composed during the eight hundred years between the fifth century B.C.E. and the third century C.E.) tell us much more about how Passover was observed in these centuries. The Book of Jubilees (second century B.C.E., Chap. 49) describes only the sacrifice and the seven-day feast of unleavened bread. Even first-century writers like the Greek-speaking Alexandrian Jewish philosopher Philo (20 B.C.E.–50 C.E.) and the Jewish historian of Roman Palestine Josephus (37–ca. 100 C.E.) speak almost exclusively about the offering of the Passover sacrifice, a little about the eating of *matsah* (and the avoidance of leaven), and a few mentions of such things as drinking wine and singing hymns to God. Employing his characteristic philosophical approach to the interpretation of the Bible, Philo gives allegorical explanations for some of the observances; thus *matsah* signifies humility in contrast to the puffed-up character of leavened food, which symbolizes arrogance and pride.[6] Philo's explanations for the ritual food may also remind us of the symbolic meanings of the bread and the wine that Jesus imparts to his disciples in the three synoptic gospels (Mark 14:17–25; Matthew 26:20–34; and Luke 22:14–20), in which the Last Supper is depicted as the ritual banquet of the Passover sacrifice. (In John 13, the Last Supper takes place the night before Passover, while in John 19:14 we are told that Jesus was crucified on the fourteenth of Nisan, literally making him into the sacrificial Paschal lamb.) None of these sources, however, mentions anything that begins to resemble the later seder, let alone the haggadah.

This silence surrounding the infancy of the seder is the first remarkable fact about its early history. The second is that our earliest description of the seder as a full-blown ritual banquet comes in the Rabbinic legal compendium, the Mishnah (edited in Roman Palestine around the year 220 C.E.). Finally, and even more remarkably, in the Mishnah's account virtually *all* of the seder's principal features and some of its most prominent texts are already referenced, even if they are not quoted verbatim or in full. No other ancient Rabbinic account describes where or how the Mishnah's seder came into existence. At one point, the Mishnah suggests that the full ritual already existed during the period of the Second Temple before its destruction in 70 C.E., but, as we shall see, most contemporary scholars believe this to have been historically improbable.

Indeed, modern scholarly reconstructions of the seder's history point specifically to the destruction of the Temple, and the impossibility thereafter of offering the Passover sacrifice (which, like all sacrifices, had to be made within the Temple), as the major impetus behind the seder's invention. To make up for the loss of the sacrifice, early Rabbinic sages looked for surrogate rituals through which to observe the Passover feast. As scattered passages in early Rabbinic literature suggest, groups of sages adapted different strategies. A tale still preserved in the haggadah today relates how one group of rabbis spent the entire night in the town of Bnei Braq telling the *story* of the Exodus (and thereby fulfilling the command to explain to one's child the "meaning" of the Passover sacrifice). While we do not know for certain how they told the story, it was most likely the way most ancient rabbis related narratives based upon the Bible—through *midrash,* biblical study, elaboration, and interpretation. As another early Rabbinic text tells us (Tosefta Pesahim 10:12), a different group of sages adopted another strategy to substitute for the lost sacrifice: they spent all night *studying* the laws of the Passover sacrifice, as though study were equivalent to performance. Such study probably included discussion of the other special ritual foods eaten during the seder, like the *matsah* and the *maror* (bitter herbs), and their significance.

By the time of the Mishnah's final composition in the third century, these two separate approaches appear to have been merged into a single ceremony. The Mishnah's seder includes both. Narrating the story of the Exodus occupies the center of the haggadah, specifically the lengthy section that offers a midrashic commentary on Deuteronomy 26, a capsule history of Israel from the time of the patriarchs through the Exodus and up to the Israelites' arrival in the land of Israel. In turn, the study and discussion of the sacrifice and other symbolic foods are encapsulated in the famous questions that the child asks his or her parents and in the answers given to those questions in the passage attributed to the second-century sage Rabban Gamliel, who explains the meaning of the Passover sacrifice, the *matsah,* and the *maror.* As it happens, this last Mishnaic passage (Pesahim 10:5) is quoted in expanded form (with the addition of biblical proof texts) in the haggadah, and it represents our earliest evidence for the process through which the seder became "textualized," that is, turned into a fixed text. We see here, in other words, the very beginning of the haggadah as the seder's script.

The overall shape of the Mishnah's seder was based upon the Greco-Roman banquet, with three main courses—an appetizer course, at which greens and raw vegetables (as well as roasted sweet breads, toasted rice, and other delicacies) were eaten with dipping sauces; a second, "bread" course, the meal's main course, consisting of two cooked dishes, such as meat as well as fowl and eggs, eaten along with bread (or, in the case of the seder, unleavened bread in the form of *matsah*); and a third and final dessert course. Traces of all three courses remain in the seder. The appetizer course is preserved in the part of the seder known as *karpas*—from a Greek loan word for leafy vegetables, such as parsley, celery, and lettuce—which were originally dipped in *haroset,* a kind of thick fruit sauce; at a later point, salt water was substituted for *haroset* (which today is reserved exclusively for the bitter herbs eaten at the beginning of the main course). Similarly, the Passover "bread," the *matsah,* is eaten with the main course, which consists of various cooked dishes along with additional ritual foods like the bitter herbs, which, as noted, are dipped into *haroset.* This second dipping of greens at the seder is also one of several instances in which the Rabbinic sages sought to distinguish their seder from a typical Roman banquet. Dipping the greens *twice*—during the appetizer course, as expected, *and* during the main course—aroused the curiosity of the seder's participants, and they were led to ask about the meal's oddities. In the seder's later development, different communities added additional symbolic foods, like the hard-boiled eggs eaten by many European Jews at the beginning of the main course. (Alas, *matsah* balls do not count as a ritual food.)

In its earliest stages, the first two courses of the meal almost certainly were eaten at the very beginning of the seder, and only after the participants had finished eating did the "recitation" and discussion begin. The unusual foods and eating practices performed at the seder—eating only unleavened bread, dipping the greens twice, eating roasted meats in commemoration of the sacrifice—thereby naturally became the subjects of questions for discussion. Only later, at some unspecified time, did the order change, and the *magid,* or recitation, section took precedence over the meal, which then came to occupy the middle part of the banquet.

The Mishnah's seder also borrows features from a special type of Roman banquet, the symposium, or drinking party, an actual social occasion that later became, in Greco-Roman literary culture, a conventional setting for an entire literary genre of symposiac dialogues (the most famous example of which is Plato's *Symposium*).[7] In these works, philosophers and other literary and intellectual types gather at a symposium to sing hymns to the gods, imbibe vast amounts of wine, and discuss arcane topics like history so ancient it is ripe material for imaginative invention; unanswerable philosophical questions like the origins of love; and exotic cultural practices like culinary habits practiced by people living on the margins of civilization—Jews, for example. Such topics are discussed at the seder as well, and hymns are also sung to God. The drinking of wine is a prominent feature of the seder. But where the amount of wine drunk at a symposium was never prescribed, the Rabbinic sages limited the cups of wine at the seder to four (or, according to some, five), and these four glasses took on the additional function of basically punctuating the seder's different sections. So, too, where a typical symposium concluded with an *epikomion*, a drunken procession of the participants from one symposium to another, the Mishnah explicitly prohibits its celebrants to conclude their seder with an *epikomion*—or, in its Hebrew form, *afikomen*. As the word's original meaning was forgotten, however, *afikomen* instead became a word for all after-dinner revelry, then for a postmeal dessert, and finally, for that last sad piece of *matsah* which is eaten at the meal's very conclusion as a poor substitute for a real dessert.

The case of the *afikomen* is only one example of how the seder and its component elements and their meaning changed as the historical and geographical situations of its participants—their languages, eating habits, and religious customs and beliefs—also changed. In the Mishnah's original seder, the meal was eaten in the fashion of a typical Roman banquet, with its participants reclining on sumptuous couches arranged in a semicircle around a removable table in the center. The main difference between the Roman banquet and the Rabbinic seder was that, in the former, the banqueters were usually from the more aristocratic and elite classes, while in the case of the seder, even "the poorest in Israel" (Mishnah Pesahim 10:1) is commanded to participate in the ritual banquet.

The meaning of reclining changed, however, as the majority of Jews moved from Roman Palestine to Sassanian Babylonia, where it was no longer customary to eat banquets while reclining on couches. As a result, the very act of reclining was "ritualized." It, too, became another part of the seder's sequence of commemorative, symbolic acts. Reclining ceased to be merely a sign of banqueting (as opposed to eating an ordinary meal while seated on a chair or standing up) and became a symbol of freedom as opposed to slavery. Similarly, the famous questions asked by a child of his or her father were originally (as attested in the best early texts of the Mishnah) three, not four, with each question addressing one of the three main symbolic foods: the Passover sacrifice, the *matsah*, and the *maror*. As eating habits changed, particularly as Jews moved from one Diaspora to another, the questions also changed. After the Roman custom of dipping greens at an appetizer course ceased to be practiced in Babylonia, the original question—"Why on all other nights do we dip greens once, but on this night, twice?"—no longer made sense, and it was therefore changed to, "Why on all other nights do we dip greens *not even once*, but on this night twice?" As the original question about eating only roasted meats on Passover ceased to accord with practice (lest, God forbid, someone mistake the roasted meat for a genuine sacrifice), that question was dropped, and the one about bitter herbs was substituted in its place. So, too, a fourth question was added: "Why on all other nights do we eat sitting on chairs, but on this night we recline?"—another addition that clearly reflected the changed seating habits of the Jewish participants.

As these few examples demonstrate, the history of the seder is not merely a history of a ritual's development over time. It is actually a story about the Jews themselves and the vicissitudes of their history, and how human invention and creativity created a religious tradition of lasting significance in response to the changing conditions and requirements of new historical moments.

By the eighth or ninth century, after Babylonian Judaism had firmly established itself as the dominant arbiter of Rabbinic Judaism, there existed two distinct versions of the seder—the original Palestinian seder (as recorded in the best early texts of the Mishnah), with three questions and a relatively brief midrash on Deuteronomy 26; and a lengthier, more elaborate Babylonian version with four questions and a more complete midrashic exposition of the Deuteronomy passage, along with several other, less prominent differences from its Palestinian counterpart. Eventually, the Palestinian version died out completely, and the Babylonian seder became the near-universal standard with slight variations in different regions and communities.

At the same time, more pieces of the seder's text came to be added to it. The Babylonian Talmud records a disagreement between two third-century sages regarding a "prologue" that introduced the midrash on Deuteronomy 26. According to one sage, the prologue began, "We were slaves in Egypt," while according to the other, it began, "Our forefathers were idolaters." Eventually, both versions came to be included in the haggadah's text. The passage about the four sons—the wise son, the wicked son, the simple son, and the son who does not even know how to ask—originally appeared in a third-century Rabbinic midrashic collection, where it explained why the pedagogical verses with similar questions and answers were repeated multiple times in the Bible.[8] When the midrashic passage was transplanted in the seder, it assumed a somewhat different meaning as it seemed to address the challenge of explaining the ceremony's meaning to different types of "sons." *Dayenu,* a song of thanksgiving with the refrain "Had God done only *x,* and not *y,* it would have been sufficient," first appears in a tenth-century haggadah, although it has the literary form of an ancient liturgical hymn. A very different kind of late addition to the seder is the passage found immediately after the Grace after Meals and the third cup and immediately before the second part of *Halel* (psalms of praise to God). This passage, known by its opening words as *Shefokh Hamatkha,* "Pour out Your fury" (Ps. 79:6), effectively constitutes a curse against the Jews' Gentile enemies "who know not God." The passage appears to have been inserted into the seder in the twelfth century, in the aftermath of the Crusader massacres that had decimated the Jewish communities in Germany and France. While some modern Jews have found the passage embarrassing or objectionable, its presence in the haggadah is a stark reminder of the extreme and violent historical circumstances in which Jews have sometimes had to persist in celebrating the Passover seder and holding fast to their dreams of redemption. Other additions to the seder, particularly at its conclusion, were also made in the late Middle Ages. These include various liturgical poems that were taken from the synagogue service, including *Hasal Seder Pesah* ("The Passover Seder Has Been Completed," originally composed by the eleventh-century French poet Joseph ben Samuel Bonfils), *Az Rov Nisim* ("Then You Performed Many Miracles," by the sixth-century Palestinian Yannai), and *Omets Gevurotekha* ("You Wondrously Showed Your Might," by the sixth-seventh century Palestinian poet Eliezer Kalir).[9] They also included several popular and anonymous after-dinner songs like *Ki Lo Naeh* ("To Him It Is Fitting") and *Adir Hu* ("All-Powerful Is He"), which entered the seder in the thirteenth and fourteenth centuries, respectively, the first possibly in England, the second in Germany.[10] The most famous of all these folk songs, the cumulative song *Had Gadya* ("One Kid"), was actually the last to be incorporated in the haggadah; it first appears regularly only in printed editions of the sixteenth century. Readers of the Washington Haggadah should not be surprised to find that it is missing from its pages.

The most meaningful addition to the Mishnah's original seder was, however, among its earliest supplements; indeed, early on this passage appears to have been deemed so central to the seder's meaning that in most medieval manuscripts of Mishnah Pesahim it was actually copied into the Mishnah's text as part of its description of the seder. The passage is found at the very conclusion of the *magid* section of the seder, after the midrashic exposition of Deut. 26 and following the quotation of Rabban Gamliel's dictum about the requirement to explain the meanings of the three ritual foods:

> In every generation a person is obligated to see himself [*lir'ot 'et 'atsmo*] as if he had gone out of Egypt. As it says: "It is because of what God did for me when I went free from Egypt" (Exod. 13:8).
>
> Not our ancestors alone did the Holy One, blessed be He, redeem, but us too He redeemed with them. As it says: "And us He freed from there, that He might take us and give us the land that He had promised on oath to our fathers" (Deut. 6:23).

This passage is actually a midrash, a Rabbinic interpretation, of Exod. 13:8. In its original biblical context, this verse is spoken by Moses to the Israelites immediately after the Exodus, when Moses repeats the commandment to keep the holiday of *matsot* in the future, adding to the command, "And you shall explain to your son on that day, 'It is because of what the Lord did for me when I went free from Egypt.'" Now, in its original context in the Bible, the father whom Moses addressed had, after all, just left Egypt, and as a result, he would have had no difficulty saying to his son, "It is because of what the Lord did *for me* when I went free from Egypt" (my italics). For a rabbi living a thousand or more years later, however, fulfilling the command in the verse was truly problematic: How could he say "what the Lord did *for me*"? This problem is the source of the midrash's exegetical "solution." Namely, "In every generation a person is obligated to see himself as if he had gone out of Egypt." By "seeing oneself" *as though* he or she had gone out of Egypt, a parent can honestly teach his or her child that the reason for observing the holiday is "because of what the Lord did *for me*." (The same exegetical operation is also at work in the implied interpretation of Deut. 6:23 at the passage's conclusion, specifically in its reading of the word "us.")

Perhaps more than any other passage in the haggadah, this text captures the essence of the seder, the goal of its ritual. It is incumbent upon the participant not only to remember the Exodus as a thing of the past but to reexperience the redemption for him- or herself in the present moment with the result that, in the words of the German literary philosopher Walter Benjamin (1892–1940), "every second of time [may be] the strait gate through which the Messiah might enter."[11]

What the passage does not explain, however, is exactly what it means "to see oneself." This phrase has been variously interpreted through the ages. By vocalizing the word slightly differently—as *le-har'ot* rather than as *lir'ot*—the twelfth-century sage and philosopher Maimonides (1137/8–1204) explained the verse as meaning "to show" or "to display" to others what it means to be redeemed, as, for example, by raising on high the *matsah* like a trophy, and by reclining like a freedman.[12] It is said that in Yemen, at the beginning of the seder one of the participants would wrap a piece of *matsah* in a napkin, put it on his shoulder, and walk around the house until the other participants asked him, "Why are you doing this?" to which he would reply, "Thus did our forefathers when they left Egypt hurriedly."[13] Others have reimagined the very terms of "slavery" in Egypt, seeing that servitude in more metaphorical senses, as reflecting other types of subjugation that Jews have known and suffered. This strategy has especially informed the many commentaries that have been written on the haggadah since the early Middle Ages (and that continue to be written to this day), in which rabbis and scholars, under the guise of explaining the "meaning" of the seder's text, invariably refract the text through the prism of their own experience.

The most moving example of this type of interpretation is found in the haggadah commentary of Don Isaac Abravanel (1437–1508), the great Portuguese-born Jewish statesman, philosopher, and exegete, who wrote it some four years after his expulsion from Spain in 1492 while he lived in Monopoli, Italy, one of the many towns through which he wandered after being exiled from his home. On "seeing oneself," Abravanel wrote that every Jew

> will experience individually in the state of his subjugation to the Gentile nations in the present time of exile the very same thing that the people of Israel as a nation experienced in Egypt . . . For it is impossible that a person living in our age of exile will not experience [in his life] some type of suffering—whether it be bodily, or financial, or having to do with his children [by having to watch them undergo forced conversion to Christianity]; or by being forced himself by the Gentiles to violate the sanctity of the Sabbath and the holidays. And since the Lord, blessed be His name, does save us daily in our time of exile by being a saviour who redeems us through miracles and signs and wonders, it is therefore fitting that every person should look upon himself as though he

> went out of Egypt. . . . because each one of us is redeemed innumerable times in his lifetime in the course of having to live in exile.[14]

For Abravanel, the miracle of daily survival amid the tribulations of exile is no less astonishing than the miraculous experience of the children of Israel when they were redeemed by God from Egypt. In the entire history of the haggadah, there is probably no more immediate testimony to the act of reading the haggadah through the prism of the commentator's own historical experience. Indeed, for Abravanel, to imagine oneself as having gone out of Egypt is to imagine oneself as having triumphed, through God's miraculous intervention, over the vicissitudes and trials of history.

As we shall see, in the career of the haggadah as a material book, the idea of "seeing oneself" as having gone out of Egypt is often literally illustrated in the pictures that accompany the text.

The History of the Haggadah

By the tenth century, the Mishnah's seder appears to have gradually developed into a form more or less approximating the traditional celebration familiar today. For most of this period, there was no written text for the seder. Nearly all the literary texts recited were relatively brief and so widely known that they could easily be memorized, like the short history of Israel encapsulated in Deuteronomy 26, or the four questions and Rabban Gamliel's dictum. The psalms sung in the seder's second half were part of the standard liturgy; if some people did not know them by heart, they may have returned to the synagogue after eating in order to hear them recited publicly.[15]

The haggadah first appears to have been committed to writing in the ninth or tenth century. No complete haggadah text survives from this period, but our earliest fragments were preserved in the Cairo Genizah. In Jewish tradition, Hebrew books are treated like people, and when they are no longer fit for use, they are not discarded or destroyed but removed from circulation and either buried or deposited in a specially dedicated space, typically in a synagogue, known as a *genizah*. The most famous "literary cemetery" of this type was located in the Ben-Ezra synagogue in Fustat, Old Cairo.[16] The Cairo Genizah haggadot are significant for two reasons. First, they tend to reflect the original Palestinian version of the seder (as recorded in the original Mishnah), which appears to have still been followed in Cairo as late as the eleventh century. Nearly everywhere else in the Jewish world, the longer Babylonian version (which is what all other haggadot from the Middle Ages until today preserve) had displaced its Palestinian predecessor. Second, these early haggadot are actually fragments of larger prayerbooks. They thus testify to a period before which the haggadah had become its own separate book.

By the thirteenth century, however, probably first in Spain, the haggadah had detached itself from the prayerbook and become a book in its own right; for obvious reasons, this was more convenient to use at the seder. Such haggadot were eventually composed in virtually every place Jews lived, and early on, the haggadah became one of the most common Jewish manuscripts that individuals possessed (because everyone observed Passover, and the book was a small one and therefore relatively easy to produce and comparatively inexpensive to purchase). By the mid-thirteenth and fourteenth centuries, decorated and illustrated haggadot were also being produced—some, for an obviously wealthy, aristocratic class (particularly in Sepharad, namely, the Iberian Peninsula as well as southern France); others, apparently for an emerging Jewish mercantile middle class (particularly in Ashkenaz, that is, Germany and northern France).

The actual literary text of the haggadah was remarkably similar in Ashkenaz and Sepharad, although there remained small differences between the rites of some communities, but the overall shape of the haggadah *as a material book* was significantly different in the two centers. These differences can be seen in the structure and full contents of the book in each region, and they are especially evident in the illustrated haggadot from the two centers because they have distinct illustration programs.[17] In Sepharad, the haggadah was almost a kind of mini-holiday prayerbook containing, at its beginning and end, the special prayers and liturgical poems *(piyyutim)* that were recited in synagogue on Passover. Similarly, the illustrations in these haggadot tend to be found in a series of miniatures that are typically located at the beginning of the codex and that retell the history of Israel, beginning either from the Creation or from the birth of Moses and concluding with pictures of contemporary Jews making preparations for the seder. As scholars have shown, these sequences were influenced by similar biblical miniatures found in Latin psalters from France and elsewhere in central Europe.

The construction of these miniature sequences is dramatically teleological: whether they begin with the time of Creation or the birth of Moses, they telescope all of Jewish history so as to culminate literally in the Passover seder being celebrated that very night. The effect of this telescoping is, again, to collapse past and present—to make readers see themselves as though they had gone out of Egypt. At the same time, these sequences may also represent a kind of Jewish response to the Christian typological use of the Old Testament as a prefiguring of the New Testament's narration of salvation through Jesus Christ.[18] Unlike the Christian narrative, the haggadah illustrations take as their subject the *national* tale of Israel's redemption as found in the Bible; the sequences tend to emphasize the importance of figures like Joseph and Moses, the agents of Israel's redemption who were also "Jewish" representatives in the courts of the pharaohs, Gentile potentates not unlike the Christian kings whom the Jewish courtiers of Spain—often the very ones who commissioned these illustrated haggadot—served in similar capacities. The conception of redemption that animates these haggadot is a communal, nationalist one, almost as though leaving Egypt were akin to leaving the exile of Christian Spain.

In contrast to the public nature of the Sephardic haggadah, the haggadah in Ashkenaz was very much a domestic book. It very frequently begins with the ritual of searching for leaven—a rite specifically performed within the privacy of the home—and almost never includes the synagogue prayers or poetry. (The Sephardic haggadot, in contrast, almost never contain the ritual text of the search for leaven even though Sephardic Jews performed this ritual as faithfully as did their Ashkenazic contemporaries.) Unlike the Sephardic miniature sequences, the illustrations in the Ashkenazic haggadot tend to be found largely in the margins of the haggadah, and typically relate to the haggadah's text on the page and to the rituals performed on those pages or to the biblical narrative of the Exodus.[19] These haggadot lack the metanarrative of national redemption that so dominates the Sephardic haggadot, even though their marginal illustrations do allude to biblical episodes mentioned in the haggadah. Instead, they seem to reflect the more private world inside the Ashkenazic Jewish home. Their quality as art is almost folksy and cartoonish in contrast to the sophisticated and urbane Sephardic manuscripts. Sometimes the illustrations are accompanied by short captions suggesting that one of the purposes these pictures served was to instruct the seder's participants as to how to perform the various rituals at given stages of the ceremony. We have little knowledge as to who commissioned illustrated haggadot in Ashkenaz, though they must have been persons of some means.

The single surviving early Ashkenazic haggadah with illustrations is the famous Bird Heads Haggadah—so called because the Jewish figures in the margins all have the heads of birds—which dates from around the year 1300 C.E.[20] There are a few other illustrated Ashkenazic haggadot from the early fourteenth century, but through that century the haggadah continued to be written in Ashkenaz as part of the prayerbook.[21] Only in the fifteenth century did the Ashkenazic haggadah regularly become its own book. The surviving Spanish haggadot nearly all come from the fourteenth century, mainly from Catalonia and elsewhere in the north of Spain.[22] The two Jewish centers in Ashkenaz and Sepharad were in contact with each other, and especially from the fourteenth century on, images and motifs from Sepharad, like the pictures of the four sons, made their way into Ashkenazic haggadot. Book production in general in both Ashkenaz and Sepharad, however, was severely curtailed by the persecutions and forced expulsions that began to disrupt Jewish life in both areas from the beginning of the fourteenth century, first in Ashkenaz, and then even more severely in Spain in the fifteenth century. Over this century, many Jews fled both centers, some to North Africa and Ottoman Turkey, others to Eastern Europe, and many to Italy, which became a haven especially for Ashkenazic refugees. Among these refugees were a number of scribes.

Italy was the home of the longest continuously inhabited Jewish community in Europe (dating back to imperial Rome, if not earlier) and had long played a formative role in Jewish book culture. It was the site of the earliest dated European Jewish manuscript (1072/3), and after the beginning of the fifteenth century it became the major site of Jewish book production. Nearly one-third of all dated medieval Hebrew manuscripts were written in Italy between 1350 and 1550.

In general, the haggadot produced in Italy follow the Ashkenazic model in terms of their overall structure as essentially domestic books. As we shall see, Germany and northern Italy were closely associated during this period with scribes and illustrators like Joel ben Simeon regularly moving between the two countries. The illustrated haggadot produced in the two areas, however, defy easy categorization. There are some, like the Yahuda Haggadah (Jerusalem IM MS 180/50) and the Second Nuremberg Haggadah (formerly Schocken MS 24.087, now in the private collection of David Sofer, London)—both from southern Germany and dating from the mid-fifteenth century—with margins packed with drawings of both biblical and ritual scenes.[23] The Floersheim Haggadah (formerly Sassoon MS 511) was composed in Florence in 1487, and also has its margins filled with illustrations, although the model on which it is based is different from that used by the Yahuda and Second Nuremberg, and its illustrations are framed in architectural borders.[24] The illustrations in all three haggadot are somewhat reminiscent of the popular, folkish style characteristic of the Bird Heads Haggadah.[25] Finally, there are the haggadot produced by Joel ben Simeon and other scribes with whom he associated, such as Meir ben Israel Jaffe of Ulm, the scribe of the First Cincinnati Haggadah.[26] These haggadot tend to resemble the fourteenth-century Sephardic haggadot in their luxuriousness, and they clearly display the absorption of Italianate features in their use of color and delicate penwork.

Despite their differences, these fifteenth- and early sixteenth-century German and Italian haggadot nonetheless share a vision of redemption that contrasts sharply with that found in the Spanish haggadot of the previous century. If the latter's conception was nationalistic, these haggadot have a much more private, even individualistic, view. As noted, following the Crusader massacres of the eleventh and twelfth centuries, Ashkenazic Jews inserted a special passage known as *Shefokh Hamatkha* that invokes God's wrath upon the Gentile nation. In its earliest version in Ashkenaz, the passage consisted solely of Ps. 79:6, "Pour out Your fury on the nations that do not know You, upon the kingdoms that do not invoke Your name," but the passage was quickly adapted in virtually every rite, including those of Sepharad, in many cases with additional verses cursing the Gentiles. Beginning in the second quarter of the fifteenth century, on the page containing *Shefokh Hamatkha,* first German and later Italian haggadot regularly included a picture of the Messiah riding on a donkey, often accompanied by Elijah blowing a shofar, arriving at the home of a Jew.[27] The meaning of the picture's placement on this page is slightly ambiguous: Was it meant to suggest that vengeance against the Gentiles would come as part of the messianic scheme? Or that Jews could *only* imagine such vengeance taking place *after* the Messiah had arrived?[28] For our interests, what is most noteworthy about the illustration is that the Messiah is frequently pictured as arriving at the private home of an individual Jewish family. This moment of the seder also happened to coincide with a ritual act of opening the front door to the home—an act that may have long preceded the insertion of the *Shefokh Hamatkha* into the haggadah, but that was interpreted by Ashkenazic Jews as an invitation to the prophet Elijah, who might actually turn up just then to herald the impending arrival of the Messiah.[29] In fact, one early sixteenth-century writer, the apostate Jew Anthonius Margaritha (born ca. 1500), records a custom among Ashkenazic Jews of having someone dressed up as Elijah fall through the open door into the room![30]

As the Jewish art historian Joseph Gutmann has shown, the history of this picture is extraordinarily complex. The idea for its imagery is based on Zechariah 9:9, "Lo, your king is coming to you. He is victorious, triumphant yet humble, riding on an ass, on a donkey foaled by a she-ass." The actual iconography of the illustration, however, derives from pictures of Christ's entering Jerusalem on a donkey as depicted in the gospels (for example, Matthew 21:2–5 or John 12:12), a narrative which itself is explicitly based on the Zechariah verse (as conflated with Isa. 62:11). Jewish artists (or Christian artists directed by Jewish scribes) adapted this iconography to the Jewish conception of the messianic arrival. Thus, whereas the head of the donkey Jesus rides is nearly always pictured bowed down in humiliation, portending the Christian Savior's imminent death, the Jewish Messiah's donkey is often not quite so depressed, and the Messiah is usually accompanied by the prophet Elijah blowing the shofar to announce the redemption. In fact, no two Jewish depictions of the scene are identical. Individual artists each developed the image in their own way, and in her essay on the Washington Haggadah's illustrations, Katrin Kogman-Appel describes in detail the singular features of Joel's version. In all cases, however, the arrival of the Messiah is imagined in dramatically familiar and intimate terms, as a kind of personal salvation, not unlike the notions of personal salvation that were beginning to penetrate pre-Reformation Christianity at roughly the same time. This, then, is another example of how the specific context of the diasporic culture in which the haggadah was produced profoundly helped shape its idea of redemption.

From what we know, haggadot were typically commissioned or bought by the increasingly wealthy members of the growing population of Jewish bankers, merchants, and doctors in Italy and southern Germany. It should be noted, however, that Italy, unlike Ashkenaz, retained the tradition of including the haggadah in the holiday prayerbook through the sixteenth century, and many Italian haggadot are found in such books as well as in the great miscellanies like the famous Rothschild Miscellany produced in northern Italy in 1470. This practice continued even into the age of print. The very first printed haggadah appeared in the Mahzor Roma, the holiday prayerbook according to the

Roman rite, printed by the Sons of Soncino in 1485–1486. Not incidentally, this edition also included the first printed haggadah illustration, an initial panel in the shape of a *matsah*, with the word *matsah* in its center (an image that probably derived from the Sephardic iconographical tradition). Such illustrations were a carry-over from the manuscript tradition and illustrate the close connections between Hebrew manuscripts and early printed books.

The history of the haggadah as a printed book continues to this day. The reader interested in more recent printed haggadot should consult the Bibliography and, in particular, Yosef Hayim Yerushalmi's book *Haggadah and History*.[31]

Joel ben Simeon and the Washington Haggadah

Among medieval Jewish scribes and illustrators, Joel ben Simeon was an unusual figure. In the first place, he was both a scribe and an artist—an unconventional combination at the time. In Joel's case, we have unillustrated manuscripts that he merely copied (the Parma Tefilla, 1449), texts written by other scribes that he illustrated (the London Haggadah), and still others, like the Washington Haggadah, which he both wrote and illustrated.[32] All told, there are ten manuscripts that Joel himself signed, and between four and nine others that various scholars have either attributed to him or associated with him. This high number of manuscripts, if not entirely unparalleled, is decidedly unusual. Cumulatively, their variety provides an opportunity to view the singular personality of a very gifted scribe and artist.

In her essay on the illustrations in the Washington Haggadah, Katrin Kogman-Appel tracks in detail the various events of Joel's biography; here I will only summarize its major movements.[33] Joel was born in Cologne in the early 1420s. His full name was Joel Feibush ben

Simeon—his middle name taken from the Old French Veives (and not, as some past scholars believed, from the Latin Phoebus)—and in some later manuscripts, written outside Germany, he recalled his birthplace by calling himself Ha-Ashkenazi ("The German"). In 1424, the Jews were expelled from Cologne, and Joel and his family moved to nearby Bonn, where Joel was raised and lived until 1445 or 1450, and where he appears to have received his early training as a scribe and artist. It is possible that he began to travel as an itinerant scribe/illustrator even before he left Bonn for good. In one of his earliest works, the undated First Nuremberg Haggadah, there is a somewhat enigmatic reference to a place named *Ferunyah*, which some scholars have taken to mean the town Brünn in Moravia, to which he may have expressed a desire to return.

He did not return to Moravia so far as we know. After being forced out of Bonn, Joel went south across the Alps to northern Italy, from where a dated and localized manuscript survives that he wrote in Cremona in 1452/3. Over the next thirty to forty years, the surviving manuscripts that he wrote—those that are either signed by him or attributed to him—include at least seven more haggadot, three prayerbooks, and one commentary to the Book of Psalms. These manuscripts certainly represent only a fraction of his output, but we have no idea how many manuscripts he actually produced. Although we know no more details about his life, it is clear that during this forty-year period he returned to Germany at least twice to write or illustrate books. During the second trip, in 1478, he wrote the Washington Haggadah, a virtually certain fact that the Israeli master codicologist Malachi Beit-Arié has determined on the basis of the manuscript's equalized parchment, quiring, pricking, and ruling techniques.[34] Joel then returned to Italy, and scholars believe that as late as 1492, when he would have been seventy or close to it, he was still working intensely, writing a beautifully decorated prayerbook known as the Moskowitz Siddur and working with a team of artists who illustrated the spectacular Rothschild Mahzor.

As Kogman-Appel points out in her essay, Joel's movements back and forth between Germany and Italy had a major impact on his artistic style. He always remained essentially an Ashkenazic scribe, as is most evident in his script. Yet while his unframed marginal drawings retained much of the flatness and two-dimensionality of the spared-ground technique typical of German illustration, he nonetheless absorbed the Italian feeling for depth and detail that is most evident in some of his more ambitious drawings (which, in general, are found less in the Washington Haggadah than in other manuscripts, like the London Haggadah). At the same time, he also adopted new motifs that he encountered in Italy, some of which had been previously introduced by Spanish haggadah manuscripts. In this way, Joel was an active agent of cultural exchange by bringing these influences back to the haggadot and other works he composed in Germany. Kogman-Appel and other scholars, such as Yael Zirlin, have spelled out some of the influence of Joel's work on later handwritten haggadot. There is no question that Joel's work—his haggadot in particular—was known and used by other contemporary scribes. A subject that remains to be explored more comprehensively by scholars is the impact that Joel's manuscripts had on early printed illustrated books. He worked precisely at the moment of the critical juncture between the age of manuscripts and the new age of printing. The first Hebrew books were published, most likely in Rome, in the 1470s, if not slightly earlier. Just as Joel was certainly aware of early printed books, so, too, early Jewish printers were fully acquainted with the heritage that the manuscript age had left them; indeed, early printers often sought to make their books look like manuscripts. Joel's haggadot would have served as perfect exemplars for such attempts.

In her essay, Kogman-Appel demonstrates the many ways that Joel's illustrations expressed the distinctive aspects of his artistic personality—his penchant for visual puns, his "signature" portrait of the traveling Jacob, and his ability to capture the social world in which he lived through vivid and sympathetic representations. While Joel's illustrations are sometimes stereotyped, he truly excelled in the artistry of scribal technique and the kinds of decoration more specifically associated with scribal virtuousity. Like most Ashkenazic scribes, Joel wrote the core text of the haggadah in a square script and used four different sizes of this script for different sections of the text—a medium size for the regular text of the haggadah, a larger one for initial words of important passages, a very large size for illuminated words at the beginnings of major sections, and a smaller size for the instructions in the margins on fol. 1r and 1v, and for some blessings, like those on 1r, 1v, and 2v–3r. In addition, he used a semicursive, calligraphic script in different sizes—in the large size for initial words (as in the rubrics on 11r), in a regular size sometimes for writing refrains (13v–14v), and in a small size for writing instructions and a few texts (as on 19r).[35] These different types and sizes of script created a visually transparent hierarchy of texts for the reader, but the variation also served a clearly aesthetic purpose in making the page less uniform and more interesting to look at. Most of the text is written in a black–dark brown ink, but Joel regularly used red, green, lighter brown, and blue inks to vary the text's color. Especially noteworthy are the large painted initial panels, which mainly have a blue background with white filigree sprigs and round white flowers with red centers, while the initial words themselves and the frames are in burnished gold leaf. One of the most beautiful of these panels is on 17v, with its alternating red and blue letters against a background of intertwined leaves, a small gem that literally turns words into ornament.

As with these panels, Joel's scribal virtuosity extended beyond the mere writing of the text to the overall aesthetics of the text page. A general concern of medieval Jewish scribes was line justification, which in the case of Hebrew texts meant justified *left* margins (because Hebrew is written right to left). In order to maintain the left margin, scribes utilized different techniques, and Joel employed nearly all of them. These include compression or dilation of letters at the end of a line (8r, line 4 and last line; 9r, line 6), abbreviation and truncation of words (6v, line 5; 9r, line 1); and elongation of letters (9r, line 9; 11v, line 10). One of the most individualistic techniques, however, was the use of graphic forms that look like Hebrew letters but are not. Joel used such a graphic filler extensively in the Washington Haggadah; there is at least one example on virtually every page, and often more—17v alone has four (on lines 1, 2, 4, and 7, not counting the initial word in the panel); depending on the line, Joel sometimes elongated the filler or compressed it. While the form of this graphic filler conforms to a basic type used by other Ashkenazic scribes, Joel made it his own by adding to its basic shape a descending stroke that curls to the left, and at other times, ascending strokes. In this way, the graphic filler became, in effect, Joel's scribal "trademark," as Malachi Beit-Arié has called it.[36] Indeed, this unique filler is so characteristic of his work that scholars have been able to use it to attribute unsigned manuscripts to Joel.

In addition, the close reader may wish to note several artistic flourishes Joel added to his script, in particular spiraling ascenders that sometimes mark ligatures (3r, line 1; 4v, line 1) and colored spiraling descenders like the one in the enlarged initial word *ma'aseh* on 4v, or in the next-to-last word on the page's final line, or the elongated final letter *khof* on the facing page, 5r. These little flourishes clearly added an element of visual diversity to the page, as did the alternating use of colors in the initial words from the bottom of 4r through 11v, where red initials (rubrics) alternate with green or blue ones. Another peculiarity of Joel's works that has intrigued scholars is his use of a three-pointed crown in several of his manuscripts; in the Washington Haggadah, one is found on 2r, line 2, over the Hebrew word *vayekhal.* Various theories have been offered to explain this enigmatic crown, but none has yet found wide acceptance.[37]

Of all Joel's distinguishing features as a scribe-artist, however, the most distinctive are his delicate filigreed panels, drawn in various colored inks, which surround the initial words of some key passages.[38] In the Washington Haggadah, some of these frames consist of intricate floral patterns—"swirling sprigs and dense curly leaves," as Bezalel Narkiss described them (as on 20r)—which show a clear Italianate influence.[39] Other touches are more humorous and witty: on the right side of a number of panels, Joel drew a grotesque face in profile, grimacing toward the outer margin, with a curlicue-like tongue and a long twisting strand of a beard. The first to appear in the book is on 1v, right next to the initial word in red, *barukh* ("Blessed"); on the facing page, at the top right, the initial *va-yekhulu* ("and were completed") is framed by a king emerging out of a worm-like long neck. On 7v, directly beneath the drawing of the traveling forefather, the grotesque profile once again leans out from the side of the Hebrew word *va-yered,* while on top of the word, a lively hare flees in the opposite direction. Finally, near the haggadah's conclusion (24r), at the beginning of the Great Halel (Psalm 136), the grotesque profile appears for the last time in an especially ornate and beautiful panel. In other works, like the London Haggadah (which Joel illustrated and decorated), the grotesques sometimes appear, almost partially hidden, inside the large colored panels that mark major sections of the haggadah. None are to be found in the Washington Haggadah's large colored panels, but even the grotesques that I have mentioned play a game of hide-and-seek with the reader. At first, we do not notice them, but when we do, they take us by surprise, making us look ever harder at a text we thought was utterly familiar.

Taken separately, all these individual scribal practices may seem to be mere details of technique, but collectively they point to the ways in which a professional scribe like Joel defined his individuality within a profession that was otherwise powerfully governed by convention. Indeed, such means of individuation transformed a figure like Joel from a mere copyist into a scribe. Even so, scribes also remained copyists in a strict sense—that is, their main job was to transcribe their texts as accurately as possible by copying them from other manuscripts. To a great extent, their skill as accurate copyists was the standard by which they were judged. Nonetheless, even when copying from another manuscript, scribes constantly faced choices as to what to copy, a task complicated by the fact that most manuscripts included marginal glosses, corrections, and other additions to the core text.

In his study of the text of the Washington Haggadah, the Israeli scholar Mordechai Glatzer has pointed out an interesting example of such a choice Joel made.[40] From early on, Ashkenazic haggadot contained a series of mnemonic abbreviations that reminded the participants of the order of rituals performed during the banquet. What eventually became the standard version, beginning with the words *Kadesh U-rehats,* is still printed today at the beginning of most traditional haggadot and frequently sung as a kind of ditty at the beginning of the celebration. This same mnemonic is also found at the bottom of the very first page (1r) of the Washington Haggadah, written out in three lines of large square script. The careful reader will note, however, that above the mnemonic, in a tiny hand, are the three words *seder aher le-pesah,* "another order for the Passover [banquet]." Why "another" order? What was the first one?

The answer to this question lies in a second, much less common mnemonic order that is also recorded in the Washington Haggadah on 19r, in the middle of the haggadah, and written in a calligraphic semicursive hand. This mnemonic order is far older than *Kadesh U-rehats*, dating back to the eleventh century. This second order details the entire sequence of rituals marking the actual banquet in the middle of the seder—the eating of the ritual foods, the *matsah*, *maror*, and so-called Hillel sandwich, the meal itself, and the Grace after Meals, followed by the pouring and drinking of the fourth cup of wine. According to Glatzer, this older mnemonic was actually the original "order" for the Washington Haggadah, but in the margins of the manuscript from which he copied his text, Joel found, on the first page, written in the margins, the later order, which was prefaced by the phrase "another order." Joel, it seems, copied the second order directly into the text of the Washington Haggadah *including* the phrase "another order" before it! By doing so, somewhat ironically, Joel conserved the marginality of this later mnemonic order even though it appears in the Washington Haggadah as the first and primary one, and also thereby preserved a small piece of the history of the medieval haggadah that would otherwise probably have been lost.

As a professional scribe, Joel typically wrote on commission. The colophon of this haggadah, however, does not mention the manuscript's patron or commissioner, an uncharacteristic omission. As earlier scholars have noted, Joel may have written this haggadah to be held as stock and sold to a future customer. This untraditional practice had in fact become more common in the last decades of the manuscript age, and it anticipates the modes of production that rule in the period of print.[41] Perhaps for the same reason, the Washington Haggadah has a relatively small number of illustrations (which could have been increased if the eventual buyer wished to have more); the same rationale would also explain the empty final pages of the last gathering, which Joel may have deliberately left in the manuscript in the event that a customer wished to have an additional text written there (as, in fact, turned out to be the case, as we shall see).

Because the manuscript was written while Joel was in Germany, it is not surprising that the haggadah's text follows the German rite. As noted, from the time of the early Middle Ages the core text of the haggadah had become standardized according to the Babylonian rite nearly everywhere in the world, but there still remained some small differences between the communal rites of Ashkenaz, Sepharad, and Italy (and sometimes their smaller communities as well). In the course of his career, Joel mainly wrote haggadot according to the Ashkenazic rite, but his oeuvre also contains two haggadot of the Italian rite. The Washington Haggadah follows the Ashkenazic rite, but it also contains one or two features which show that Joel had absorbed certain Italian customs, while at other points its text contains several early features of the Ashkenazic rite that have since fallen out of usage, a fact that doubtless shows Joel's native comfort and familiarity with that tradition as the one with which he grew up.[42] These various features—both Italian and early Ashkenazic—include the following:

(1) At the very beginning of the haggadah, at the top of 1r, inside a delicately pen-drawn unraveled scroll, Joel wrote two formulaic scribal formulae, "With good luck [*betuv gadda*] I shall write the order of the Passover [seder]," and "For your honor, God." The first formula is known to have been used by scribes in Ashkenaz and Provence, and occasionally by Ashkenazic scribes in Italy. The second formula is exclusively used by Italian scribes, and as was suggested by Moritz Steinschneider, it may have been borrowed from Latin scribal eulogies like *Deo laus et honor* or *Deo laus, honor, et gloria*.[43] The presence of both formulae in the Washington Haggadah marks Joel's own position between the two different scribal cultures.

(2) Before eating the *karpas*—the greens that, in the seder, represent the appetizer course of the meal—it is customary to wash one's hands in remembrance of the laws of purity that obtained during the Temple period. Because this ritual washing is largely symbolic, however, there was a long-time dispute as to whether or not it was necessary to recite a blessing before undertaking the ritual washing. Eventually—by the sixteenth century at the latest—it was conclusively decided that a blessing was not required, and that is the custom followed today by observant Jews. In medieval Ashkenaz, however, opinions were divided, and in the Washington Haggadah (3r, in the instruction written in the smaller hand in the middle of the page), as in all of Joel's haggadot, he states that the blessing *is* required.

In the same instructions, Joel also writes that one dips the *karpas* in *haroset,* the dipping sauce made from fruit and nuts. This was indeed the original custom in Ashkenaz. At a later period, salt water or vinegar was substituted for the *haroset* in order to differentiate the *karpas* from the bitter herbs, the *maror,* which are eaten later in the seder and which are still dipped in *haroset* today, while the *karpas* is dipped in salt water.

(3) As noted, the third of the four questions—the one about dipping greens twice at the seder—has a complicated history involving a number of changes to the original question as recorded in the early manuscripts of the Mishnah, which was, "Why on all other nights do we dip once but on this night twice?" In the Babylonian Talmud (Pesahim 116a), the Mishnaic text was initially emended to read, "on all other nights we are not obligated [*en anu hayyavin*] to dip even once," and still later, in the same Talmudic discussion, it was further emended to read, "on all other nights we do not dip even once."

Many medieval rabbis, both in Ashkenaz and in Sepharad, ruled that the correct reading was the second one, and this reading was followed in all Italian haggadot. Many Ashkenazic haggadot, including Joel's (and the Washington Haggadah, on 4r), however, preserve the first Talmudic version of "we are not obligated." Exactly why this version was preserved despite the Rabbinic rulings to the contrary is unclear. It should be noted, however, that Joel's two haggadot written according to the Italian rite both follow the second version in the Talmud. In these cases, obviously, Joel delivered what his client wanted.

(4) In the "second order of the seder" on 18v (see my comments above), Joel writes that for *Barekh* [= *Karekh*], the *matsah* "sandwich" eaten in remembrance of the Temple according to the custom of Hillel, one uses horseradish *(meerrettich)* rather than the lettuce *(lituga)* earlier prescribed for the *maror* or bitter herbs.[44] This instruction is one of our earliest pieces of evidence for the transition to the use of horseradish as the bitter herb—today eaten almost universally—in place of the traditional bitter lettuce that goes back to the seder in the Talmudic period.

(5) Like many Ashkenazic haggadot, the Washington Haggadah contains only a single verse, Ps. 79:6, for the curse against the Gentile nations, *Shefokh Hamatkha* (19v), discussed earlier in this introduction. At the top of the page, a later hand added another nine verses; and still another hand, a tenth verse. These additional verses accord with the northern French rite, which, presumably, a later owner of the haggadah followed. It is worth noting that *Shefokh Hamatkha* was not originally recited in the Italian rite and was first introduced into use by Joel himself in the Second New York Haggadah (JTSA Mic. 8279), written in 1454.[45]

(6) Following the Great Halel, *Hodu* (Ps. 136), at the very bottom of 25r, Joel copied an additional Psalms verse, Ps. 33:1, "Sing forth [*Ranenu*], O you righteous, to God, it is fit that the upright acclaim Him." In fact, this addition is found in many Ashkenazic haggadot, dating back to the Bird Heads Haggadah. As Mordechai Glatzer has ingeniously explained, the presence of this odd verse in the haggadah probably derives from the period when, as we have seen, the Ashkenazic haggadah was

still part of the holiday prayerbook.[46] In the morning service according to the Ashkenazic rite, the recitation of Ps. 136 is indeed followed by the recitation of Ps. 33 (as it still is today). In these prayerbook codices, scribes would not necessarily have recopied the Great Halel in the book's haggadah section, because it is after all a fairly lengthy passage; they would merely have noted to the celebrant an instruction such as, "and recite over [the cup] the Great *Halel*, 'Praise GOD; for He is good, His steadfast love is eternal' (Ps. 136:1), and recite it up to 'Sing forth, O you righteous, to God, it is fit that the upright acclaim Him' (Ps. 33:1)"—an instruction that is indeed found in one manuscript.[47] The scribe originally meant that one should recite Ps. 136 *until* (but not including) Ps. 33:1. An early scribe, however, misunderstood the instruction and thought that the recitation *included* Ps. 33:1, and therefore wrote out that verse in his haggadah. All of Joel's haggadot include this verse. As Glatzer also notes, because the Sephardic and Italian morning prayer rites do not follow the Great Halel with Ps. 33:1, scribes in those two realms never made the mistake, and the latter verse is never found in their manuscripts.

(7) The earliest of the after-dinner songs sung at the conclusion of the seder is *Ki Lo Naeh, Ki Lo Yaeh* (32v–33v). There are, however, differences in the wording between the Ashkenazic and the Italian rites. Not surprisingly, the Washington Haggadah follows the Ashkenazic wording, but in the refrain it rather unusually switches the order by having *lekha af lekha* precede *lekha ki lekha* (except in the final stanza!).[48] The Washington Haggadah is also one of the earliest haggadot to add the song *Adir hu* on its final page (34r), where Joel wrote the first stanza in full, and then simply listed the initial words (which form an alphabetic acrostic) for all the following stanzas of the song.

(8) The scribe's colophon on 34v reads, *va-tishalem ha-melakha vedayo*, "and the work was completed." The final word in the line, *ve-*

dayo, which is found in several of Joel's manuscripts, may be an allusion to Exod. 36:7, meaning, "and it is enough" or "sufficient."[49] The American Jewish art historian Franz Landsberger suggested that the word might also be a pun on the similarly written *u-deyo,* which would make the phrase mean "and the work was completed, and so was the ink."[50] Given Joel's penchant for visual puns, a verbal one would not be surprising.

Aside from consciously written variations in the haggadah, Joel also committed some mistakes in transcribing the book's text, a reality of scribal life that happens to even its most skilled practitioners. In the Washington Haggadah, there are a few errors of this kind, including those on 6v, 12v, 20r, and 20v, where Joel skipped words in the text and later added them to the margin.[51] On 22v, he skipped Ps. 118:8 and apparently never noticed it, but a later Ashkenazic owner who did added it to the margins in a rather ugly hand.

The most prominent errors in the Washington Haggadah are those found on the book's final pages. As noted, the last three folios of the final quire (36r–38v) were originally left empty, possibly because Joel had not written the haggadah on commission and wished to leave room to add additional prayers or texts that a future client might want to have in the codex. In this case, the customer who finally bought the haggadah requested that Joel add two special texts, *'Eruvei Hatserot* and *'Eruvei Tavshilin.* Both prayers are ritual ceremonies performed in the event that the two days of Passover fall on Thursday and Friday, thus making preparation for the following Sabbath on the holiday legally forbidden; by performing these ceremonies *before* the advent of the holiday, the celebrants are permitted to prepare for the Sabbath on Friday even though it is a holiday.

According to the logic of the holiday's chronology, these two texts should actually be found at the very beginning of the haggadah, immediately following the text of the search for leaven, and this is where they are typically found in most Ashkenazic haggadot. The fact that they are found on the haggadah's final folios contributes to the likelihood that they were added after Joel had written the haggadah and at a specific customer's request. As Myron Weinstein has noted, 1478 was indeed a year when Passover began on Wednesday night and continued through Thursday and Friday, thus necessitating the recitation of the two ceremonies that year.[52] If Joel completed his haggadah on January 29, 1478, he probably began it in late 1477 and was not yet aware of the exact weekdays on which Passover would fall in the coming year. By the time he completed and sold the haggadah, his customer certainly would have known that he would need the texts, and therefore asked Joel to write them at the codex's conclusion.

The text of *'Eruvei Hatserot* (35r) begins in Hebrew but is mostly in Aramaic, while that of *'Eruvei Tavshilin* (35r–v) is mainly in Aramaic. In the latter text, Joel made several errors—in one case, importing several words from the Aramaic text of the *'Eruvei Hatserot* into the *'Eruvei Tavshilin;* in the other case, he added a phrase saying that it is permissible to prepare on the Sabbath for the holiday, which is actually forbidden. According to Glatzer, Joel may have copied his text from an ancient and irregular version of the legal ceremony which he (or an earlier scribe whose text he was copying) misunderstood.[53]

The Afterlife of the Washington Haggadah

The corrections by later owners of the Washington Haggadah and the marginal additions they made to the text not only highlight features of the original haggadah but also provide us with clues to the haggadah's history as a book after it left the hands of its scribe-illustrator. As we have seen, it appears that Joel wrote the haggadah for stock rather than as a previously commissioned book for a specific client. We have no idea as to who first bought the haggadah, but from several faint traces of Hebrew words written as practice phrases in an Ashekenazic hand on fol. 38v, which appear to have been added not long after Joel wrote the manuscript, it seems quite certain that the first owner was a German Jew; the marginal correction of the missing verse from Ps. 118:8 is in a seventeenth-century Ashkenazic hand, a telling detail because it again suggests that the haggadah was still in Germany a hundred years later (although it is not impossible that the lines were written by an Ashkenazic Jew living in Italy).[54]

Moreover, the absence of any signatures of Christian censors from the sixteenth or seventeenth century, which would almost certainly be found in the book if it had been in Italy during this period, strongly suggests that the haggadah remained in Germany until the eighteenth century. This likelihood is further confirmed by the fact that the additional verses of malediction added to the *Shefokh Hamatkha* written by hand (19v) and a single missing word added to the margin on 8r are both in eighteenth-century Italian script.[55] We know for certain that by the late nineteenth century the haggadah was owned by the Provençali family in Mantua, an eminent family with a lineage that dated back to Moses ben David Provençal (1503–1575), one of the most distinguished Talmudists of the Renaissance period, and his brother David ben Abraham Provençal (b. 1506), who attempted to establish a Jewish university in Mantua.[56] On the inner front flyleaf (not reproduced in the facsimile) and on 36v are faint lines that name four of the members of the Provençali family in the late nineteenth century—Amelia, Zeffira, Umberto, and Attilio—and on 37v, there is a remarkable note by one Ettore Finzi in German, dated April 7, 1879, which was indeed Passover eve that year, in which he writes that they are sitting at the seder table, where they have just sung the first part of the "Gada," and are awaiting the food. After the food arrives, they start eating, and he signs off, "Guten Appetit."[57] Stains that probably stem from wine drops on 18v and 19r confirm the fact that the haggadah was actually used at seders.[58] This haggadah was not, in other words, a trophy book that its owners kept locked up in a case for display. Despite its beauty and its monetary value, it was actually used for the purpose for which Joel ben Simeon had originally written it—as a haggadah for a seder.

All this changed in the early twentieth century. While we do not know the exact facts for certain, on June 10, 1902, the book dealer Ephraim Deinard, who was in Mantua at the time, wrote to Judge Mayer Sulzberger in Philadelphia that he was sending him eight rare books and manuscripts he had bought in Italy, including an illustrated haggadah written in 1478. The asking price for the haggadah was $500, he wrote, though in a letter written in August, Deinard conceded that his original asking price may have been too high and hinted that he was willing to bargain.[59] Apparently, Sulzberger was still not interested enough to purchase the haggadah, and it remained in the dealer's stock for another fourteen years.

Ephraim Deinard (1846–1930) was one of the most exceptional figures in the history of the Jewish book in the last two centuries.[60] Bookseller and bibliographer, publisher and author or editor of some fifty books of his own, Zionist activist and publicist, and vitriolic polemicist against a myriad of persons and causes not to his personal liking—which included Hasidism, Kabbalah, Reform Judaism, communism, and the great Rabbinics scholar and later chancellor of the Jewish Theological Seminary Solomon Schechter—Deinard was a seminal and still insufficiently recognized figure in laying the foundations for Jewish scholarship in America. Born in the Baltic region of the tsarist empire in the mid-nineteenth century, he grew up in Lithuania, moved to White Russia, and then went to Crimea, where he became the amanuensis and factotum of the Karaite book dealer and collector Abraham Firkovitch (1786–1874). In his very first book, *Toledot Ibn Reshef* (Warsaw 1875), a biography of Firkovitch, Deinard described how the Karaite dealer pressured his poverty-stricken coreligionists and stole and finagled valuable books out of them, in addition to forging manuscripts and artifacts in order to prove the antiquity of Karaite settlement in the region.[61]

For all his apparent distate for Firkovitch, Deinard appears to have learned more than a little from his employer's methods. Over time Deinard proved to be an extremely shrewd book dealer who was deeply mistrusted even by some of his most loyal customers. In the 1880s he was the proprietor of his own bookstore in Odessa, though he spent much of his time traveling through Europe and the Near East unearthing and saving valuable manuscripts and books. He corresponded with all the great scholars and bibliographers of the time, both Jewish and Christian, and sold books to all the great European libraries. His indefatigability in obtaining manuscripts and rare printings became legendary early on. As Alexander Marx, the librarian of the Jewish Theological Seminary of America, and the greatest expert on Jewish books during his lifetime, wrote about Deinard: "How he managed to obtain some of these unique volumes I do not know, but undoubtedly a considerable number would have perished in the disorders of the last decades if Deinard had not found them a safe resting-place in great Jewish and general libraries."[62]

In October 1888, with his wife, four young daughters, a niece, and eleven pieces of luggage that he stuffed with manuscripts and books, Deinard arrived in the United States, where he would live for the remaining forty years of his life, with the exception of one brief, aborted attempt to settle in Palestine and many trips abroad in search of books and artifacts to sell. In the course of those forty years, Deinard lived in

Newark; St. Louis; and, for the last twelve years of his life, New Orleans. In all these places he published newspapers (including one of the first Hebrew newspapers in America), journals, and books. Following a time-honored tradition of using fictional places of imprint in Hebrew publishing, Deinard cited Baltunowka ("Chattertown") and Sodom as places of publication for books that were actually printed in Newark. The Sodom title, moreover, was said to have been produced "in the printing press of Raziel the Angel fifty years before the Creation of the World."[63]

Deinard's chief and lasting contribution, however, was certainly in his role as a collector and dealer in manuscripts and books that would become the foundations of some of America's greatest public and institutional collections of Hebraica and Judaica. Early on—possibly even before he emigrated to the United States—Deinard recognized that America was likely to become a center for the modern critical Jewish scholarship that was then developing in Western Europe (*Wissenschaft des Judentums*, now known as Jewish Studies), and that there would be a need for great Jewish research libraries in the New World to support that scholarship. His main goal, he wrote in one of his later works, was "to establish libraries in all the leading cities of our land. It is my hope that in the course of time I shall succeed in disseminating Jewish literature in this barren country . . . If a Jewish scholar needs an ancient text [now], he must go to Europe, to the British Museum or the Bodleian in Oxford."[64] To remedy that situation, Deinard began by persuading professors like Richard Gottheil of Columbia University to establish Hebraica collections in their university libraries, and private collectors like Judge Sulzberger to build collections that they would eventually donate to public institutions (in Sulzberger's case, mainly to the Jewish Theological Seminary of America). He also sold an important collection of Judaica objects he had gathered to the Smithsonian Institution in Washington, D.C., whose librarian at the time was Cyrus Adler, later to become the president of Dropsie College in Philadelphia, the first nonsectarian institution of higher learning in Ancient Near Eastern and Jewish Studies in America.[65] His final sale was that of his own private collection—twelve thousand printed volumes, including sixteen incunables and twenty-nine manuscripts—which he sold to Harvard University, just months before his death in 1930, thereby establishing the foundation for Widener Library's magnificent collection.[66]

Deinard's greatest dream, however, was to establish a major Judaica collection in America's national library, the Library of Congress, that would rival the great national libraries of Europe, like the Bibliothèque nationale in Paris, the British Library in London, and the National Library in Berlin. It was a happy coincidence that precisely at this time the Library of Congress itself was in the process of becoming a major research library that sought to cover all of world literature and culture. The library had been founded to serve the particular needs of Congress. In 1814, however, the original library was destroyed in a fire set by British troops, and Congress decided to reconstitute it by purchasing the private library of Thomas Jefferson, America's third president and first bibliophile, whose 6,487 volumes covered the truly encyclopedic range of Jefferson's eclectic humanistic and scientific interests. Among its many treasures, Jefferson's library also contained seven books of Judaic or Hebraic interest, including the 1737 first edition of William Whiston's translation of *The Genuine Works of Flavius Josephus, the Jewish Historian*, as well as a copy of *De Legibus Ebraeorum: Baba Kamma, Mi'masekhet Nezikin* (Leyden: Elzevir, 1637), with the Hebrew text and a Latin translation and commentary by Constantin L'Empereur (1591–1648) of the University of Leiden.[67]

These few books hardly constituted a serious Judaic collection, as Deinard well understood. In 1904 Herbert Putnam, the Librarian of

Congress and a man of broad cultural and creative vision who was the driving force behind the library's expansion into a major research library, acquired a huge collection of classical Indian literature, and shortly later, equally impressive collections of Russian, Chinese, and Japanese literature. Although he had tried nearly fifteen years earlier to sell the Library of Congress a collection of Hebraica, Deinard now sensed that the time was ripe for a new attempt, and in 1909 he turned again to Putnam with an offer to sell him a collection "of the oldest and rarest books which are to be found only in the British Museum, and some of them are not to be found even there."[68]

Putnam's response was slow in coming, but in 1912, he approached (with Cyrus Adler's assistance) the German-born New York financier and Jewish philanthropist Jacob H. Schiff to ask if he would be willing to purchase Deinard's collection as a "gift to the Nation" that would serve as "a recognition of the part which Hebrew history, literature, and tradition, as well as the Hebrew race, play and will play in the affairs of this country."[69] Schiff finally agreed, and the Library of Congress purchased Deinard's collection, which consisted of 10,000 books and pamphlets. This purchase came to be known as the First Deinard Collection. In 1914, Schiff again bankrolled the purchase of a second collection of 4,200 volumes from Deinard, which he presented to the Library of Congress as the Second Deinard Collection. In 1916, the library purchased with its own funds a third collection of 2,300 items, and in 1916, a fourth collection of some 3,000 volumes. Altogether, then, Deinard sold the Library of Congress some 19,500 volumes and laid a strong foundation for its future growth into one of the world's great Hebraica and Judaica collections.

The Washington Haggadah most likely arrived at the Library of Congress as part of the Third Deinard Collection in 1916.[70] And there it remains today, one of the library's treasures and a highlight of its by-now truly extensive, even exhaustive, Hebraic Section. Deinard's dream has indeed been realized. The Washington Haggadah, however, is no longer a "functioning" haggadah, no longer a ritual text used at a seder. It is a Hebrew illustrated manuscript of invaluable worth, available to scholars for research, a window into the world in which it was created and its scribal book culture. And now, through this reissued facsimile edition, it is an accessible book that can be read, studied, looked at, and even brought to the seder table and used by any interested person. It is genuine proof that the Jews—and the Jewish book—have truly arrived in America.[71]

NOTES

1. Much of the information in this introduction is based on the definitive studies of the Washington Haggadah written for the Commentary volume that accompanied the original facsimile edition (Washington, DC: Library of Congress, 1991): "Introduction," by Myron Weinstein (pp. 1–25); "The Art of the Washington Haggadah," by Bezalel Narkiss (27–101); "Codicological Description and Analysis of the Washington Haggadah," by Malachi Beit-Arié (103–135); "The Ashkenazic and Italian Haggadah and the Haggadot of Joel ben Simeon," by Mordechai Glatzer (137–169); and "The Washington Haggadah: A Conservator's Perspective," by Doris A. Hamburg (171–195). Hereafter these separate studies will be referred to by their authors' names alone (for example, Weinstein, Beit-Arié) and page numbers. For a full transcription of the colophon and its significance, see Beit-Arié, 105–109.

2. For the localization of the manuscript's composition in Germany, see Beit-Arié, 122–126. The colophon does not explicitly state the place of composition.

3. For the most recent bibliography of haggadot through 1960, see Yudlov. Since 1960, I would estimate that at least another five hundred editions have appeared.

4. Numerous studies over the past several decades have addressed the histories of

both the seder and the haggadah, a number of which are listed in the Select Bibliography; the following discussion draws on the important discoveries and formulations in these works. See in particular Bokser; Goldschmidt; Guggenheimer; Kasher; Raphael; Safrai and Safrai; and Tabory.

5. On the biblical background, see Segal, *The Hebrew Passover;* and *The JPS Torah Commentary: Exodus, with Commentary by Nahum M. Sarna* (Philadelphia: Jewish Publication Society, 1991), 57.

6. Philo, *On the Special Laws,* Bk. 1:293–295, in *Philo,* with an English trans. by F. H. Colson (Cambridge, MA: Harvard University Press, 1968), VII: 269–270; Philo, *Questions and Answers on Exodus* I:15, in *Philo,* with an English trans. by Ralph Marcus (Cambridge, MA: Harvard University Press, 1970), 23–25.

7. On the symposium connection, see S. Stein, "The Influence of Symposia Literature on the Literary Form of the Pesah Haggadah," *Journal of Jewish Studies* 8 (1957): 13–44.

8. *Mekhilta de-Rabbi Ishmael, Pisha* 18, ed. J. Z. Lauterbach (Philadelphia: Jewish Publication Society, 1933; repr. 2004), 166–167.

9. Joseph ben Samuel Bonfils's well-known poem is not in the Washington Haggadah; according to Tabory (60–61) it was first introduced into the haggadah by Rabbi Shalom of Neustadt, Austria, in the second decade of the fifteenth century, but it had not yet become universally recited even in the Ashkenazic world.

10. For discussion of the background to these songs, and for the lexical difficulties in the refrain to *Ki Lo Naeh,* discussed later in this introduction in relation to the Washington Haggadah's text, see Tabory, *JPS Commentary,* 62–64.

11. Walter Benjamin, *Illuminations,* ed. with an introduction by Hannah Arendt, trans. Harry Zohn (1968; repr. New York: Schocken, 1969), 264.

12. Maimonides, *Mishneh Torah,* Laws of Hametz and Matzah 7: 6–7.

13. Jacob Sapir [Halevi], *Even Sapir* (Lyck: Mekitzei Nirdamim, 1866), I:89a. I wish to thank Professor Tzvi Langermann and Dr. Uri Melamed for assisting me in finding this and other sources for the Yemenite custom. Other communities (particularly from the Middle East and North Africa) observe comparable rituals. According to an article in the *New York Times* (March 24, 2010, D7) about the contemporary seders of Iranian Jews now living in New York City, "Before singing the song, 'Dayenu,' the assembled guests get up from their chairs, take their scallions, and begin whacking one another with them to simulate the whips of the slave drivers in Egypt."

14. *Zevah Pesah* (Constantinople: Nahmias, 1505/1506): 31v.

15. See Tosefta Pesahim 10:8.

16. On the Cairo Genizah and its history, see Stefan C. Reif, *A Jewish Archive from Old Cairo* (Richmond, Surrey: Curzon Press, 2000). The texts of these early haggadot were first published by E. D. Goldschmidt, 75–84, and by Jay Rovner in "An Early Passover Haggadah According to the Palestinian Rite," *Jewish Quarterly Review* 90 (2000): 337–396.

17. A fuller description of the differences between the Sephardic and the Ashkenazic haggadot in the Middle Ages can be found in my forthcoming book *The Jewish Library: Four Classic Jewish Books and the Jewish Experience* (University of Washington Press, 2012).

18. For a recent study of the typological significance of these miniatures, though somewhat different from my approach, see Sarit Shalev-Eyni, "Jerusalem and the Temple in Hebrew Illuminated Manuscripts: Jewish Thought and Christian Influence," in *L'interculturalità dell'ebraismo*, ed. Mauro Perani (Ravenna: Longo, 2004), 173–191; and Shalev-Eyni, "Who Are the Heirs of the Hebrew Bible? Sephardic Visual Historiography in a Christian Context," in *Medieval Encounters* 16 (2010): 23–63.

19. Marginal illustrations, it should be noted, are not entirely absent from Sephardic haggadot: for example, the pictures of the four sons. And there always are, of course, exceptions to the rule: the Barcelona Haggadah, one of the most sumptuous haggadot produced in Spain, adheres to the Spanish model inasmuch as it is a kind of mini-holiday prayerbook, but it lacks the sequence of miniatures preceding the text, and nearly all its illustrations are marginal and heavily influenced by Gothic art.

20. A facsimile edition of the *Bird's Head Haggadah of the Bezalel National Art Museum in Jerusalem*, with an Introductory Volume of essays, ed. Moshe Spitzer, was published by Tarshish Books (Jerusalem, 1967). The Bezalel Museum is now the Israel Museum, which holds the haggadah as MS 180/57.

21. For other French and Ashkenazic haggadot in prayerbooks, see Garel, nos. 62, 96, 97, 98. As yet, there has been no full-scale study of the Ashkenazic haggadah, illustrated or not.

22. On these haggadot, see Kogman-Appel, *Illuminated Haggadot from Medieval Spain*.

23. The Second Nuremberg Haggadah is now accessible on the National Library

of Israel website (formerly JNUL) at http://jnul.huji.ac.il/dl/mss-pr/mss_d_0076/open_eng.html, together with two articles by Katrin Kogman-Appel on the Nuremberg Haggadah and the Yahuda Haggadah: "The Iconography of the Biblical Cycle of the Second Nuremberg and the Yahuda Haggadot: Tradition and Innovation," originally published in *The Old Testament as Inspiration in Culture: International Academic Symposium—Prague, September 1995*, ed. Jan Heller, Shemaryahu Talmon, Hana Hlaváčková, and Martin Prudký (Prague, 2001); and "The Second Nuremberg Haggadah and the Yahuda Haggadah: Were They Made by the Same Artist?" in *Proceedings of the Eleventh World Congress of Jewish Studies, Jerusalem, 1993, Division D* (Jerusalem: Magnes, 1994), II: 25–32. See as well Kogman-Appel's book *Die Zweite Nürnberger und die Jehuda Haggada*. For a related haggadah, see BnF Hebreu 1333, described and reproduced in Garel, no. 108.

24. A facsimile edition of the Floersheim Haggadah, with a descriptive booklet, was published in Zurich/Dielsdorf by Lichtdrucht in 1985. For a detailed study of the haggadah and its context, see Yael Zirlin, "Discovering the Floersheim Haggadah," *Ars Judaica* 1 (2005): 91–108.

25. For a very early example of what is most likely an Italian haggadah, see Hamburg Cod. Heb. 155 (thirteenth century?), Italy (according to the catalogue of the Institute of Microfilmed Hebrew Manuscripts in the National Library of Israel). A plate from the book is reproduced and described in *HIM*, pl. 22, pp. 84–85 (where it is called the Dragon Haggadah and attributed to France). As Narkiss notes, the haggadah was originally part of a prayerbook.

26. On this haggadah, see Narkiss, *HIM*, pl. 130. The haggadah is available on CD from Hebrew Union College. Meir ben Israel's father was Israel ben Meir Jaffe of Heidelberg, the scribe of the Darmstadt Haggadah (Middle Rhine, c. 1450), a sumptuous but somewhat problematic haggadah that has also been published in facsimile, twice in fact: Bruno Italiener, *Die Darmstädter Pessach-Haggadah Codex orientalis 8 der Landesbibliothek zu Darmstadt aus dem vierzehnten Jahrhundert*, 2 vols. (Leipzig, 1927–1928); and *Die Darmstädter Pessach-Haggadah; Codex orientalis 8 der Hessischen Landes- und Hochschulbibliothek Darmstadt*, ed. Joseph Gutmann, Hermann Knaus, Paul Pieper, and Erich Zimmermann, 2 vols. (Berlin: Propyläen Verlag, 1972).

27. On the history of this illustration, see Joseph Gutmann, "The Messiah at the Seder: A Fifteenth-Century Motif in Jewish Art," in *Sefer Refa'el Mahler* (Merhaviah: Sifriyat Poalim, 1974), 29–43.

28. For discussion of the repercussions of this illustration, see Yuval, 123–130.

29. The opening of the door possibly dates back to some of the earliest moments of the seder's history, when the banquet may have ended at precisely this point and the door would have been opened to signal to guests that it was time to go home. For an early interpretation linking the opening of the door to the messianic arrival, see the passage from R. Joseph Yuspa Hahn's *Sefer Yosif Ometz* quoted in translation in Gutmann, "The Messiah at the Seder," 29.

30. Anthonius Margaritha, *Der ganze Jüdische Glaube* (1530; Leipzig, 1705), quoted in translation in Gutmann, "The Messiah at the Seder," 30.

31. For a bibliography of printed editions until 1960, see Yudlov; and for discussion and facsimile plates, see Yerushalmi.

32. For texts merely copied by Joel, see Parma, Biblioteca Palatina, Ms. Parm 3144; cf. as well David Kimhi's Commentary on the Psalms, Modena, 1485, Parma, Biblioteca Palatina, Ms. 2841. In both cases, parts of the manuscript were also copied by a second scribe. For texts that Joel illustrated but did not copy, see British Library Ms. Add. 14762; some of Joel's illustrations were painted over by Johannes Bämler, who added illustrations as well.

33. In addition to Kogman-Appel's essay in this volume, see as well the essays by Beit-Arié and Glatzer in the Commentary volume accompanying the earlier facsimile from the Library of Congress.

34. Beit-Arié, 122–127.

35. For a full description of all the different scripts Joel used, see Beit-Arié, 114–115.

36. Beit-Arié, 116.

37. Weinstein, 9; but see Zucker, xxiii–xxiv.

38. The fullest description of Joel's penwork is in Zucker, xxii–l. For the grotesque profiles (or, as Zucker calls them, "masks"), see xlvii–l.

39. Narkiss, 54.

40. Glatzer, 150–151.

41. Beit-Arié, 105–106.

42. The following paragraphs are largely based on the scholarly discoveries put forward by Mordechai Glatzer in his chapter in the supplement volume, 139–169.

43. On these formulae, see Beit-Arié, 134–135, note 39, who cites Steinschneider, *Vorlesungen über die Kunde hebräischer Handschriften* (Leipzig, 1897), 47.

44. Weinstein, 12; cf. as well the comments of Narkiss, 74, regarding the illustration in the Hileq and Bileq Haggadah.

45. Glatzer, 145–146.

46. Glatzer, 155–156.

47. New York, JTSA Mic. 4454; cited by Glatzer, 169, note 82.

48. Glatzer, 147, and 164, note 34.

49. Beit-Arié, 130, note 1.

50. Landsberger, 80.

51. These cases should be differentiated from those where Joel could not complete a word on the line and simply wrote its end in a minuscule hand in the margin next to it, as on 1r, 4r (last line), or 6r (last line). On 26r, I do not understand why he wrote *hineh* in the margin.

52. Weinstein, 10–11.

53. On both texts, see Glatzer, 156–157.

54. Weinstein, 22, note 32.

55. Weinstein, 8, and 22, note 33. As noted earlier, the additional verses to *Shefokh Hamatkha* seem to accord with the northern French Ashkenazic rite.

56. Weinstein, 8, 21–22, note 31. On the members of the Provençali family, see *Encyclopaedia Judaica* (Jerusalem: Keter, 1972), 13:1257–1264.

57. Weinstein, 20; see also the note on the inner back flyleaf, also not reproduced in the facsimile, which names the members of the Provençali family who jointly "offer the 'Gada.'" As Weinstein notes, the word "Gada" is not Judeo-Italian but appears to be borrowed from the colloquial language of German Jews.

58. Hamburg, 176.

59. The letters—all to be found in the Alexander Marx–Mayer Sulzberger File of the Papers of Ephraim Deinard in the Library of the Jewish Theological Seminary of America—are cited by Weinstein, 7–8.

60. For Deinard's biography, see Simcha Berkowitz, "Ephraim Deinard: Bibliophile and Bookman," *Studies in Bibliography and Booklore* 9 (1971): 137–152; Berkowitz, "Ephraim Deinard: A Portrait," *Jewish Book Annual* 37 (1979–1980): 125–131; Myron M. Weinstein, "The First Deinard Collection of the Library of Congress," *Judaica Librarianship* 12 (2006): 31–48.

61. For a taste of Deinard's eccentric literary style, see Brad Sabin Hill's wonderful essay "Ephraim Deinard on the Shapira Affair," *The Book Collector: Special Issue* (1997), 167–179.

62. Alexander Marx, "Jewish Libraries in America," *Menorah Journal* 31 (Winter 1943): 1, 80; quoted in Berkowitz, "Ephraim Deinard: Bibliophile and Bookman," 137.

63. See Yosef Goldman, *Hebrew Printing in America, 1735–1926* (Brooklyn: YG Books, 2006), 1: 370–371, entries no. 407 (Baltunowka) and no. 408 (Sodom). For the translation of Baltunowka as "Chattertown," see http://en.wikipedia.org/wiki/Ephraim_Deinard.

64. Ephraim Deinard, *A History of the Jewish Settlement at Kearny-Arlington, N.J., Arukhat Bat 'Ami* (St. Louis, 1920), 17–18; cited in Berkowitz, "Ephraim Deinard: Bibliophile and Bookman," 17–18.

65. On Deinard, the Smithsonian, and the LOC, see in particular Grace Cohen Grossman, *Judaica at the Smithsonian: Cultural Politics as Cultural Model* (Washington, DC: Smithsonian Institution Press, 1997), Chap. 8, "The Ephraim Deinard Collection: A New Factor," 69–79.

66. Harry A. Wolfson, *Harvard Alumni Bulletin* (April 29, 1932), 7; cited in David Wilk, "Ephraim Deinard and the Establishment of Hebrew Judaica Collections in America's Libraries," *Proceedings of the 35th Annual Convention of the Association of Jewish Libraries* (2000), 124–125.

67. On Jefferson's Hebraic/Judaic collection as granted to the Library of Congress, see Abraham J. Karp, *From the Ends of the Earth: Judaic Treasures of the Library of Congress* (Washington, DC: Library of Congress, 1991), 1–9.

68. Letter from Deinard to Putnam, October 5, 1909, quoted in Weinstein, "The First Deinard Collection," 36. As Weinstein notes, an equally important factor in Deinard's decision to reapproach the Library of Congress was the fact that Cyrus Adler, who had opposed the earlier attempt by Deinard, had by this time left the Smithsonian for Dropsie.

69. Letter from Putnam to Schiff, April 1, 1912, quoted in Weinstein, ibid., 38–39.

70. Weinstein, 6–7. As Weinstein notes, the bookplate in the Washington Haggadah is also not the correct one for either of the Schiff donations. For the difference between the bookplates used for the 1912 and 1914 purchases, and those used for the 1916 and 1919 ones, see Hamburg, 191, note 9.

71. I wish to thank Katrin Kogman-Appel, Sarit Shalev-Eyni, Kathryn Hellerstein, and the anonymous reader for Harvard University Press for reading earlier versions of the essay and making many valuable corrections and suggestions for revision.

The Illustrations of the Washington Haggadah

KATRIN KOGMAN-APPEL

> The work was completed, and it is sufficient. And today is the twenty-fifth day of the month of Shevat in the year 238 according to the short enumeration. The word of the least of the scribes, Joel, the son of Simeon of blessed memory.

This signature appears at the end of the Washington Haggadah whose facsimile is contained in this volume. It informs us that it was written in 1478 by Joel ben Simeon, a scribe and artist fairly well known to students of medieval Hebrew book production. In another colophon, in the so-called London Haggadah of c. 1460, we read:

> My heart counsels how to reply to him who asks and says, "Who painted these [pages]?" I shall answer him: "I am he, Feibush, called Joel, for Jacob Mattathiah, may he live long, the son of MHRZ, a pious man."[1]

Even though Joel says nothing about painting in the Washington colophon, his hand is easily recognizable in the style and layout of the small drawings on the margins of the text, which can be compared to that of other books associated with him.[2]

Who is this man, Joel ben Simeon, who completed the Washington

Haggadah on January 29, 1478? Although scribal signatures are not rare in medieval Hebrew manuscripts, it was quite uncommon to sign a haggadah. Joel, who signed several more manuscripts as scribe, must thus have been a man of well-defined professional identity. Yet more unusual is the fact that he left signatures stating explicitly that he illustrated books in whose production he was involved.

Joel ben Simeon left sufficient traces for modern scholars to attempt a reconstruction of his professional biography. This can rarely be done for medieval craftsmen, most of whom remain anonymous to the modern reader and viewer. In 1454, while already residing in Italy, Joel noted in the colophon of a manuscript now in New York (the Second JTS Haggadah) that he originated from Cologne.[3] Born around 1420, he must have been a young child when he experienced the expulsion of the Jews from that town in October 1424. In another colophon in a prayerbook now in Parma (Parma Siddur), dated 1449, however, he indicates that he was from Bonn. It is thus quite likely that after the expulsion from Cologne he spent some time in nearby Bonn. It is here that he may have made his first steps into the profession. Scholars also speculate that prior to his move to Italy he may have spent some time in Moravia, Swabia, or in the Upper Rhine region.[4]

During this early period of his career he produced two manuscripts: the so-called First Nuremberg Haggadah (Fig. 1) and the First JTS Haggadah. From the colophons we know that he wrote both these haggadot, and it is assumed that he also executed the drawings. Unfortunately, both manuscripts were badly trimmed and thus our knowledge of his artistic work from this period is limited.

It is possible that around 1445 Joel was for the second time in his life expelled from the town of his residence, this time Bonn. In 1449 he signed the Parma Siddur, perhaps already in Italy.[5] In any event, in 1452 at the latest, he can be traced to Italy, where he signed a Mahzor (prayerbook) in Cremona. He was now a young professional who, like

אותנו גאל עמהם שנ׳ ואותנו הוציא משם
למען הביא אותנו אל הארץ אשר נשבע
לאבותינו:

וכל אחד ואחד ירים
הכוס שלו ויאמר:
לפיכך בקול רם:

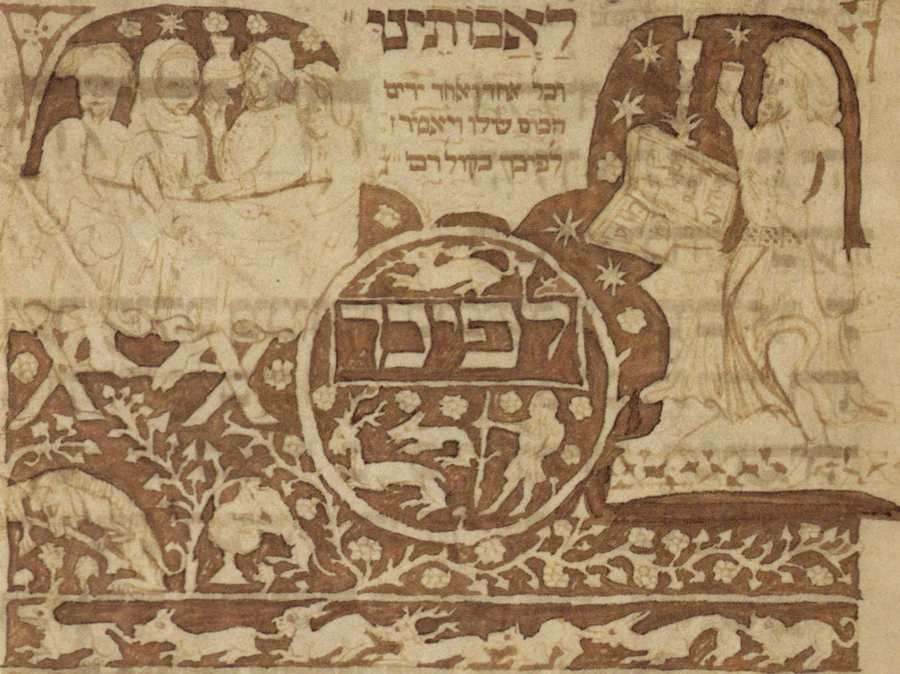

לפיכך

אנחנו חייבין להודות להלל לשבח
לפאר לרומם להדר לברך לעלה
ולקלס למי שעשה נסים לאבותינו ולנו
את כל הנסים האלו הוציאנו מעבדות
לחרות מיגון לשמחה ומאבל ליום
טוב

many of his Ashkenazi coreligionists, had decided to try his luck farther south, to cross the Alps, and to settle in Italy. For a young Jew who had grown up in the German lands facing the threat of persecution and expulsion, northern Italy seemed like the perfect alternative. In contrast to Central Europe, where Jews were often expelled or suffered constant harassment, violent persecution, and forced baptism, early-modern Italy facilitated acculturation and cultural exchange.

Whereas in Sicily and Rome Jews had lived continuously since the Roman period, only an occasional Jewish presence can be observed in northern Italy before the second half of the thirteenth century. This situation began to change rapidly in the later years of the century, when northern Italy became a preferred destination for immigrants, not only from the south, but also from France, whence the Jews had been expelled several times throughout the fourteenth century. Since approximately 1350 an increased immigration of Jews can also be observed from southern Germany. During this period the cities of northern Italy enjoyed a time of expansion and economic development. Jewish physicians and bankers played an important role in those years of growth. The Jewish population increased significantly. Interaction between Jews and Christians, in particular on a financial basis, was frequent and natural.

Tension resulting from religious animosity and economic competition was milder in Italy than in other countries. Occasional anti-Jewish acts did occur during this early period of Jewish settlement in the north, but they did not attain the same degree of vigor as in contemporary Germany and Spain. Outbursts of violence increased during the fif-

1. *Lefikhakh.* First Nuremberg Haggadah, Jerusalem, Israel Museum, MS 181/60, formerly Schocken Library, MS 24086, southern Germany, c. 1440, fol. 14r. (Copyright © Israel Museum, Jerusalem)

teenth century, especially in the second half, usually in response to public sermons by mendicant preachers. The deterioration of the Jewish conditions of life that had been taking place in the German lands for more than three centuries began to affect the Jews of Italy only relatively late and not with the same intensity.[6] Despite such early signs of a changing Christian attitude toward the Jewish population, northern Italy was still a place where a young Jewish professional of the book trade could hope for additional artistic training, a wealthy clientele, and an atmosphere that, in comparison to what he had seen in the Rhineland, was open-minded, seemed promising in terms of personal security, and could enable his professional development.

Only a few of Joel's Italian colophons mention places, and it is quite clear that he did not settle anywhere for long, but rather continued to move, seeking work in various locations. From the sharp change in style observable in his subsequent work, including the Washington Haggadah, it becomes clear that in all likelihood he did receive some training after arriving in Italy. His figures became securely drawn and realistically proportioned, and they display delicate facial traits. They are dressed in the fashion of early-modern Italy, wearing short colorful coats or long luxurious mantles, elaborate headgear, berets, and pointed hats (see, for example, fols. 16r and 17r). His approach to perspective reflects the trend of Italian art, even though issues of perspective would never play the same role as they did in Italian (manuscript) painting. A love for realistic detail can now be observed in his work: some of his figures suffer from goiters (fol. 14v); the young man stirring the fire uses a pair of bellows (fol. 1r); and a dog in the kitchen scene hopes for leftovers (fol. 14v).

After some training in drawing and painting, then, Joel ben Simeon began to produce new work. Later he would return to Germany at least twice and take part in the creation of at least two manuscripts: the

London Haggadah in c. 1460, and the Washington Haggadah in 1478.[7] Between these periods and after 1478 he went back to Italy, where he died apparently at some time around 1492. One of the high points of his work is a prayerbook he made in 1469 for Menahem ben Samuel and his daughter, "the honored and learned, the pleasant virgin Lady Maraviglia." Other manuscripts lack a colophon, but their decoration is attributed to Joel in full or in part on the grounds of stylistic observations. Among these we can count a haggadah from c. 1470 now in Stuttgart; the so-called Rothschild-Weill Mahzor of approximately the same period, now in the National Library of Israel; the Rothschild Mahzor, produced in Florence in 1492 by the scribe Abraham Judah ben Yehiel of Camerino and a large team of artists, Joel among them; and the Moskowitz Mahzor in Jerusalem, dated around the same time.[8]

The Washington Haggadah thus reflects Joel's work at the peak of his career. By the time he signed it, he was a mature scribe and artist who had traveled between cultures. In his migrations between the two regions Joel was in a sense an agent of cultural exchange, importing elements of Ashkenazi haggadah illustration into Italy and taking back stylistic devices acquired in the region south of the Alps. During these years he developed a highly personal repertoire of haggadah motifs and an iconographic program that recurs in several variations.

The Manuscript and Its Decoration

Like most other medieval Passover manuscripts, the Washington Haggadah in the Hebraic Section of the Library of Congress is a small, thin book (9.3 x 6.25 in.). It consists of thirty-eight parchment folios bound in five gatherings. Its text version, as already demonstrated in David Stern's essay, follows the Ashkenazi rite, which was common not only in the German lands during the second half of the fifteenth century but also among Ashkenazi immigrants in northern Italy, including Joel ben Simeon himself. Scholars have observed, however, that the particular type of parchment used for the production of the Washington Haggadah is found almost exclusively in the German lands, whereas Ashkenazi scribes and patrons in Italy used local parchment of a different type. This indicates that by 1478 Joel was back in some area north of the Alps and that the Washington Haggadah was produced there. This can be supported by the observation that Joel normally used Italian parchment while working in Italy.[9] Moreover, in Italy he occasionally notes in his signatures that he is "from Ashkenaz," an addition that—superfluous in Ashkenaz itself—is not found in the Washington Haggadah.

The Washington codex contains ten painted initial panels and fifteen colored drawings in the margins. The former follow a recurring pattern of initial letters written in gold and floral design on a blue background framed in gold (fols. 1r and 3v, for example). Pen flourishings usually extend from the frame to the outer margins. The text on each page leaves ample margins for the drawings. Originally these margins were still broader; they were trimmed during later rebinding. These marginal drawings, executed in brown ink with a thin pen, were colored in a somewhat richer palette than the initial decorations. Joel commonly mixed his colors and used a rather sophisticated technique of superimposed layers of color, highlighting in white or yellow, and shading in brown and purple to produce volume.

The series of marginal illustrations begins on fol. 1r with two images that depict the search for leaven and the burning of the final leftovers of leaven found in the house. On the left a man is shown scrutinizing a cupboard, while on the right a youth is using a pair of bellows to stir a fire. Several other images follow a similar approach: a man pouring wine illustrates the text, "In what ways is this night different from all other nights?" on fol. 4r; two women and a man are busying themselves with the preparation of the meal as an illustration to the *dayenu* prayer on fol. 14v, as a reminder that the time has come to get the meal ready; a somewhat grotesque monkey seated on a red cushion holds a *matsah* on fol. 15v; on the following page an apparently unhappy couple represents the *maror*, the bitter herbs, and by extension the bitter life in Egypt; a luxuriously dressed man raises a cup illustrating the text, "Therefore, we are obligated to thank, acclaim, and praise," on fol. 17r.

As in all other haggadot made by Joel ben Simeon, the questions of the four sons are illustrated by four figures, each representing a certain social type (fols. 5v–6r): the wise son is shown as a seated scholar with an open book; the wicked son as a knight; the simple son as a man in a somewhat worn cloak seated on the floor; and the fourth son, "who does not know how to ask," as a jester. An elaborate composition illustrates the text, "Pour out Your fury on the nations that do not know You," on fol. 19v. Joel left a particularly large margin at the base of this page to allow sufficient space for the image. It shows a castle-like structure on the left with a youth peeking through the door and inviting Elijah (or the Messiah?), who, riding a donkey, approaches from the right. He is accompanied by an entire family seated behind him on the donkey's rear. The last image of this series, on fol. 30r, shows Daniel in the lion's den as an illustration to the poem, "Then You performed many miracles at night," or rather specifically the sentence, "the one who was saved from the lion's den solves the frights of night."

Since his early work in the German lands Joel ben Simeon had taken a liking to verbal puns, expressions from the text translated literally into a visual language. Such visual references to verbal expressions are also quite common in Christian manuscript illumination, especially in Latin psalters. However, whereas the latter tend to be quite sophisticated links to adjacent text portions, those applied by Joel seem to be more naïve, catchy references, often to just one or two words, occasionally to a short verse. A typical example appears on fol. 7v near the text, "Go forth and learn what Laban the Aramean sought to do to our ancestor, Jacob." The marginal illustration shows a man in traveling gear: a short mantle, a *chaperon*—a hood covering the head and neck—a rather high hat with a feather, leggings, and high boots. Over his shoulders he carries a lance, a water container, and a bag. Emphasizing the act of "going forth," he moves forward energetically on a small piece of green land. On fol. 22r the text of the *halel* reads, "in distress I called on God." The word "distress"—*matsor*—can also be understood as "siege," and the verse would read, "From the siege I called on God." Joel drew a walled town with a large tower, in whose window the face of an imprisoned man—David, the author of the psalm—can be discerned.

On the whole, the manuscript is well preserved. All the pages are still extant and most of the miniatures are fully legible in detail. Most of the colors survived unchanged; some, however, have reacted to age and environmental circumstances. One such color is verdigris, a shade of green made from copper patina. It is very stable when used with oil but less so in the media commonly employed in manuscript painting, gouache or watercolor. When no varnish is applied this color tends to flake off, as can be observed in the Washington Haggadah at several points (see, for example, fol. 1r, the hat of the figure on the right). The green color was particularly vulnerable at the corners of pages, which would be frequently touched in reading (for example, fol. 3v, lower right). Joel used other green hues as well, mixing blue and yellow. The blue color also tends to flake off where cohesion of the color to the parchment has been affected, and occasionally only a thin layer of blue remains. Because of the yellowish color of the parchment such layers now look green (see, for example, fol. 4r, the cup held by the man pouring the wine). Some facial details were painted in white produced from lead. Like colors that contain silver, those with lead tend to blacken as a result of oxidation (see, for example, fol. 5v, at the noses of both figures, or fol. 7v).

Haggadot are read during the Passover meal when a variety of dishes and wine are consumed, and occasional traces of food and wine can still be found on the pages. On some folios of the Washington Haggadah there are signs that the ink became wet, causing imprints on the opposite page when the book was closed. This is the case on fol. 16v, where traces of red ink from the initial word *lefikhakh* on fol. 17r can be seen (see also fols. 24v and 25r; 27v and 28r). On fol. 2r the red ink of the initials *wayekhullu* at the top and *barukh* at the foot appears to have been smeared, apparently after the page got wet and a careless hand accidentally rubbed it.

Parchment was made from the skin of young animals. Owing to local production methods, Ashkenazi parchment tends to be extremely thin. Not only are the corners of the parchment pages somewhat worn off with handling, but occasionally the illuminations shine through and are visible on the other side of the thin folio (see especially, for example, fols. 4r–4v). During the production process, flesh and hair residues are scraped off the skin. Ashkenazi parchment was scraped to such an extent that the hairy and fleshy sides of the folios are no longer distinguishable, and hair follicles can occasionally be observed on both sides. This process made Ashkenazi parchment rather darker and harder than the Sephardic type, which, while thicker, is significantly softer and brighter. On some pages, finally, we can see where the ink has eaten through the parchment, leaving holes more or less in the shape of the letters (see, for example, fol. 2r, the first line, or fol. 9v, the second line from the end).

Despite its flaking colors and oxidizing lead white, the Washington Haggadah still offers insight into the life of a wealthy Jewish family in late medieval southern Germany. We can easily imagine the family gathered around the table passing food and wine. The "master of the household," as he is often referred to in medieval texts, holds the book, recites from it, explains the text to the young members of the family, and shows around the images.

An Artist between the Cultures

Joel ben Simeon was active in an age of tremendous economic, social, and cultural change. Traveling between southern Germany and northern Italy, he lived between two cultures, each quite different from the other. His artistic profession also provided him with the ability to look beyond the borders of his own minority culture and to familiarize himself with the artistic fashions of the Christian environment. In recent decades cultural historians have given much thought to the phenomenon of cultural exchange among the different religious communities in medieval Europe. Abandoning the notion of earlier anthropologists that acculturation of minorities (or immigrants) in modern societies was (and is) merely a matter of cultural diffusion, since the 1960s scholarship has developed different models to help us better understand the specifics of acculturation.

Acculturation and cultural exchange take place when elements from one culture are transmitted to another, whereas assimilation involves the integration of a minority into the majority's social system. These processes occur whenever two cultures come into contact, and a whole range of different cultural, political, and social circumstances determine their dynamics and the degree to which they happen. Moreover, the transmission of cultural goods from one society to another is a continuing and dynamic process. Scholars are now aware that cultural interaction exists even between conflicting societies. It would thus appear that Ashkenazi culture was less isolated than was once assumed.[10]

A number of factors determines which of the cultural goods transmitted will be adopted by another culture. The process is also determined by the people engaged in the making of culture repertoires, who can be referred to as "cultural agents": scholars, writers, artists, and patrons with their various tastes and fashions.[11] Joel ben Simeon undoubtedly functioned as such a "cultural agent," adopting elements of early-modern Italian art and transmitting them to Ashkenazi culture during his repeated returns to the German lands.

At the time that Joel made his first attempts at decorating a manuscript there was already a fairly well established tradition of haggadah illustration in Ashkenaz, a field that was to become his expertise. While still living in the Rhineland, he had received training as a scribe; whether he also had some formal training in the arts, however, is another matter. His drawings are rather crudely executed, but he certainly knew the Ashkenazi repertoire of motifs. He may also have developed some themes of his own devising. Given that our knowledge of the Ashkenazi haggadah tradition and of Joel's two trimmed manuscripts from this phase of his career is only partial, it is hard to say to what extent he was innovative.

The scanty remains on the trimmed margins of the First Nuremberg and the First JTS Haggadot suggest that Joel decorated his text with images of men raising cups of wine (Fig. 1); depictions of a family seder table; portraits of the rabbis mentioned in the text of the haggadah; references to the erection of the Egyptian treasure cities—shown as typical medieval towns whose roofs are still discernable in the First JTS Haggadah—and the bondage of the Israelites. A man appears in the First Nuremberg Haggadah near the text that mentions the *maror*, and we can assume that he held a bundle of bitter herbs in what can be defined as typical Ashkenazi iconography. This is in clear contrast to most Sephardic parallels, which tend, instead, to show a large decorative vegetable in the shape of an artichoke, normally not held by any figure. Similarly, the *matsah* is shown in Iberia as a huge decorative disc, whereas Ashkenazi haggadot display a realistic *matsah* in the hand of a man. Most likely such a figure appeared also in Joel's haggadot. The text of *Shefokh Hamatkha* (Pour out Your fury) in the First JTS Haggadah is illustrated by a man riding a donkey in a somewhat simpler version than its counterpart in the Washington Haggadah. Since all these motifs are known from earlier haggadah illustration, it can be inferred that Joel knew this tradition well and made wide use of it.[12]

As noted, Joel ben Simeon also developed some motifs of his own. We have seen that he particularly enjoyed the use of verbal puns. He produced several such puns already in both the First Nuremberg and the First JTS Haggadah. The latter preserves an early version of the young traveler to illustrate the verse, "Go forth and learn"; in subsequent years, this figure would become a kind of trademark of Joel's iconography. Near the verse *behatsi halailah* ("In the middle of the night") in the First Nuremberg Haggadah he added the image of a man fast asleep in his bed; and near the mention of the hand of God—*ta'oz yado* ("May Your hand be strong") in the First JTS Haggadah we find a little drawing of a hand. Another such pun appeared near the text, "Out of the straits I called the Lord," in the First JTS Haggadah. The margins are trimmed, but the traces of a building with a flag are still visible. A look at fol. 22r of the Washington Haggadah suggests that the JTS drawing may have shown a building, perhaps a tower, with an imprisoned David.

Joel's work is well embedded not only in the tradition of haggadah illustration but also in the more general visual culture of the German lands. For example, a typical feature of southern German illuminated books of the late medieval period is the almost exclusive preference for marginal illustration. The popularity of unframed, quickly drawn marginal pictures is a by-product of social shifts, changes in reading practices, and the resulting developments in the book trade. Such drawings began to appear in the late thirteenth and fourteenth centuries in secular manuscripts, and they were particularly popular in the German lands. They replaced the carefully executed gouache paintings typical of lavish illuminated manuscripts of the early and high Middle Ages. Whereas during the earlier Middle Ages the haggadah formed part of the general prayerbook, at some time during the thirteenth century it began to circulate as a separate entity. A small, thin, and handy book, it soon became popular in wide circles of Jewish society beyond the upper classes, making it suitable for new, simpler methods of production. Quite naturally, when the first haggadot were made around the same period, the practice of unframed marginal illustration was also adopted in this field. The custom spread beyond Ashkenaz and is found in Italy as well.

Another characteristic typical of late medieval German book art is the design of numerous small figures, animals and other motifs, in the color of the parchment against a background of brownish ink. This technique was popular in the German lands in both Jewish and Christian books throughout the fourteenth and most of the fifteenth centuries, but rarely used elsewhere. The initial panels of the First Nuremberg Haggadah (Fig. 1) contain a variety of hunting motifs and other decorations in this popular technique.

Toward the middle of the century Joel ben Simeon set out to cross the Alps for the first time. Four haggadot associated in some way or another with Joel have come down to us from his early years in Italy. Only one of them, the Second JTS Haggadah, is dated; it was signed by Joel in 1454, and states explicitly that Joel not only wrote and vocalized but also decorated the manuscript. Another signed haggadah is kept in the Bodmer Collection in Cologny, Switzerland (Bodmer Haggadah). Another, unsigned copy, usually referred to as the Rothschild or Murphy Haggadah, is now in the National Library of Israel and can be accessed on the Internet (http://jnul.huji.ac.il/dl/mss/heb6130/index_

eng.html). The last of the four manuscripts is housed in Parma (Parma Haggadah). The changes in style discussed above are easily observable in all four manuscripts.

Joel was now confronted with a somewhat different tradition of haggadah illustration, which had some roots in Iberian Jewish art. An Ashkenazi repertoire of motifs was here occasionally combined with Sephardic elements. Unfortunately, very few Italian haggadot survive, and the local tradition seems not to have been as rich as the one Joel had known north of the Alps.[13] Some of the Passover motifs that we encountered in Ashkenaz, such as the images of a man raising a cup and the family seder table, are universally employed and also appear in Iberia and Italy. Other elements distinctively different from the Ashkenazi pool of motifs originate in Sephardic haggadah illustration of the late thirteenth and early fourteenth centuries and were imported into Italy most likely by immigrants from Iberia. For example, most Italian renderings of the *matsah* and the *maror* follow the Sephardic model, showing the former as a decorative disc rather than as realistic unleavenend bread. Joel, however, remained faithful to the Ashkenazi iconographic tradition and always used the Ashkenazi imagery of a man holding the *matsah* or the *maror* (Rothschild Haggadah, fols. 20v and 21r). Interestingly, this applies not only to haggadot of the Ashkenazi rite intended for Ashkenazi immigrant patrons but also to the Bodmer and Second JTS Haggadot belonging to the Italian rite.

Joel did, however, also borrow some imagery that, at least from what we can see in the surviving material, was hitherto uncommon in Ashkenaz. For example, he seems to have elaborated on the four sons, an imagery that would become one of the most popular features of haggadah illustration. Although the four sons are occasionally found in earlier Ashkenazi examples, it appears that Joel followed the Sephardic and Italian models that he had come to know after his immigration (Rothschild Haggadah, fols. 4v–6r). He adopted and adapted them, adding new motifs to the iconography, such as the attributes of the jester representing the fourth son. I shall come back to these figures in more detail in the concluding section of this introduction. The motif of raising an enormous seder plate also now appears in his books (Rothschild Haggadah, fol. 2v); very likely he had seen it in an Italian manuscript.

He also introduced illustrations of the search for leaven. Images of the family cleaning the house before the Passover while the man performs the search for leaven appear first in Sephardic haggadot (Fig. 2), of which two examples still survive.[14] These images are more elaborate and show a full composition of an interior setting. Joel reduced the Sephardic rendering to a small image of a man in front of a perspectively drawn cupboard with the doors of the upper section open. The man holds a candle, a bowl, and a feather and performs the search (for a later version of this motif see fol. 1r in the Washington Haggadah). Other examples are new verbal puns, which Joel had encountered in Italian haggadot. The verse *beyad netuyah* ("with an outstretched arm") shows a raised hand holding a sword (Rothschild Haggadah, fol. 13v). The verse *erom ve'eryah* ("you were still naked and bare," Ez. 16:7) is accompanied in the Rothschild Haggadah (fol. 10r) by the image of a naked woman—undoubtedly an idea that Joel developed by looking at early-modern art in Italy. This pun occurs earlier in the Schocken Haggadah, an Ashkenazi haggadah produced around 1400 in Lombardy, which shows a naked man rather than a naked woman.[15]

The art of these manuscripts swarms with lively images taken from everyday observation of society: the busy building scenes in the treasure cities (Rothschild Haggadah, fol. 10v); the water-carriers meant to show Israelites in bondage, but depicting workers in a fifteenth-century Italian city (Rothschild Haggadah, fol. 2v); the four sons, each representing a different social type (Rothschild Haggadah, fols. 4v–6r); the cleaning of the cupboard, apparently a typical Italian piece of furniture. Even though these images with their graphic quality of somewhat flat

ותקח מרים הנביאה אחות אהרן את התף בידה

בעל הבית מצוה לחלק מצות וחרוסת לתינוקות

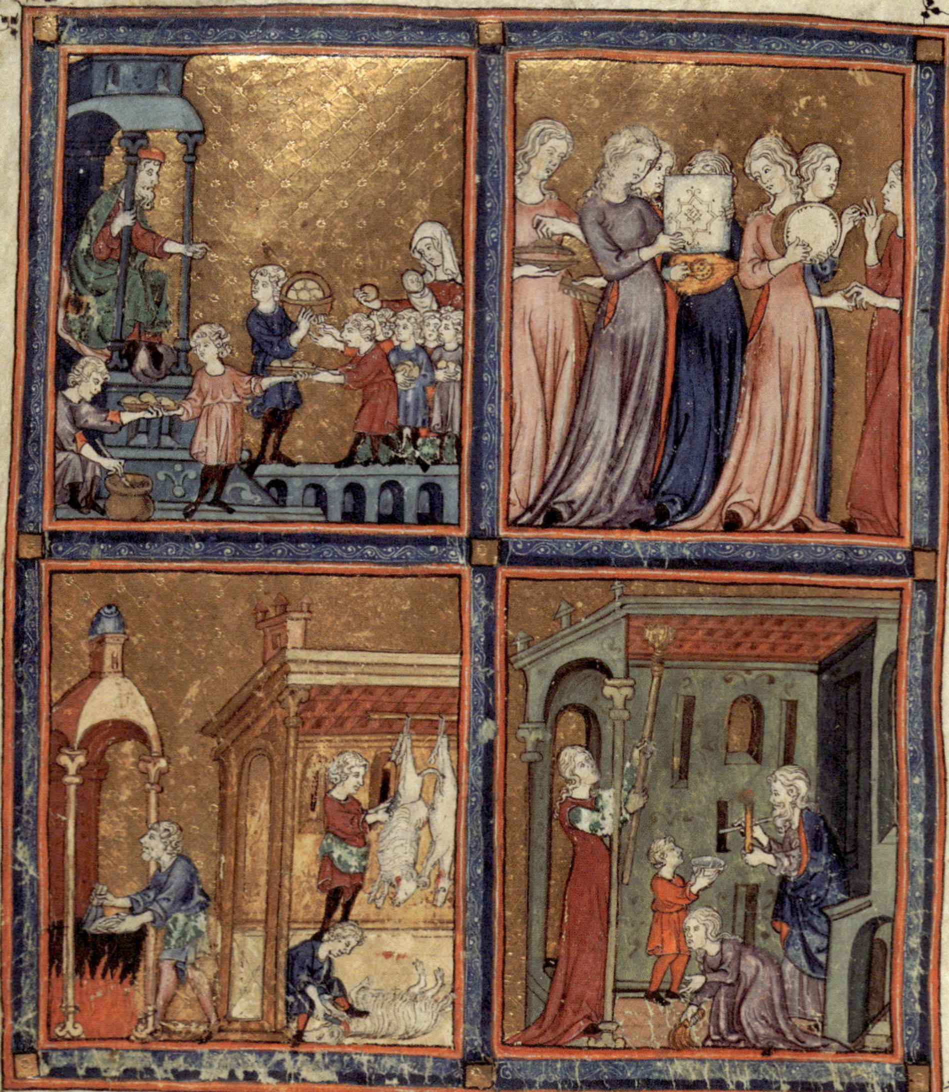

בודק את החמץ לאור הנר

[illegible]

מתקנין צרכי הפסח

drawings preserve some characteristics of southern German book art of the time, the keen observations of everyday life are indebted to the realistic style of early-modern art in Italy that Joel now confronted.

To this we can add another of Joel's icongraphic developments of these years, an elaborate composition of the thematic high point of the haggadah, the Crossing of the Red Sea, spread over a double page (Rothschild Haggadah, fols. 32v–33r). On the right-hand page a massed Egyptian army approaches. On the left folio Moses follows the column of fire leading the Israelites safely through the waters. The idea of showing the Crossing on one page while the Egyptian army pursues on the preceding (opposite) page is not new, and we know similar versions from earlier Ashkenazi manuscripts (Fig. 3). Joel enriched the iconography with innovative pictorial details. More striking, however, is the spatial representation of the two crowds of people reaching relatively deep into the picture space. Earlier Ashkenazi work had known nothing of the kind. Old Testament illustration has a long tradition in Italy, dating back to the early Christian period when the churches of Rome were decorated with elaborate narrative cycles of the history of the Israelites. The Crossing of the Red Sea figures prominently in this tradition. Cosimo Roselli's composition of the Red Sea scenario in the Sistine Chapel from c. 1480 is a good example (see Fig. 4). It postdates Joel's work but gives us a sense of how fifteenth-century Italian artists would have approached the subject. Although in the details of his figure style Joel never fully acquired early-modern Italian perspective and three-dimensional articulation, his organization of the picture space, as in this image, is indebted to Italian art to a rather high degree.

2. Cleaning the House of Leaven. Golden Haggadah, London, British Library, MS Add. 27210, Barcelona (?), c. 1320, fol. 15r. (Copyright © British Library Board)

73.

אור ישע

מאושרים

ימוור זה מוכשרים	ש	
שיר השירים		אהודנו כי דודיו כשרים
יחלוח עיזה שוקקות	ל	איילת אוהבי השוקות
ישקני מנשיקות		אספי שבע להשקות
ושלי גנוכי מבמניך	מ	רוכי מעלמיה משמניך
לריח שמניך		בשמהב המדריך כממניך
נב חור שחריך	ה	בני ביתך והודיך
משכני אחריך		ביה מדין יעחדיך

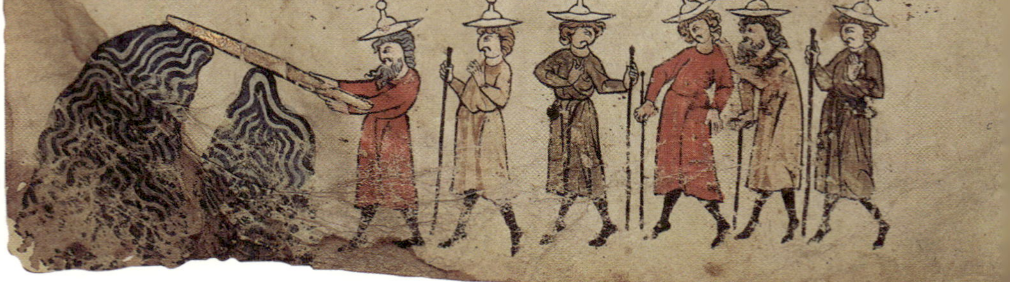

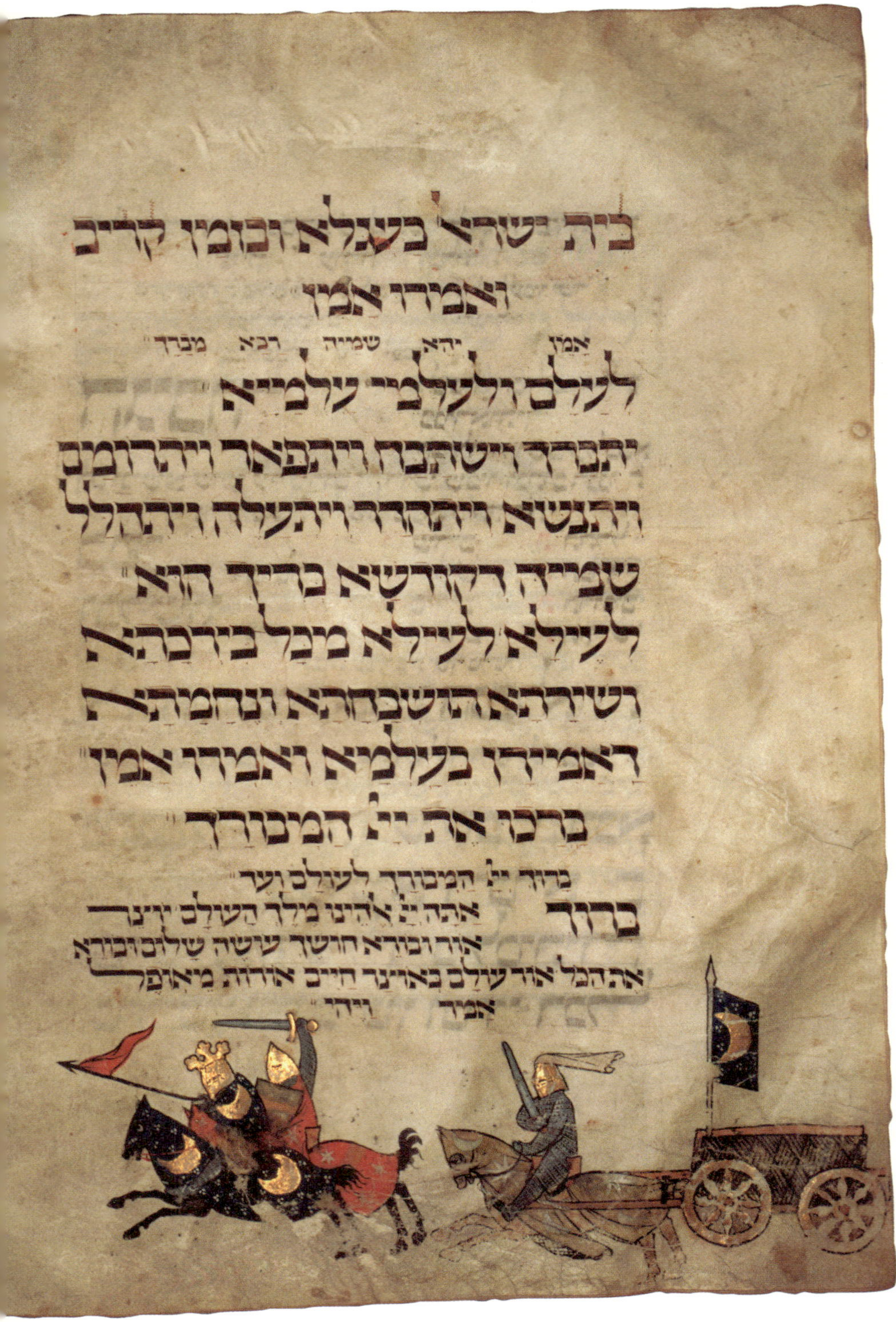

3. Israel Crossing the Red Sea. Leipzig Mahzor, Leipzig, Universitätsbibliothek, MS V 1002/I, Worms, c. 1310, fol. 72v–73r.

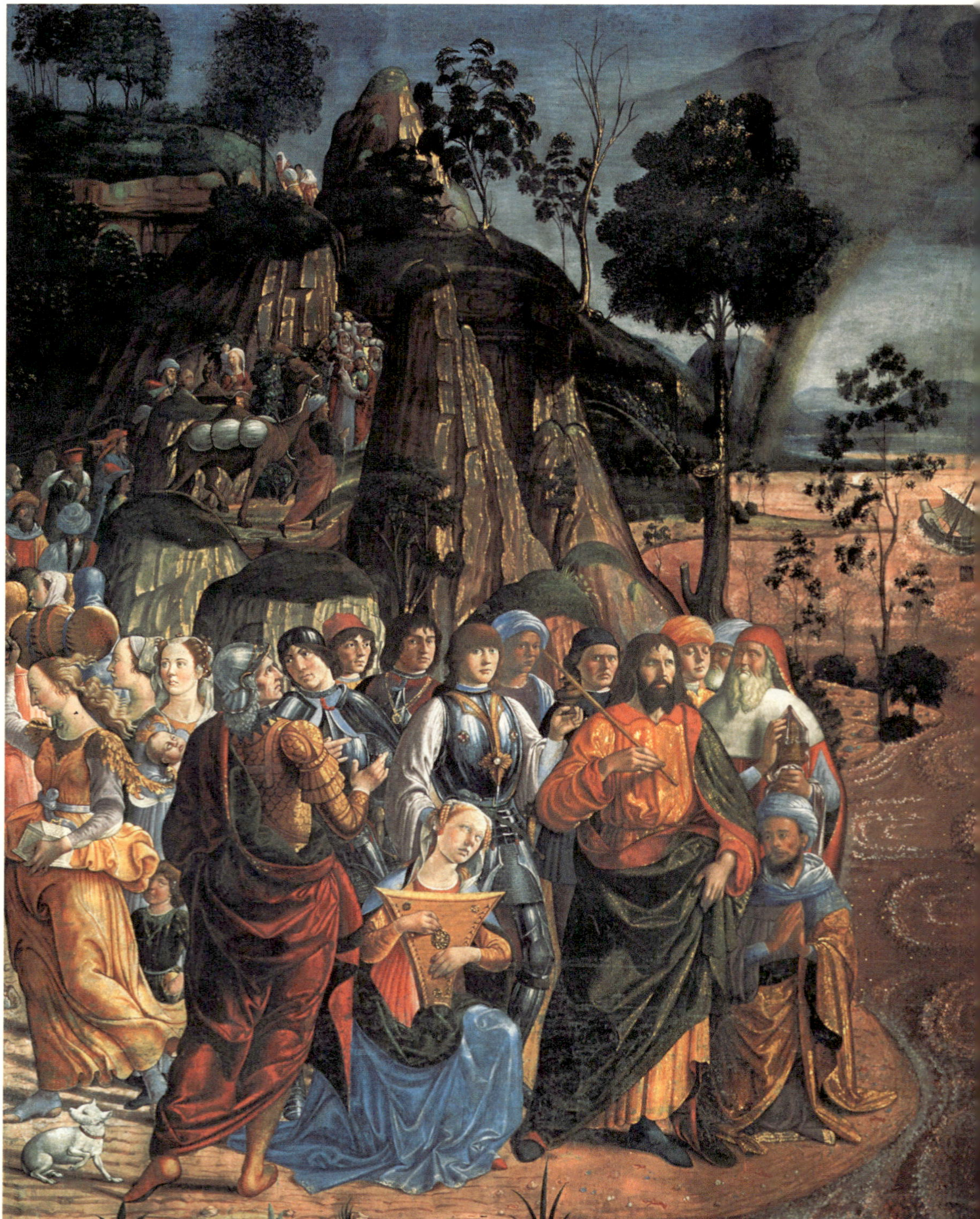

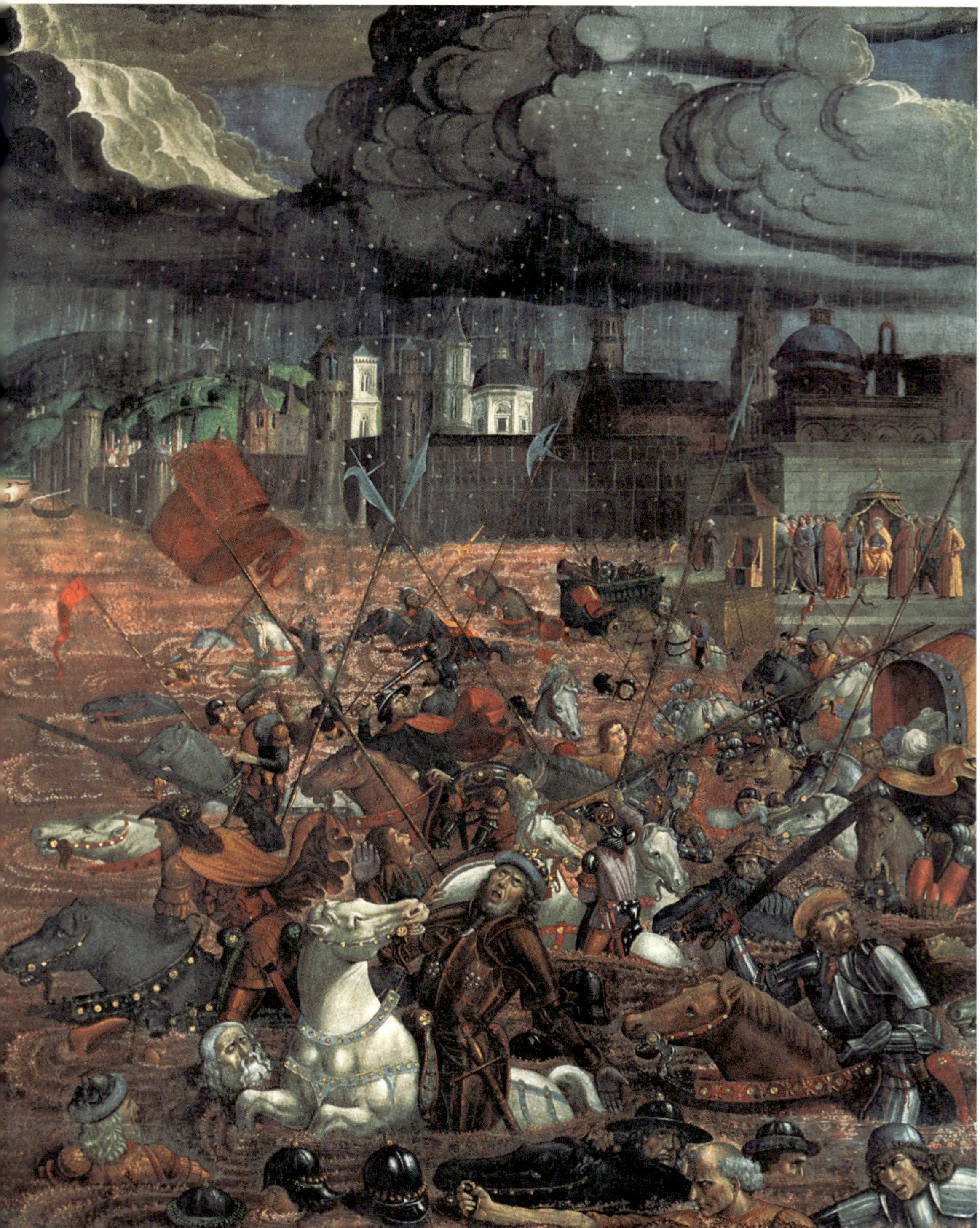

4. Israel Crossing the Red Sea. Cosimo Rosselli (1439–1507), fresco, Sistine Chapel, Vatican Palace, Vatican State, c. 1480. (Copyright © Scala/Art Resource, N.Y.)

In this group of haggadot from the 1450s Joel developed his basic approach to the genre. The later haggadot, the Washington manuscript among them, are variations of this basic program. Around 1460 Joel moved back to Germany and introduced some of his new repertoire there. The London Haggadah is a product of this stage in his career. The script has been recognized as that of Meir Jaffe, a scribe and bookbinder in Ulm.[16] In a colophon Joel ben Simeon states, as we have seen at the beginning of this chapter, that he *painted* the haggadah for a patron by the name of Jacob Mattathiah. Several of the marginal illustrations indeed bear the imprint of Joel's art. Others, especially at the beginning of the manuscript, are different in style, and it has been suggested that they are the work of Johannes Bämler, a southern German publisher of manuscripts and printed books between the 1450s and 1475.[17] Some scholars maintain that the London Haggadah was completed by Bämler at some later stage, perhaps after Joel had left again. The fact that traces of his work are found primarily at the beginning of the book suggests, however, that he did not compose the images but painted over earlier drawings by Joel ben Simeon. Perhaps the patron wanted the modestly colored drawings replaced by fully painted, more lavish miniatures. Another possibility is that the haggadah needed repair after some years of use. If so, the iconographic program of the London Haggadah reflects Joel's work.

By means of the London Haggadah some Italian motifs found their way into Ashkenaz. An example is the group of rabbis who discussed matters of Passover at Bnei Braq all night long until their students alerted them that it was time to say the morning prayers (Fig. 5). This motif was very common in fourteenth-century haggadot from Catalo-

5. Rabbis at Bnei Braq. London Haggadah, London, British Library, MS Add. 14762, Ulm, c. 1460, fol. 7v. (Copyright © British Library Board)

הקב״ה את אבותינו ממצרים
הרי אנו ובנינו ובני בנינו משעת
משעבדים היינו לפרעה במצ
במצרים ואפלו כלנו חכמים
כלנו נבונים כלנו זקנים כלנו
יודעים את התורה מצוה עלינו
לספר ביציאת מצרים והמספר
ביציאת מצרים הרי זה משובח׃
מעשה ברבי אליעזר
ור׳ יהושע ור׳ טרפון
ור׳ אלעזר בן עזריה
ור׳ עקיבא שהיו מסבין בבני

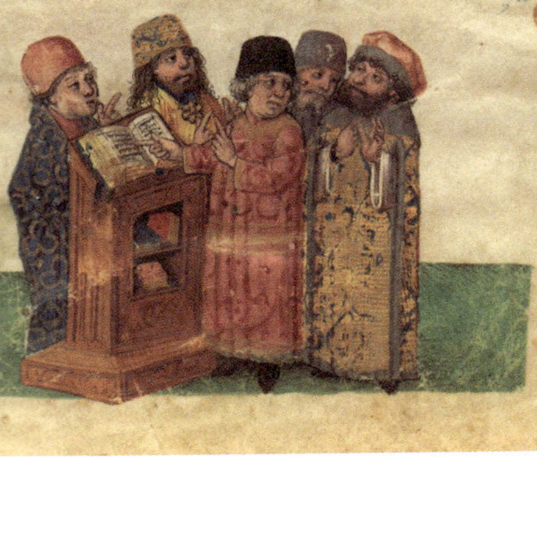

nia and Aragon, and may have been introduced in Italy by Sephardic immigrants. Earlier Ashkenazi haggadot and earlier works by Joel himself (the Rothschild Haggadah, fol. 3v) usually portrayed a single rabbi as illustration of this text. The London Haggadah also contains illustrations of the four sons (Fig. 6), the traveler for "go forth and learn," and a particularly elaborate composition of the Crossing of the Red Sea.

It is plausible that Joel was involved in still more projects while he was in Germany. Some of his motifs appear in Ashkenazi haggadah illustration shortly after 1460. Among them are a few that are not found in the London Haggadah but do appear elsewhere in Joel's work. Three Ashkenazi haggadot produced within a few years after Joel's sojourn in southern Germany have survived. They all show somewhat crude marginal drawings, to some degree recalling the style of early woodcuts. Two of them were probably made in Franconia around 1465. They are closely related and were done in the same workshop by a team that grasped the new needs of the book trade and issued copies of texts in an accelerated production process. One of these two, the so-called Second Nuremberg Haggadah, in the private collection of David Sofer in London, can now be seen on the website of the National Library of Israel (http://jnul.huji.ac.il/dl/mss-pr/mss_d_0076/). A similar manuscript of uncertain date and provenance is now kept in Paris and is often referred to as the Hileq and Bileq Haggadah.[18]

These manuscripts reveal a significant degree of familiarity with Joel's repertoire of haggadah motifs. Most strikingly, for example, the illustrator of the Second Nuremberg Haggadah reproduced the composition of the Crossing of the Red Sea (fols. 20v–21r) and translated the

6. Fool (fourth son of the Haggadah). London Haggadah, London, British Library, MS Add. 14762, Ulm, c. 1460, fol. 9v. (Copyright © British Library Board)

ממצרים לי ולא לו אלו היה
שם לא היה נגאל

תם מה הוא אומ'
מה זאת ואמרת
אליו בחוזק יד
הוציאנו יי' ממצרים מבית
עבדים

ושאינו יודע
לשאל את
פתח לו שנאמר והג'
והגדת לבנך ביום ההוא לא
לאמר בעבור זה עשה יי' לי
בצאתי ממצרים

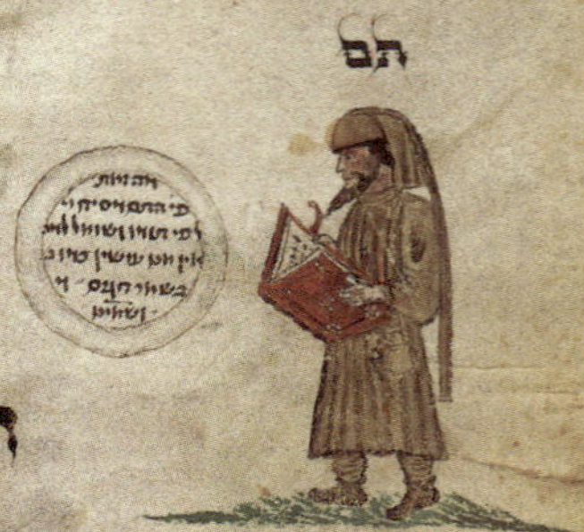

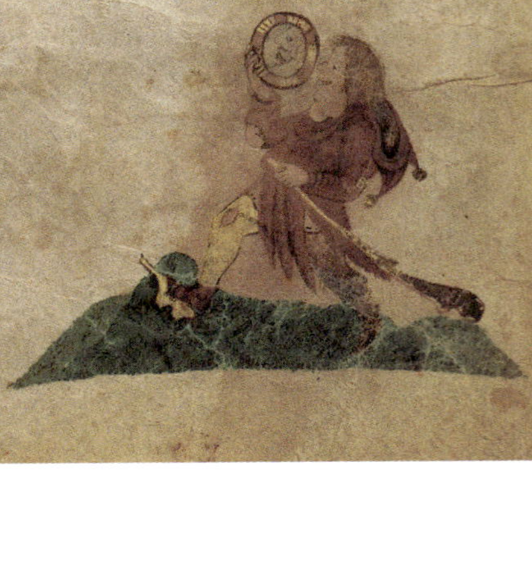

delicate visual language indebted to the Italian treatment of the picture space into a much plainer composition in significantly flatter articulation, still ensconced in the medieval tradition and typical for the graphic idiom of late medieval German book illustration.

This "translation" can also be observed in the cleaning scenes at the beginning of the three Ashkenazi haggadot. The search for leaven is part of a series of several more actions: women are involved in the cleaning; the cellars are searched; leaven is collected in a hermetically sealed container to be kept until it is burned; the last act is to burn the leaven (Second Nuremberg Haggadah, fols. 3r–v). This detailed representation, however, has no relation to any specifically realistic approach to illustration. The flat idiom of these little drawings, which turns the beautiful Italian Renaissance cupboard into a somewhat odd structure of undefined form, indicates the opposite. These added acts of cleaning seem, rather, to be a by-product of the halakhic approach found typically among Ashkenazi authorities. Halakhic codices of the time are very detailed and leave no questions open about preparing one's home for the holiday.

Several more of Joel's motifs can be observed in the Ashkenazi haggadot. In the Hileq and Bileq Haggadah the seder plate is raised in a manner recalling Joel's Italian works (Rothschild Haggadah, fol. 1v), and all three haggadot show numerous men drinking, introduced, it would seem, by Joel into the Ashkenazi repertoire and seen for the first time in the Rothschild Haggadah (fol. 1r). The water-carriers included in Joel's Italian haggadot as part of the depiction of the bondage in Egypt (Rothschild Haggadah, fol. 2v) figure in all three Ashkenazi haggadot, where they, on the contrary, carry water for the preparation of *matsot* (Second Nuremberg Haggadah, fol. 2r). The traveler so frequently met in Joel's haggadot (Rothschild Haggadah, fol. 8r) reappears in the Franconian haggadot translated into the figure of Moses on his way from Egypt to Midian (Second Nuremberg Haggadah, fol. 11v). It is also possible that it was Joel ben Simeon who introduced the full series of depictions of the Egyptian plagues to Ashkenazi haggadah illustration. Such series are known in the fourteenth century in the Sephardic haggadot, where they are part of the biblical miniature cycles at the beginning of the books. Both the Rothschild and the London Haggadot display the plagues in small vignettes in the margins of the text discussing the plagues (Rothschild Haggadah, fol. 14v). The three Ashkenazi haggadot translate these into unframed marginal drawings (Second Nuremberg Haggadah, fols. 15v–17v). In the earlier Ashkenazi tradition such full series of plagues do not occur.

Not all the motifs that Joel introduced into the Ashkenazi repertoire were fully adopted in local work. The naked beauty in the Rothschild Haggadah (fol. 10r) illustrating the phrase "you were still naked" was transformed in the London Haggadah into a skinny, elderly man. Depictions of naked women, even though occasionally found in Iberia, where Pharaoh's daughter's maidens are shown standing naked in the water rescuing the infant Moses, may not have been to the taste of Ashkenazi patrons. To the north of the Alps both the princess and her maidens remain dressed (Second Nuremberg Haggadah, fol. 8r), and perhaps that is why the man in the London manuscript replaces the naked woman of the Italian parallel. No other haggadah from the German lands ever added an image of a naked figure, female or male, to illustrate this particular text. Neither was nudity included in the Washington Haggadah.

In 1469 at the latest, Joel ben Simeon was back in Italy and signing Maraviglia's prayerbook. During the 1470s and 1480s he was involved in the production of several other manuscripts, noted above. At this stage Joel did not add much to his already well-established repertoire; in all these later works the whole range of figural motifs encountered in his earlier work is represented: the rabbis, the four sons, the workers in the bondage scenes, the traveler, and many more. The Rothschild-Weill Mahzor includes a particularly fine and elaborate example of the Red Sea composition.

The year 1478 found Joel back in Germany, where he delivered the Washington Haggadah. Although Joel did not reinvent the genre and used his established pool of motifs, it is clear that he recognized the specific needs and tastes of the potential Ashkenazi patron he had in mind when he made this manuscript. Whereas numerous motifs had appeared in his earlier Italian works, here there are some elements specific to the Ashkenazi realm.

We have seen, for example, that Ashkenazi illustrators tended to elaborate on the cleaning scenes. Whereas Italian haggadot show only the search of the cupboard, the Washington Haggadah, even though it does not contain the entire Ashkenazi scenario, has not only the search but also the burning of leaven (fol. 1r). The three Ashkenazi haggadot of the 1460s show scenes of cooking as an illustration to the *dayyenu* prayer (Second Nuremberg Haggadah, fol. 18r), a feature found also in the Washington Haggadah (fol. 14v).

The Hileq and Bileq Haggadah in Paris introduced an intriguing detail in the depiction of the *maror*, known earlier—even though rarely—only in Sephardic contexts. At the mention of the bitter herbs and the bitter fate in Egypt, a couple appears and the man points a finger at his wife. A variation of this motif recurs in a somewhat unusual manner in the Washington Haggadah (fol. 16r), where the man seems to be forcing the bitter herbs into his wife's mouth. As this motif was not common in Italy, Joel may have understood this detail as characteristic of Ashkenaz.

The most striking of the typically Ashkenazi features of the Washington Haggadah appears near the section *Shefokh Hamatkha*—"Pour out Your fury on the nations that have not known You," a selection of verses with curses against the Gentiles. The verses were added to the haggadah at some point in medieval Ashkenaz, perhaps after the First Crusade. They are recited immediately after the fourth cup of wine is poured and the door is opened to welcome the prophet Elijah. Israel Yuval has shown that the Ashkenazi perception of the messianic era implies that God will take vengeance on the persecuting Gentiles when the time comes.[19] The addition of "Pour out Your fury" is an expression of that perception. Sephardic and Italian patrons and artists did not really develop a typical iconography of the theme of God's fury and the messianic hopes associated with it. The Rothschild Haggadah (fol. 28r) has a man who raises a cup, referring laconically to the fourth cup to be poured just before reciting "Pour out Your fury."

In Ashkenaz, on the other hand, a specific imagery began to appear around the 1430s at the latest. Illustrations of these verses focus on messianic hopes and show Elijah approaching a house or the Messiah on a donkey escorted by the prophet proclaiming his arrival (Fig. 7). In several slightly later examples, including the Washington Haggadah, the figure on the donkey is accompanied by followers, some seated on the donkey behind the Messiah, and others seizing the donkey's tail. A sixteenth-century text written by a baptized Jew reports a Jewish folk belief about the coming of the Messiah: "According to the lies of the Jews, when the Messiah comes he will ride upon an ass and seat all the Jews upon the ass, while all the Christians will sit on the ass's tail. Then the Messiah will ride with all his passengers into the sea, and when he comes to the depths of the sea, the donkey will drop its tail and all the Christians will fall into the sea and drown. And indeed, this will have to be a very big ass. But an even bigger ass is a person who believes such things!"[20] Yuval identifies the last person in the Washington Haggadah, on the right, trying to hold onto the tail, as a Christian maidservant and suggests that the image refers to the belief about the Messiah riding into the sea.

In his early years Joel ben Simeon had already known the motif of

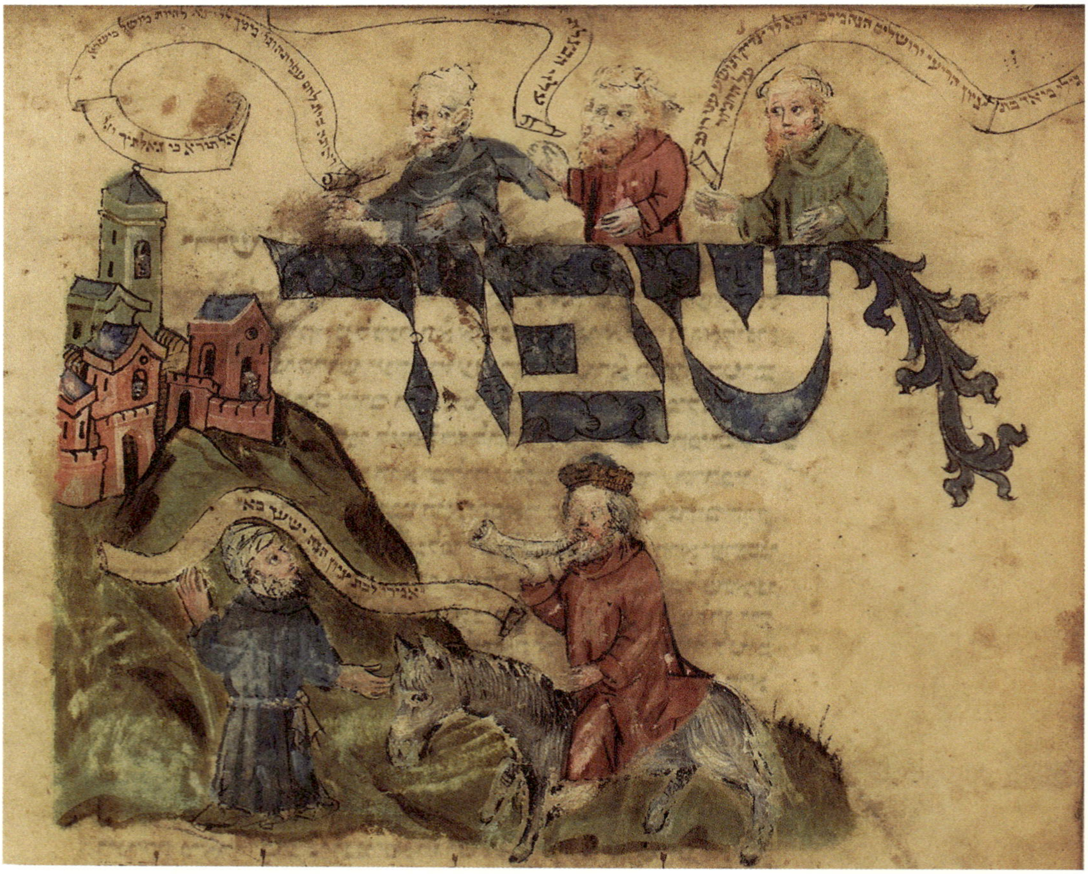

7. Messiah. Hamburg Miscellany, Hamburg, Staats- und Universitätsbibliothek, cod. heb. 37, Mainz, c. 1425–30, fol. 35v.

the Messiah on a donkey. It appears in the so-called Hamburg Miscellany in Mainz around 1430 (Fig. 7), and Joel himself included it in the First JTS Haggadah, where it is one of the few images that can be clearly made out. The Second Nuremberg Haggadah included two variations of the theme. The text of *Shefokh Hamatkha* shows Elijah riding and blowing a *shofar* (fol. 29v). At the end of the cycle we find a more elaborate version of the Messiah, also on a donkey accompanied by Elijah and a crowd on the donkey's rear (Second Nuremberg Haggadah, fol. 41v). The Washington Haggadah follows this full iconographic version (fol. 19v). It thus seems that when Joel considered a patron in the German lands, he studied the local tradition. While he had known the basic imagery of the Messiah/Elijah theme in his youth, he now realized that it had undergone certain developments, and he incorporated the new motifs into his work.

In considering Joel ben Simeon's role as an agent of cultural exchange, it is worth taking a look at another Ashkenazi haggadah written about the same time as the Washington codex. The so-called Cincinnati Haggadah was copied in Germany by Meir Jaffe of Ulm, the scribe of the London Haggadah.[21] Its illustration program owes a large debt to the legacy of Joel ben Simeon's art as it was known from his activity in Germany. At the beginning of the manuscript there is a depiction of the search for leaven in the typical Joel ben Simeon fashion. A few pages later another illustration copied from the London Haggadah appears representing a hunting scene adjacent to the text of the *havdalah* (Fig. 8), the blessing recited at the end of the Sabbath. If Passover eve falls on a Sabbath, the recitation of the *havdalah* is performed at the beginning of the seder. As this is an unusual case, occurring only in some years, Meir Jaffe added a mnemonic abbreviation to determine the sequence of blessings: *yayin*—the blessing over wine; *qiddush; ner*—referring to the candle used for the *havdalah* ceremony; *havdalah*—the actual blessing; *zman*—the blessing usually recited on any holiday. The first letters of these words form the expression *yaqneha"z*, which in a German-speaking region could be heard as *jag den has* ("hunt the hare"). Hunting scenes are extremely common in Jewish art. They often appear as an allegory of the vulnerable people of Israel equated, as in the Song of

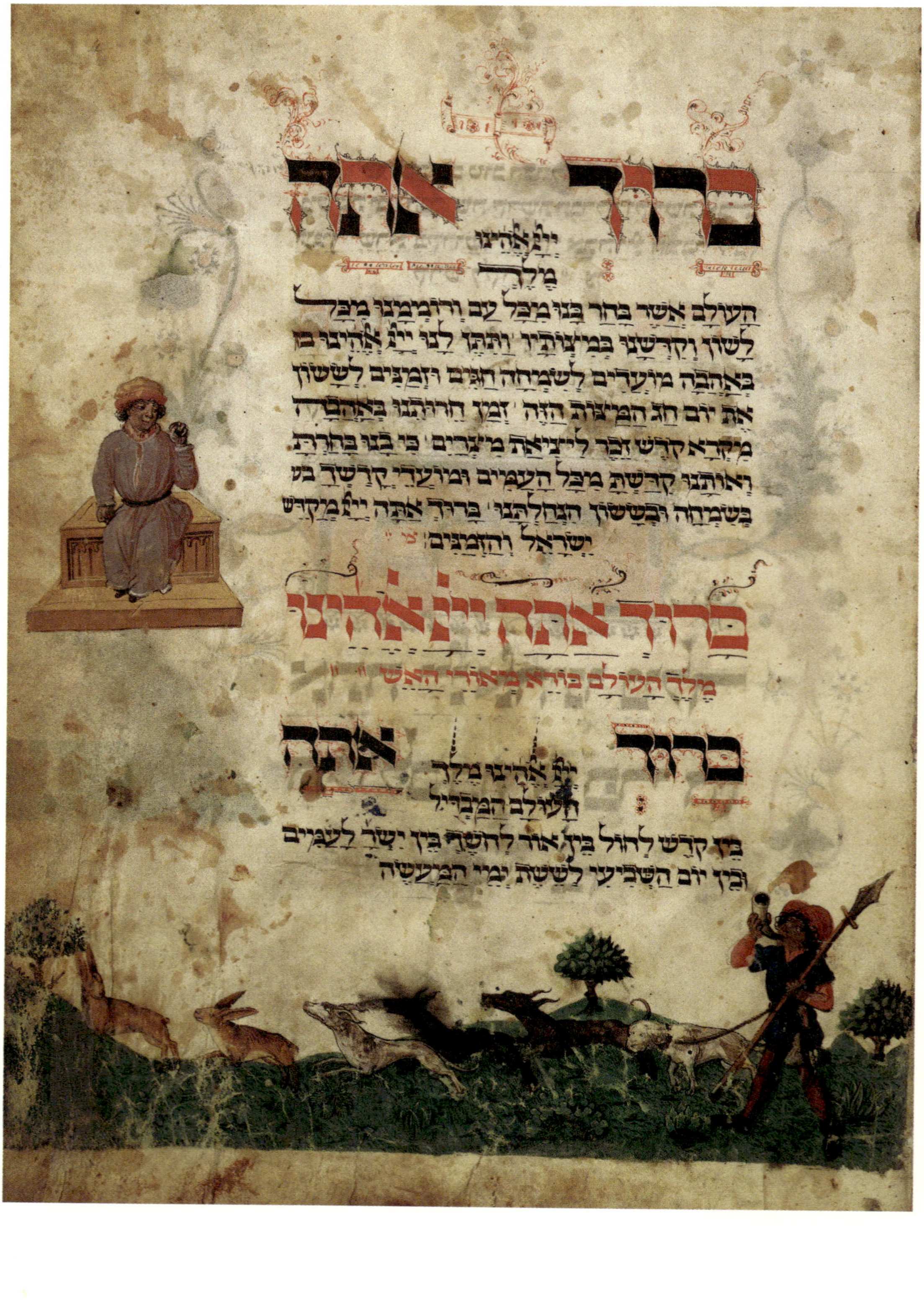
ברוך אתה
ייי אלהינו
מלך
העולם אשר בחר בנו מכל עם ורוממנו מכל
לשון וקדשנו במצותיו ותתן לנו ייי אלהינו בו
באהבה מועדים לשמחה חגים וזמנים לששון
את יום חג המצות הזה זמן חרותנו באהבה
מקרא קדש זכר ליציאת מצרים כי בנו בחרת
ואותנו קדשת מכל העמים ומועדי קדשך בש
בשמחה ובששון הנחלתנו ברוך אתה ייי מקדש
ישראל והזמנים:
ברוך אתה ייי אלהינו
מלך העולם בורא מאורי האש
ברוך אתה
ייי אלהינו מלך
העולם המבדיל
בין קדש לחול בין אור לחשך בין ישראל לעמים
ובין יום השביעי לששת ימי המעשה

Songs, with a doe being pursued by a Gentile hunter. The juxtaposition of the hunting motif with the *havdalah* and the *yaqneha"z* acronym, however, made sense only to those who spoke a German idiom. It is not known in haggadot prior to the London Haggadah, and perhaps it was introduced by Joel ben Simeon.

A man of versatile skills, active in an age of great movement in the book trade, and moving between two cultures, Joel ben Simeon must thus have seen a great deal. He was perhaps twice expelled from German towns, and he was a young man when he set out for Italy. Still, he must have had some sense of the tremendous changes in German economic life. An early fifteenth-century native of the Rhineland, he belonged to a Jewish community, which was persecuted in a region where the political and economic situation of the Jews had gradually deteriorated since the twelfth century. When he emigrated to Italy he certainly sensed a change of cultural atmosphere, got a taste of early-modern humanism and changing artistic styles, and was able to witness dynamics of close Jewish-Christian relations to a degree that a German Jew would not have been able to witness.

Joel began to build up his repertoire of haggadah motifs early in his career while still in the German lands. Aware of the local tradition of haggadah illustration, he developed a cycle of which, unfortunately, we have only a scant idea, as the margins of the two books from this period are so badly preserved. On his arrival in Italy he saw early-modern Italian art, echoes of which can be found in his subsequent work. Later he introduced some of these more recent motifs in haggadot he made while temporarily working in Germany. The Washington Haggadah demon-

8. Hunting Scene. London Haggadah, London, British Library, MS Add. 14762, Ulm, c. 1460, fol. 4r. (Copyright © British Library Board)

strates this process beautifully. Drawn in the delicate figure style Joel had acquired during his early years in Italy, and displaying several typically Italian motifs, it shows that in anticipation of an Ashkenazi purchaser he now focused on some typical Ashkenazi features.

Indeed, the fact that the Washington colophon does not mention a patron by name indicates, as we have seen in Stern's essay, that the book was not produced to order, but rather that it was intended to be sold on the free market, a feature increasingly found in the late medieval book trade.[22] Whereas for the greater part of the Middle Ages a wealthy patron would commonly order a lavish manuscript for his own use, and scribes and artists worked only on commission, the fourteenth, and especially the fifteenth, centuries witnessed significant economic and social developments that affected the book market, its clientele, and the way books were used. Patterns of book production began to change. The southern German book trade played a prominent role in these developments, and it appears that Joel ben Simeon was well aware of them. Far-reaching social shifts occurred during that period, when an ever-increasing wealthy middle class began to consume cultural goods that had hitherto been confined to the nobility. This educated urban middle class grew into an influential clientele for the book trade, which in consequence underwent dramatic developments that would ultimately lead to the printing press. Decades before Johannes Gutenberg invented his press in 1455, the makers of books had already begun to adapt to the evolving situation and, among others, to produce paper manuscripts of secular literature in the vernacular. This trend led to an entirely different approach to illustration and to the appearance of simple, quickly executed, only partly colored pen drawings, enabling the illustrators to work on greater numbers of copies. Another move toward accelerated book production was the appearance of the woodcut. One of the consequences of this development was the fact that books were no longer exclusively produced to order, but were made in several copies for the open market and to be kept in stock.

Like their Christian colleagues, Jewish scribes and illustrators were well aware of these new possibilities. The colophon in the Washington Haggadah, which lacks the name of a patron, together with the nature of the marginal illustrations, exemplifies these tendencies. As an active agent of the late medieval book trade Joel was aware of these changes; he certainly knew of Gutenberg's invention and had seen some printed books.

Joel's work continued to be influential even after his death. As Evelyn Cohen demonstrates, a sixteenth-century Italian haggadah now in a private collection in New York still quite faithfully relied on Joel's repertoire and repeated many of the themes he had introduced decades earlier.[23]

Society as Depicted by Joel ben Simeon

Although Joel acquired several stylistic features of early-modern Italian art, he never became a truly realistic illustrator. He adopted numerous genre motifs taken from Italian fashion, architecture, and interior design, and he embraced the love for details from daily life. He was influenced to some degree by the spatial concepts of Italian perspective but never really adopted the methods of three-dimensional illusion. Rather, his spatial design remains faithful to the style typically employed in German marginal illustration. Though he was not a realistic painter in the sense of early-modern Italian art, something in the way Joel portrayed certain figures betrays a keen and lively eye directed at the society in which he lived. His observation of people cuts through several social strata, and in what follows we shall take a closer look at how he viewed some of the representatives of the communities he encountered. In this context the depictions of the four sons of the haggadah are of particular interest. Representing different types of men, they—together with some further figures embellishing the margins of Joel's manuscripts—were highly suitable to sketch a socially diverse picture. They will be approached here not in their traditional order as they appear in the haggadah, but rather from the point of view of social groups.

The Wealthy

Commissioning an illuminated manuscript in the Middle Ages was a costly affair. The examples Joel ben Simeon delivered to his patrons and those he produced on stock for future buyers were not necessarily among the most luxurious: they did not use a great amount of gold, and the relatively few marginal drawings cannot be compared with the fully painted miniatures in the larger books that had been common during the thirteenth and fourteenth centuries. Still, even the production of a haggadah in the style Joel offered could be paid for only by a relatively wealthy client.

We can easily imagine that the owners of the haggadot are meant to be represented in some of the drawings: they show men holding wine cups, the *matsah,* or the *maror* (see, for example, the Rothschild Haggadah, fol. 20v). Some haggadot represent the family seated at the seder table, illustrating mostly the *ha lahma* and *lefikhakh* sections (Rothschild Haggadah, fols. 2v, 28r). The fact that in Maraviglia's prayerbook, known to have been owned by a woman, the person holding the *matsah* is a young lady indicates that indeed such figures were meant to represent the patrons and their families. The image that accompanies the *ha lahma* initial in the Rothschild Haggadah (fol. 2v), although badly preserved, still offers a close look at a large family seated at a table lavishly set with golden dishes. All the people are well dressed, but the luxurious garment of the woman in the center certainly stands out. Another particularly wealthy patron is shown raising a cup of wine next to the initial *lefikhakh* in the Washington Haggadah (fol. 17r).

Joel represented these patrons time and again on the pages of his haggadot. Some of his patrons are known by name, others not, and it has been suggested that the books were produced to be offered to occasional buyers. These "portraits" thus define a social type rather than specific people, and sketch the particular social circle of Joel's clientele.

Scholars

Numerous scholars are shown on the margins of Joel's manuscripts. This is a common feature in both the Sephardic and the Ashkenazi tradition of Haggadah illustration. They represent the Mishnaic rabbis mentioned in the haggadah text: the five rabbis of Bnei Braq, as well as Rabbi Eleazar ben Azariah, Rabbi Judah, Rabbi Yosse the Galilean, Rabbi Eliezer, Rabbi Aqiba, and Rabban Gamaliel. These men are usually shown as elderly figures, often with long white or gray hair and a beard. Since the second half of the fourteenth century they usually appear with their heads covered. Joel adopts these figures in all their variations, and we find numerous scholars in all his haggadot (Rothschild Haggadah, fols. 15r, 16r, and Washington Haggadah, fol. 5v). They appear either standing or seated, and always with a book in their hands. The book, the typical attribute of the scholar, can be shown open, often on a lectern, or closed, in the man's hand.

In several haggadot this iconography designates also the first of the four sons, the wise. Earlier scholarship suggested that the four sons are fashioned according to the four ages of a man's life, the wise representing old age.[24] This is certainly true for numerous early-modern printed haggadot, where the four sons are also distinguished by size. In medieval haggadot, however, this iconography had not yet been established; instead, each son is characteristic of a particular social type. In Joel's work two variants of the wise son can be observed: one is a respectable middle-aged man, without a book, pointing at his nose (Rothschild Haggadah, fol. 4v). This can be understood either as a gesture of sudden understanding or as one of Joel's verbal puns. The text of the haggadah reads: "The wise one, what does he say? 'What are the decrees, laws, and rules that God, our Lord, has enjoined upon you?' (Deut. 6:20). And so [*af*] you should explain to him some of the laws of Passover, [such as] 'After the Passover meal, one may not indulge in revelry.'" The word *af* in the Hebrew also means "nose," and it is possible that Joel indeed intended a word game.

In other manuscripts, as in the Washington Haggadah (fol. 5v), Joel represented the wise son as a scholar, an imagery likely of Sephardic origin that he may have encountered in Italy. The wise son is shown as an elderly man with all the attributes of the rabbi, seated in front of a lectern supporting an open manuscript. It is significant that this same scholar represents a social type distinctly different from that of the wealthy owner of the manuscript, who is perhaps shown near the initial *lefikhakh* (fol. 17r). Whereas the latter wears a particularly lavish and luxurious outfit, the scholar seems to be a more humble person, in a plain mantle and a simple cap.

Joel's love for detail, and also his profession as a maker of manuscripts, are apparent in the rendering of the book shown on the lectern: it lies open; the letters are graphically hinted at by small strokes; the clearly visible lines of ruling and the red rubrics at the right of each line as in Hebrew script are strikingly realistic. The book is given a red binding whose clasps are clearly discernable on the left.

Commoners

The haggadah describes the third son, the simpleton, as a humble commoner who has no knowledge but is eager to understand. In social terms he would be an honest but poorly educated member of the middle or lower classes. Jewish artists employed a variety of iconographic features to express these characteristics: he can be shown without a book, or with a book with empty pages; occasionally he appears together with a person who is apparently attempting to teach him. Joel, who was instrumental in establishing the iconographic tradition of the four sons in the Ashkenazi and the Italian realms, introduces several options: the simple son can appear as a vagabond (see below); the London Haggadah shows a man with an open book, his somewhat hesitant body language expressing significantly less respect than the wise man. His clothes are different and he wears a short mantle. The simpleton of the Washington Haggadah is the most intriguing of them all, having no parallel in any other manuscript (fol. 6r). He is an elderly man with a facial expression distinctly conveying a lack of knowledge; his eyes are wide open and he stares into an open book. He wears a simple, somewhat worn hooded coat. Seated on the floor, he clearly indicates much humility and some degree of misery.

Such figures of the third son represent members of Jewish society of whom we know significantly less than of wealthy patrons and the intellectual elite. They stand for what in the fourteenth and fifteenth centuries began to be defined as a mostly urban middle class: small merchants, craftsmen, apothecaries, and the like. They were upright and pious members of the Jewish community who had acquired a trade but lacked religious learning.

Workmen

"We were slaves to Pharaoh in Egypt," the text of the haggadah begins. This mention of the Egyptian bondage has led to various iconographic treatments since haggadot were first illustrated. Some of these images refer quite accurately to the actions reported in the Bible and depict various stages of brick production, including the making of mortar, molds, and rows of bricks set out to dry in the sun. Other images, however, including those invented by Joel ben Simeon, present the bondage of the Israelites and the erection of the Egyptian treasure cities as genre scenes of medieval life.

The people inhabiting these building scenes are all shown in simple clothing, mostly of dark colors. In the Rothschild Haggadah their modest outfits are clearly contrasted with the rather elaborate costume of the overseer (fol. 10v). Young men with short hair wearing short mantles and leggings are shown climbing up ladders, carrying bricks, stones, or baskets with material on their backs, applying mortar to buildings, and so on. A recurring motif is that of the water-carriers (Rothschild Haggadah, fol. 2v).

The variety of motifs Joel used in these renderings of the treasure cities shows how keenly he observed his environment. The scenes are set in delicate designs of late Gothic and early-modern Italian architecture. With much precision they portray the workers, their costumes, their body language, their tools, and a rich variety of tasks to perform. Joel clearly is less concerned with the particulars of the biblical narrative than with his immediate environment.

phemy, he also functioned as a critic of those he was supposed to entertain. In the Jewish tradition as well questions about fools and unbalanced behavior have no clear-cut answers, and the definition of the line between normal and abnormal behavior is problematic. Christian society occasionally approached the fool as some kind of holy figure through whom God could speak, a notion that was alien to the Jewish tradition.[26]

Jesters were not found only at the court; the natural fool as entertainer, in particular, could be observed in all parts of society, appearing in towns, at fairs, and at markets. We gain a sense of how the jester figured within the human landscape of Joel's surroundings by looking at the Egyptian army in the Rothschild (fol. 22v) and London Haggadot. On the roof of the carriage at the right edge of the illustration appears a jester beating a drum and blowing a fife—both acts closely associated with the kind of entertainment a jester was supposed to provide. Early-modern Italy also witnessed the earliest versions of the *purimshpil*, a comic theatrical staging of the Book of Esther involving various types and figures, including jesters.

Medieval iconography created the image of a fool first as an illustration to Psalm 53:1: "the fool has said in his heart." Originally this *insipiens*, as the fool was referred to in Latin, was shown with the typical attributes of a mentally impaired individual: bald, in ragged clothes often exposing much of his body, and carrying a club. His body language often indicates irrational behavior, his facial expression a lack of intelligence. During the fifteenth century the figure of the jester was occasionally employed to designate the *insipiens*. In this context the jester was thus not necessarily a witty, political free-speaker employed by the court but a natural fool or imbecile whose unusual behavior may have been perceived as amusing.

Joel must have had this type of jester in mind in designing the iconography of the son who does not know to ask. Perceived as a person lacking wisdom and the ability to acquire knowledge, the popular figure of the jester could easily be employed as a prototype for this character. It is possible that Joel was actually the first artist to invent this iconography, which after 1450 became increasingly popular in Ashkenazi manuscripts of the haggadah. Joel of course was aware of all the attributes attached to the foolish jester: he apparently knew that often the jester/fool could be considered a blasphemous person of dubious morality, stupid, and overly fond of himself. The hood with donkey's ears, for example, is linked to this characterization. In a medieval German song a donkey wished to appear in the disguise of a lion, but its large ears gave it away. Like the fool, the donkey represented blasphemy, lack of knowledge, and immoral conduct. Another common prop of the jester was a mirror, a *Spiegel*, perhaps the root of the name of one of German folklore's most popular jesters, Till Eulenspiegel. Overly fond of himself, the fool looks in the mirror, a mark of pride and blasphemy. In contrast, the witty court jester's association with the mirror was his function as free-spoken critic. Obvious physical impairment in jesters symbolized, as some sort of mirror, the not so obvious intellectual impairment of the people of the court.[27]

Most of Joel's jesters present the fourth son in the guise of a comical entertaining natural fool. The foolishness is emphasized in the Rothschild Haggadah (fol. 6r), where the jester has bare legs and lacks a shoe, and his facial expression is quite idiotic. In the Washington Haggadah (fol. 6r) he points to his open mouth, perhaps alluding to the need to open the fourth son's mouth. Like many other medieval jesters he also plays the drum. The figure in the London Haggadah seems to combine the ambivalent features that medieval society had attached to the jester/fool. He suffers from goiter, a disease that was closely linked to dwarfism and hunchbacks; he wears a jester's costume, but it is ragged and torn; his expression makes him appear particularly inept (but not idiotic as in the Rothschild Haggadah); his grinning face looks into the mirror (Fig. 6). The London fool displays the features of a miserable vagabond, and as such I shall revisit him in the next section.

At the Margins of Society

The haggadah text opens with the following words: "Here is the bread of distress which our ancestors ate in the land of Egypt. Let anyone who is hungry come and eat. Let anyone who wishes come and participate in the Passover. Today we are here; next year, in the Land of Israel. Today we are slaves; next year, we shall be free men" (fol. 3v). Several figures in Joel's repertoire suggest that they are meant to represent those "who are hungry," those who are invited to come and eat.

In several of Joel's manuscripts either the third or the fourth son is shown not as a jester but as a miserable, poorly dressed figure. In the Parma Haggadah the simpleton wears a short, worn-out, ragged hooded costume indicating that he wanders around, homeless. In the London Haggadah the fourth son appears as a fool, but likewise in a ragged costume, thus merging the iconographies of the jester and the vagabond (Fig. 6). A similar figure with bare feet and a ragged hooded garment appears in both the Rothschild (fol. 18v) and the Washington Haggadot (fol. 14v) as the man who roasts the Passover lamb. In both images he is seated on the ground, one hand turning the spit over the fire—no doubt a lengthy and tiresome procedure. In his other hand he holds a cup of wine, while a bottle appears next to him for when his cup needs to be refilled. In the Washington Haggadah he appears next to the elegantly dressed women busying themselves with the preparation of the Passover meal. They peer somewhat arrogantly at his part of the composition and perhaps, as the gesture of one of the women shows, offer him some food.

This ragged vagabond seems to represent the homeless and hungry who are invited to the seder "to come and eat" and were perhaps offered the thankless job of turning the spit with the lamb.[28] Sometimes this vagabond is also physically impaired, suffering from goiters clearly indicated in the area of the neck. This is the case in both the Rothschild and the Washington Haggadot, where the man who roasts the lamb suffers from goiters; in the Parma and the London Haggadot (Fig. 6) the fourth son is shown with the same ailment.

The fact that four poverty-stricken figures suffer from this condition calls for some attention. The recurrence of the goiter motif indicates that it was not simply a realistic detail but rather an iconographic sign of deprivation, of vagabond life, and of foreignism. Poverty often went hand-in-hand with physical impairment. Joel ben Simeon was not the only fifteenth-century artist to include goiters in his iconographic repertoire. Historians of medicine have observed that representations of goitrous figures began to be fairly frequent in the early-modern period in both southern Germany and Italy.

A goiter is an enlargement of the thyroid gland that usually appears as a heavy swelling of the neck. The enlargement is due to iodine deficiency in drinking water and salt typical of alpine areas, remote from the sea. The disease is thus specifically associated with alpine populations, and it remained as such until goiter prophylaxis was introduced in alpine areas in the 1920s by means of adding iodine to the drinking water and iodizing salt in certain regions.[29] Goiters primarily affected several regions in Switzerland, the Aosta Valley in northeastern Italy, the French Alps, Carinthia, Styria, Bavaria, and some parts of the Apennines, such as Lombardy, Tuscany, and the Monti Sabini in southern Italy. Ancient and medieval physicians mentioned goiters and ways to treat the disease, and several of them were aware of its regionally determined appearance.

Since the thirteenth century other, nonmedical encyclopedic sources list the goitrous among the monstrous races. Such works were extremely popular throughout Europe during the late Middle Ages and often circulated as illuminated books. The goitrous are occasionally shown in such manuscripts as imbeciles with fools' clubs and stupid facial expressions, recalling the fool in the London Haggadah or the vagabond in the Parma Haggadah. Unlike the fabulous monsters of the East with whom they were listed, those suffering from goiters were actually encountered by travelers, pilgrims, and migrants, in particular those who crossed the Great St. Bernhard from the Upper Rhine region into Italy, a path that was very likely taken also by Joel ben Simeon. Goiters were more frequent in this area than anywhere else. To the medieval mind, nourished by popular encyclopedias, such people, although encountered in reality, were still linked with monsters. This perception remained valid until the early sixteenth century, when humanist chroniclers offered their own observations instead of reproducing earlier views about the monstrous races. In some late medieval sources, finally, the disease was understood as a punishment for sin.

Joel ben Simeon may have encountered people suffering from goiters on the Great St. Bernhard and while living in Lombardy and Tuscany, but most likely not in the Middle Rhine region where he had grown up. He may, indeed, have read or heard the view that goitrous people are considered monsters, or, at least, that they had limited intelligence.

Apart from common notions about goiters, Joel was also influenced by an iconographic tradition depicting the condition. In addition to the illustrated encyclopedias of the late Middle Ages, representations of goiters in art became more frequent in the second half of the fifteenth

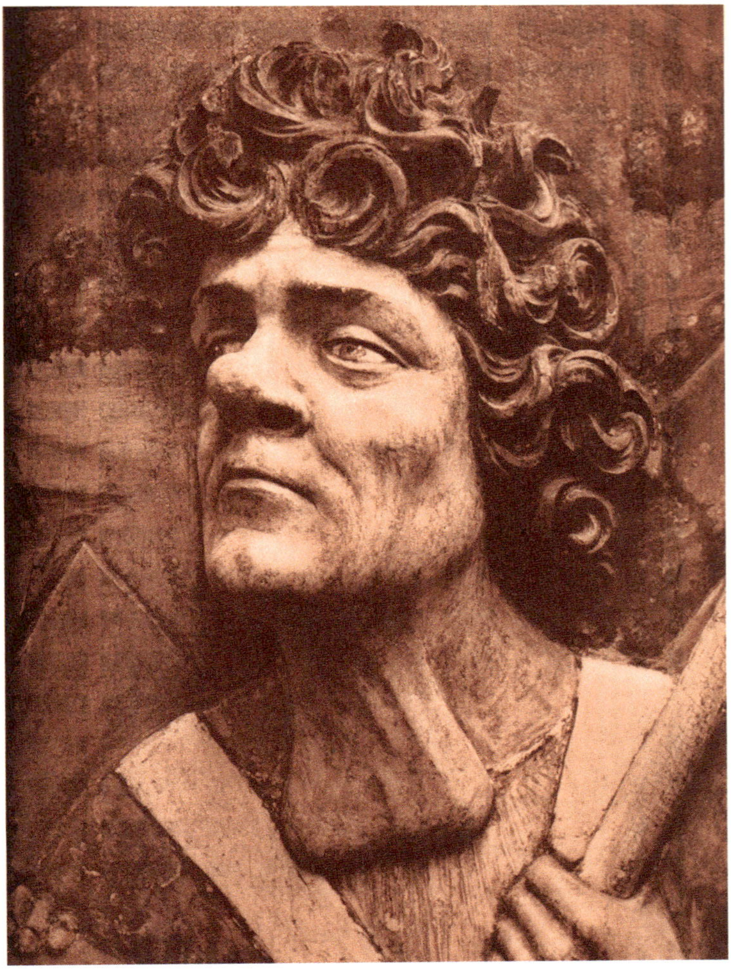

9. Flagellation of Christ. Veit Stoss, Cracow altarpiece, Cracow, Church of St. Mary, 1477–1489. (Veit Stoss, *Oltarz Krakowski* [Warsaw: Panstwowy Instytut Wydawniczy, 1951])

century. There are mainly two contexts in which images of goitrous people appear. First, continuing the earlier medieval tradition associating the goitrous with the monstrous races, goiters are often seen as an iconographic sign of a wicked and evil personality. This representation is particularly common in the northern parts of the Alps, in the Upper Rhine region, Austria, Bavaria, and in Switzerland. Here numerous depictions of the Flagellation of Jesus or other scenes of the Passion show some of the torturers and soldiers with goiters, in an attempt to emphasize their ugliness and thus their wickedness (Fig. 9). Similarly, the goitrous are found in chronicles on the side of the enemy and the wicked. These representations originate in the earlier medieval tradition that linked the goitrous with the monstrous races, and in particular in views that perceived the disease as a punishment for sinful acts.

Second, goiters appear as a by-product of early-modern realism, at times perhaps with the intention of eliciting sympathy for the poor and the sick. In such examples of realistic imagery goiters by no means indicate wickedness. This iconography was particularly common in Italy (Fig. 10).

A certain difference in mentality can be observed in these groups. The wicked goitrous of the north and the realistic Italian representations speak of different mindsets, and the latter seem to be linked to the humanistic world view that began to govern European consciousness since the early fifteenth century. Joel ben Simeon lived between these two different states of mind; he migrated between the two worlds, and

10. Abbess Lucrezia Agliardi Vertova of Bergamo (1490?–1558). Giovanni Battista Moroni (1525–1578), Bergamo, 1557. Oil on canvas, 36 x 27 in., Collection, Bequest of Theodore M. Davis, 1915 (30.95.255), Metropolitan Museum of Art, New York. (Image copyright © The Metropolitan Museum of Art / Art Resource, N.Y.)

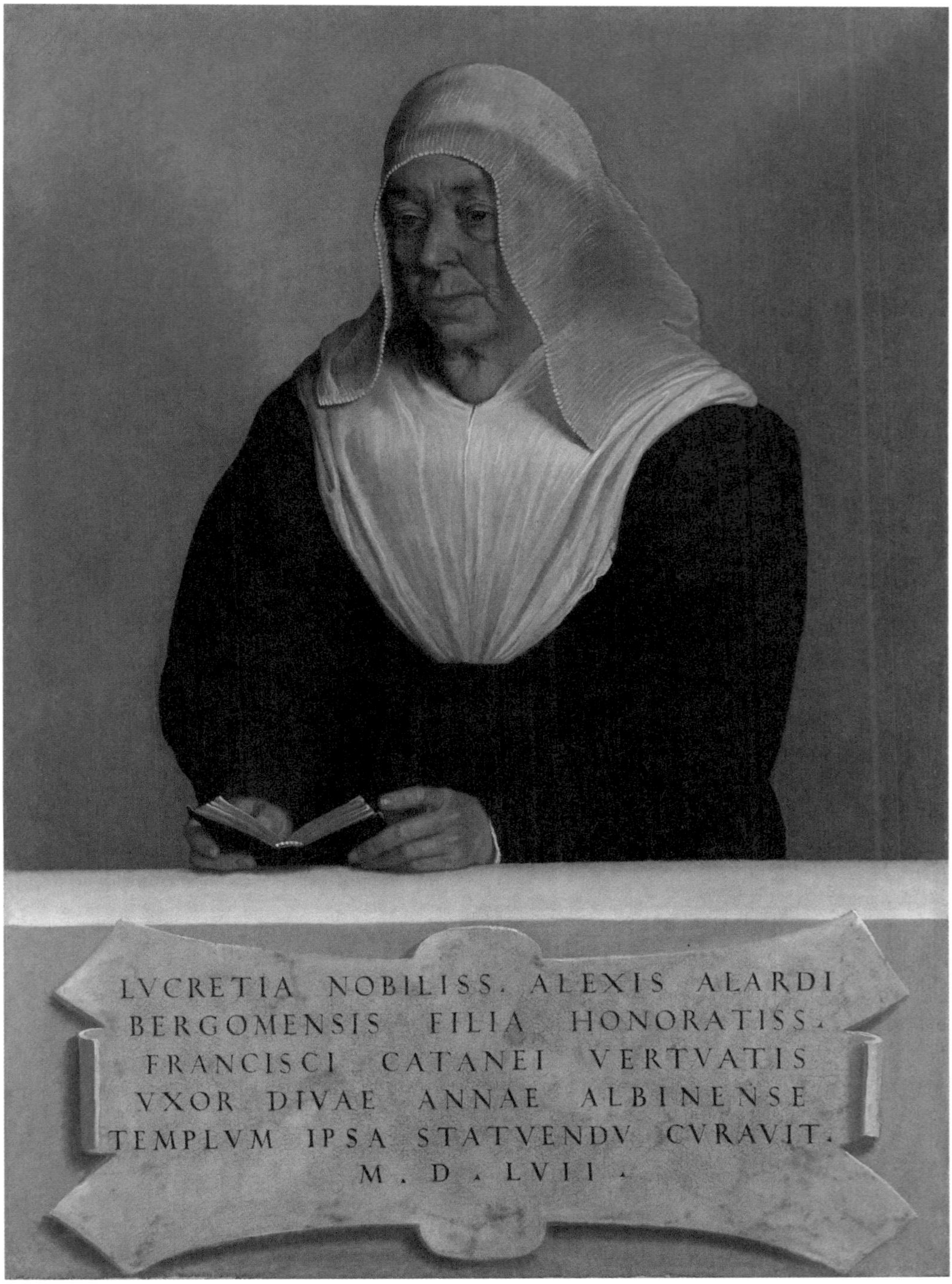
LVCRETIA NOBILISS. ALEXIS ALARDI
BERGOMENSIS FILIA HONORATISS.
FRANCISCI CATANEI VERTVATIS
VXOR DIVAE ANNAE ALBINENSE
TEMPLVM IPSA STATVENDV CVRAVIT.
M. D. LVII.

the question is, what exactly did he associate with the goitrous people he drew?

Joel's figures of the goitrous are not evil, and they are not grotesque. They are poor and miserable, ignorant and perhaps stupid; delineated as hungry vagabonds, they are quite likely to have been intended to represent those poor souls invited to partake in the seder meal. Joel most likely knew that the disease was associated with stupidity. It is, however, doubtful that he knew the upper Rhenish tradition of the wicked goitrous involved in Passion scenes. On the contrary, had he been aware of this he would perhaps have chosen another imagery to represent the hungry guest. It seems more plausible to assume that Joel had come to know Italian realistic imagery. He may have encountered images of goiters in Italy, but by the same token, he may have seen actual people suffering from the disease. He represents aspects of both mentalities: looking at the goitrous as imbeciles, but not going so far as to perceive them as monstrous, he approached them as an anecdotal detail enabling him to add a realistic emphasis to his sketches of a certain social type. To his mind, goiters, which he had not seen before his arrival in Italy, may also have become a sign of foreignism.

Non-Jews

The wickedness of the second son is defined by his alienness: "The wicked one—what does he say? What does this rite mean to you? (Ex. 12:26). 'To *you*,' and not to *him*. And since he excluded himself from the community, he has denied a fundamental [belief]. You should set his teeth on edge and say to him, 'It is because of what God did for me when I went free from Egypt' (Ex. 13:8)—'for *me*,' not for *him*. If he had been there, he would not have been redeemed." The wicked son is thus understood as an apostate and is usually shown with iconographic characteristics of a non-Jew. Several haggadot show him as an overdressed dandy with a halberd, an imagery that perhaps has an Italian origin and was also adopted in the fifteenth century in some Ashkenazi haggadot. Joel ben Simeon, like some other Ashkenazi haggadot makers, however, follows the Sephardic tradition of representing the wicked son as a knight (Rothschild Haggadah, fol. 5r, Washington Haggadah, fol. 5v).

Jewish costume was usually simple and not in any particular way fashionable. Clothing restrictions arose both from the non-Jewish sumptuary laws and from Jewish *halakhah*. The fifteenth-centuy Ashkenazi scholar Israel ben Petahiah Isserlein of Wiener-Neustadt (d. 1460), for example, bans dandified clothing, such as the colorful *mi-parti* costume and pointed shoes. In 1404 the Cologne authorities issued a law restricting the forms and fashions of Jewish clothing. What really marks these figures as non-Jews, however, is the halberd they carry. The characterization of the wicked son as a knight emphasizes not only alienness but above all aggression. In some examples, the wicked one is shown in the act of attacking an unarmed victim. The wicked son represents the Gentile aggressor and is a symbol of anti-Jewish persecution.

Until the thirteenth century the Jews of Ashkenaz carried arms and even occasionally took part in the defense of their towns. The right to protect themselves was later restricted, and the royal protection of the Jews, usually regulated in charters given to local authorities permitting them to allow Jewish dwellings in their vicinity, was linked to the fact that the Jews were not supposed to carry weapons. The Jews began to perceive themselves as unprotected victims and to associate the use of arms with Gentile aggression. The iconography of the knight emphasizes this perception of the non-Jew as aggressor.

Joel ben Simeon never chose to depict the dandy with the halberd, but always defined the wicked son as a knight, thus characterizing the wicked Gentile in unmistakable terms. Although he spent most of his working life in Italy, where Jewish-Christian relations were less contentious than those in the German lands, Joel seems to have carried on with a perception of non-Jews that grew out of his early days across the Alps. Similar knights appear in a crowded mass representing the Egyptian army, another symbol of anti-Jewish oppression and persecution.

The hunting scene in the London Haggadah speaks a similar language (Fig. 8). Although it could be understood simply as a verbal pun referring to the abbreviation *yaqneha"z*, by the fifteenth century the hunter and his dogs had acquired a definitive anti-Christian meaning. Jews did not hunt, and most animals associated with hunting are unfit for consumption. In Jewish eyes the sport of hunting was associated primarily with the nobility. More important, however, the doe mentioned in the Song of Songs was understood as an allegory of Israel, turning the hunting motif into an allegory of persecution.[30]

Joel ben Simeon's visual references to non-Jews thus employ several aspects of the typical iconographic repertoire used to define non-Jewish persecutors and oppressors. This imagery is found primarily in Iberia and in the German lands, reflecting the ever-increasing pressures on the Jewish population in these regions toward the end of the Middle Ages. Even though Joel must have been aware that in Italy Jews and Christians interacted at levels that no other Christian country had known, he continued to define the Gentiles as any Jew from the German lands would have done. He thus carried the collective memory of Jews from southern Germany who commemorated the victims of repeated waves of persecution since the first massive attack during the First Crusade in 1096. One can easily imagine that reports of the anti-Jewish incitement of mendicant preachers, becoming more and more common in Italy during Joel's lifetime, had a sharper effect on him than on his Italian coreligionists. Such preachers had been part of the southern German landscape since the thirteenth century, when Berthold of Regensburg, for example, preached the harassment of the Jews. When Joel was a young man the Italian mendicant Giovanni di Capestrano was heard in the German lands and adjacent areas until his death in 1456.[31] In the second half of the fifteenth century wandering mendicants began to increase their preaching in Italy as well. Having grown up to the north of the Alps and sharing the collective memory of Rhenish and Franconian Jews, Joel knew all too well that wandering preachers could easily stir up anti-Jewish violence.

The Traveling Immigrant

Near the text "Go forth and learn," Joel ben Simeon added the figure of a traveler, a verbal pun he may have invented himself. This motif appears already in the First Nuremberg Haggadah and recurs in almost all his later works (Rothschild Haggadah, fol. 8r, Washington Haggadah, fol. 7v). Of all the figures in Joel's haggadot, this is perhaps the one with whom he most identified. Throughout most of his life he was on the move. As a child he first left Cologne. As a young man he lived for some time in Bonn. Unlike other, especially Christian, scribes and artists who maintained organized workshops at permanent locations—some of them establishing printing workshops during the second half of the fifteenth century—Joel practiced his profession in various places. Before his move to Italy he may have worked along the Rhine Valley and perhaps also farther to the east, in Swabia and Moravia. Even after coming to Italy he apparently did not live in any permanent location for long. His constant movement was due not just to fear of persecution but also to the way he chose to practice his craft.

Joel reached Italy sometime between 1449 and 1452, when he signed a Mahzor in Cremona, in Lombardy. In 1460 he crossed the Alps again; he apparently did not go up north to the Middle Rhine but remained in Ulm, where he joined forces with Meir Jaffe. In 1469 he was back in Italy in some unknown location, and he signed the prayerbook for Maraviglia. He may also have taken part in the decoration of a Mahzor written during the 1470s by a scribe from Cesena, in Emilia-Romagna. In 1476 he may have collaborated in the production of a Halakhic Miscellany in Padua, in the Veneto. Two years later he was back in the German lands to produce the Washington Haggadah. In 1485 he perhaps can be followed to Modena, in Emilia-Romagna. That year he wrote a copy of David Qimhi's *Commentary to the Psalter* and noted in the colophon that he worked for a patron from that town. The year 1492 found Joel, an old man by now, in Tuscany, where he contributed to the decoration of the Rothschild Mahzor in Florence. These places, stations in the life of a wandering scribe, are only those mentioned in the surviving colophons, but they give a fairly clear picture of the area he covered during his career. The small images of the young traveler who "goes forth to learn" may thus very well be associated with Joel himself, who, having left his native Rhineland, set out for Italy to develop there professionally and seek a well-to-do clientele.

Illustrations from the Washington Haggadah

FOL. 1R

Searching for Leaven: A middle-aged man appears in front of a two-tiered cupboard. With a feather he removes leaven from its upper section. In his left hand he holds a bowl to collect the crumbs; a candle is attached to its rim. According to the *halakhah*, everybody in the household can participate in cleaning the house, but the head of the house must perform the final search.

Burning the Leaven: A young man, having lit a fire, is using a pair of bellows to stir it. The bowl with the leaven appears amid the flames.

FOL. 4R

Pouring the Second Cup of Wine: A man standing behind a small table pours wine from a large golden pitcher into a golden goblet on the table. In his right hand he holds a second cup, apparently about to be filled.

FOL. 5V

The Wise Son: An elderly scholar is seated in front of a lectern with an open book.

The Wicked Son: A young knight in full armor has a sword at his left side and a lance in his right hand.

FOL. 6R

The Simple Son: An old man in a long, worn-out, hooded garment sits humbly on the floor in an outdoor setting. He holds an open book in his hands.

The Son Who Does Not Know to Ask: A jester with somewhat grotesque facial features points with his right index finger to his mouth, indicating lack of knowledge. With his left hand he beats a drum.

FOL. 7V

Go Forth and Learn: A young, clean-shaven man in travel costume wanders across the margins. He carries a lance, a bag, and a water container.

FOL. 14V

Preparation of the Meal and Roasting of the Lamb: To the right a young goitrous man in a short, ragged hooded tunic sits on a small stool and turns a spit with the rack of a lamb. He is drinking wine; there is more wine in a flask behind his back. To the right are two elegantly dressed women occupied with the preparation of the meal; one of them seems to offer the vagabond either another cup of wine or some of the broth she is stirring.

FOL. 15V

The Matsah: A yellowish monkey seated on a red cushion raises the *matsah*. Although monkeys are common in the repertoires of grotesques in medieval illuminated books, this depiction of a monkey holding the *matsah*, replacing the commonly shown man, is unique and quite strange.

FOL. 16R

The Bitter Herbs—Maror: Instead of the typical man raising a bundle of bitter herbs, the Washington Haggadah refers to a scene of domestic conflict. The wife, an expression of despair on her face emphasized by her looking away from the husband, holds a two-edged sword in her right hand. The young man, significantly taller than the woman, pushes at her head and attempts to force the bitter herbs into her mouth. Whereas references to the bitterness of married life are quite common in medieval haggadot, both Sephardic and Ashkenazi, this particular setting is unique. It has been suggested[32] that the imagery reflects two verbal puns based on biblical verses. Eccles. 7:26 reads: "and I find more bitter than death the woman, whose heart is snares and nets, and her hands are bound; who so pleases God shall escape from her; but the sinner shall be taken by her." Prov. 5:3–5 reads: "For the lips of a strange woman drop honey, and her mouth is smoother than oil; but her end is bitter as wormwood, sharp as a two-edged sword. Her feet go down to death; her steps take hold on the underworld."

FOL. 17R

Raising the Second Cup of Wine: Next to the initial panel of *lefikhakh* (Therefore [it is our duty to thank and praise . . .]) appears a lavishly dressed man raising a cup. The beautiful, large golden cup is balanced on the man's palm, following a common custom based on Gen. 40:11: "I gave the cup onto Pharaoh's palm."

FOL. 19V

Pour Out Your Fury: An old man riding a donkey—either Elijah heralding the coming of the Messiah, or the Messiah himself—approaches a building whose door is being opened by a youth. This detail refers to the custom of opening the door at the end of the seder ceremony to let Elijah into one's home. The Messiah is accompanied by a family—a man, a woman raising a cup of wine, and two children seated on the donkey's rear and tail; at the very right an old woman tries to hold onto the tail.

FOL. 22R

Out of the Straits I Called upon the Lord: Next to this citation from Ps. 118:5 appears a walled town. One of the buildings, a large round tower, has a window through which a man—the psalm's author, King David—can be discerned in profile, raising, as it seems, his hands in prayer.

FOL. 30R

Daniel in the Lions' Den: This image illustrates the poem *az rov nissim* (Then You performed many miracles at night), composed in the Late Antique period by Yannai. The poem alludes to a number of biblical miracles. One of the lines reads: "The one who has escaped the lions' den." Joel linked this sentence to the story of Daniel, and pictured the prophet, his hands raised in prayer, in a pit-like den with four lions.

NOTES

1. The translation follows Goldstein, 40.

2. In his introduction to the Commentary of the 1992 facsimile edition of the Washington Haggadah, Myron Weinstein suggested that a certain Tsevi Cohen was employed in Joel ben Simeon's workshop and that he finished the haggadah (Weinstein). Weinstein's conclusion was based on scribal decoration observed on fol. 2r marking letters that form the words "and finished" and "Tsev[i]." The fact that the decoration contains a crown led Weinstein to assume that Tsevi was a Cohen. Such scribal decorations are common in Hebrew manuscripts, and they are hidden allusions to dates, names of authors, scribes, or patrons. They were applied by the scribe; it is doubtful, therefore, that this particular sign would mark an illuminator's name. Moreover, the notion of a workshop run by Joel ben Simeon is somewhat problematic, as he was constantly on the move. It is more likely that he joined workshops during his trav-

Jesters

The "son who does not know to ask" appears in almost all of Joel ben Simeon's haggadot as a jester. We do not know if this was the case already in the two early works produced before his move to Italy. Some traces in the margins of the First Nuremberg Haggadah indicate that the sons were represented there, but no details can be made out. In any event, in almost all the early Italian works, the Bodmer, the Rothschild, and the Parma Haggadot, the cheerful jester represents the fourth son (Rothschild Haggadah, fol. 6r). The same applies to the later haggadot in London (Fig. 6) and Washington (fol. 6r).

Fools and jesters were a regular part of medieval and early-modern life, and they figure prominently in the iconography of illuminated manuscripts and other visual arts.[25] European monarchs employed jesters for entertainment at their courts. During the Middle Ages these jokers wore bright, multicolored costumes with a hood extending into donkey's ears, and a tail. They carried a long stick, a heavy club, or a *marotte*, a short rod with a carved head. Jesters were either natural fools and simple comedians entertaining the common folk, or smart, funny, and eloquent outsiders employed to amuse the upper classes and members of the court. The borders between those types are not always entirely clear. Hunchbacks and dwarfs, physically impaired, often filled the role of jesters, and they were considered particularly witty and funny. This group was often ironic and critical and enjoyed some freedom of speech. Unconventional in their behavior, they were not part of any usual system of hierarchies and norms.

The attitude of medieval society to the fool and the jester was somewhat ambivalent. He could be a sinner or an innocent; he could be believed to be close to the devil or close to God; in no way was he bound to conventions and norms. Representing immoral behavior and blas-

the Sephardic rite in Hamburg, Staats- und Universitätsbibliothek, cod. hebr. 155, from c. 1310; the Wolf Haggadah, now in the National Library of Israel, cod. 8°7246, was written in the second half of the fourteenth century in southern France, but perhaps decorated slightly later in Italy (for photographs see http://cja.huji.ac.il/manuscripts/Wolf%20Haggadah/Overview_document.html); the Schocken Haggadah, formerly Jerusalem, Schocken Library, MS 24086, a haggadah of the Ashkenazi rite, written c. 1380–1400 in Lombardy; the decoration of a southern French haggadah in Paris, Bibliothèque nationale de France, cod. hébr. 642, betrays some Italian influence. Unlike Ashkenazi Mahzorim, Italian prayerbooks often contain the haggadah; some examples survive, but they are relatively sparsely decorated. See a Siddur now in London, British Library, MS Add. 26968; Schocken Library, MS 13873.

14. Some of these motifs appear in a manuscript now in Parma, Biblioteca Palatina, MS Parm 2895. This book was begun in 1450 in Ulm and completed in 1453 in Treviso. Mendel and Thérèse Metzger believed its decoration to be of German origin (Metzger and Metzger). The style of the illustrations, although somewhat stiff in comparison to Italian early Renaissance art, reveals a spatial concept unlike the flat, somewhat naïve approach of German book art of the time and seems to point to an Italian origin. The comparison can be supported by several motival parallels to Joel ben Simeon's works from these years. The manuscript has never been studied in depth.

15. Formerly Jerusalem, Schocken Library, MS 24085.

16. In the commentary to the 1991 facsimile of the Washington Haggadah, Mordechai Glatzer identified the scribe and declared that the haggadah was written in c. 1469 (Glatzer in Weinstein). Whereas the attribution to Meir Jaffe is very convincing, the date Glatzer offers is rather doubtful. Yael Zirlin identifies a type of scribal decoration in the London Haggadah as suggesting the year 1460 (Zirlin, "Joel Meets Johannes"). This is certainly possible, as we know that the patron of the London Haggadah, a certain Jacob Mattathiah ben Isaac, commissioned another manuscript in the same city in 1459. Glatzer concludes that Joel returned only once to Germany between 1469 and 1485 and that during those years he worked on both the London and the Washington Haggadot and that the two are close in date. It is more likely that Joel returned to Germany twice and that the date proposed by Zirlin and others before her for the London Haggadah is indeed 1460.

17. Edmunds. Johannes Bämler may have been a painter in the 1460s in Ulm; in 1472, however, he is known to have run a printing workshop in Augsburg.

18. Paris, Bibliothèque nationale de France, cod. hébr. 1333.

19. Yuval, chap. 3.

20. Antonius Margarita, *Ein kurzer Bericht und Anzaigung* (Vienna, 1541), fol. 11v; the translation follows Yuval, 125.

21. Cincinnati, Hebrew Union College–Jewish Institute of Religion, Klau Library.

22. First noted by Beit-Arié in Weinstein.

23. Cohen.

24. Mira Friedman.

25. For a recent study on court jesters, see Otto; on the iconography of jesters and fools in medieval art, see Gifford.

26. Shoham-Steiner, chap. 6.

27. In his study of marginal figures in Jewish society Ephraim Shoham-Steiner observed that descriptions of abnormal behavior in the Middle Ages can be understood as some sort of mirror image of ideal, normative behavior (Shoham-Steiner, chap. 4).

28. I owe this notion to Ephraim Shoham-Steiner. I wish to thank him for the conversations we had on this image and the ideas he shared with me.

29. For a detailed historical study on goiter, see Merke; he suggested that iodine deficiency and the appearance of goiters in certain Alpine areas have to do with glaciation in the Quaternary and the resulting geological conditions.

30. The hunting scene is among those that bear signs of Johannes Bämler's painting style, but scholars now agree that such illustrations were designed and composed by Joel, whereas Bämler worked on the coloring. For background on the Jewish approach to hunting, see Offenberg.

31. That Joel ben Simeon may have witnessed such preachers was suggested in Zirlin, "The Early Works of Joel ben Simeon"; on Giovanni di Capestrano preaching in Germany see, among others, Ruß.

32. Landsberger, 76; Narkiss in Weinstein, 73.

Bibliography

The Manuscripts of Joel ben Simeon in Chronological Order

First JTS Haggadah. Southern Germany, c. 1445. New York, Jewish Theological Seminary of America, MS Mic. 4481.

First Nuremberg Haggadah. Southern Germany, c. 1445. Jerusalem, Israel Museum, MS 181/60, formerly Schocken Library, MS 24086.

Parma Siddur. Southern Germany or northern Italy, 1449. Parma, Biblioteca Palatina, MS Parm 3144.

Turin Mahzor. Cremona, 1452–1453 (damaged in a fire in 1904). Turin, Biblioteca Nazionale Universitaria, MS A. III. 14.

Second JTS Haggadah. Northern Italy, 1454. New York, Jewish Theological Seminary of America, MS Mic. 8279.

Bodmer Haggadah. Northern Italy, c. 1450–1460. Cologny-Geneva, Fondation Martin Bodmer, Cod. Bodmer 81.

Parma Haggadah. Northern Italy, c. 1450–1460. Parma, Biblioteca Palatina, MS Parm 2998.

Rothschild Haggadah. Northern Italy, c. 1450–1460. Jerusalem, National Library of Israel, MS Heb. 4°6130.

London Haggadah. Ulm (?), c. 1460. London, British Library, MS Add. 14762.

Pentateuch Commentary by Levi ben Gershon from Avignon, 1430, with later illustrations by Joel ben Simeon. Northern Italy, c. 1460–1470. London, British Library, MS Add. 14759.

Six leaves with representations of the Temple implements. Northern Italy, c. 1460–1470. New York, Jewish Theological Seminary of America, MS 0822.

Maraviglia Prayerbook. Northern Italy, 1469. London, British Library, MS Add. 26957.

Rothschild-Weill Mahzor. Northern Italy, c. 1460–1470. Jerusalem, National Library of Israel, MS Heb. 8°4450 (vol. 1) and Georges Weill Collection (vol. 2).

Stuttgart Haggadah. Southern Germany, 1470–1480. Stuttgart, Württembergische Landesbibliothek, Cod. Or. Q 1.

Washington Haggadah. Southern Germany, 1478. Washington, DC, Library of Congress, MS Heb. 1.

David Kimhi's Commentary on Psalms. Modena, 1485. Parma, Biblioteca Palatina, MS 2841.

Moskowitz Mahzor. Northern Italy, c. 1490–1492. Jerusalem, National Library of Israel, MS Heb. 4°1384.

Rothschild Mahzor. Florence, 1492. New York, Jewish Theological Seminary of America, MS Mic. 8892.

Select Bibliography

Beit-Arié, Malachi. "Codicological Description and Analysis of the Washington Haggadah," in Weinstein, 104–135.

———. "Joel ben Simeon's Manuscripts: A Codicologer's View," *Journal of Jewish Art* 3–4 (1977): 25–39; repr. in *The Making of the Medieval Hebrew Book: Studies in Palaeography and Codicology*, ed. Malachi Beit-Arié. Jerusalem: Magnes Press, 1993, 93–108.

——— "The Washington Haggadah, Written and Illuminated by Joel ben Simeon," in *The Making of the Medieval Hebrew Book: Studies in Palaeography and Codicology*, ed. Malachi Beit-Arié. Jerusalem: Magnes Press, 1993, 216–248.

Bokser, Baruch. *The Origins of the Seder: The Passover Rite and Early Rabbinic Judaism*. Berkeley: University of California Press, 1984.

Bonfil, Robert. *Jewish Life in Renaissance Italy* (Hebrew). Berkeley: University of California Press, 1994.

Cahn, Annabelle, and Walter Cahn. "An Illuminated Haggadah of the Fifteenth Century," *Yale University Library Gazette* 41 (1967): 166–182.

Cohen, Evelyn M. "Joel ben Simeon Revisited: Reflections of the Scribe's Artistic

Repertoire in a Cinquecento Haggadah," in *A Crown for a King: Studies in Jewish Art, History and Archeology in Memory of Stephen S. Kayser*, ed. Steve Fine, William Kramer, and Shalom Sabar. Berkeley, Jerusalem, and New York: Judah L. Magnes Museum, 2000, 59–72.

Edmunds, Sheila. "The Place of the London *Haggadah* in the Work of Joel Ben Simeon," *Journal of Jewish Art* 7 (1980): 25–34.

Even Zohar, Itamar. "The Making of Culture Repertoire and the Role of Transfer," *Target* 9/1 (1997): 373–381.

Fooner, Michael. "Joel ben Simeon, Illuminator of Hebrew Manuscripts in the XVth Century," *Jewish Quarterly Review* N. S. 27 (1936–1937): 217–232.

Friedman, Mira. "The Four Sons of the Haggadah and the Ages of Man," *Journal of Jewish Art* 11 (1985): 16–40.

Friedman, Shamma. *Tosefta Atiqta-Pesah Rishon: Synoptic Parallels of Mishnah and Tosefta Analyzed with a Methodological Introduction* (Hebrew). Ramat Gan: Bar-Ilan University Press, 2002.

Garel, Michel. *D'une main forte. Manuscrits hebreux des collections françaises—exhibition catalogue.* Paris: Bibliothèque nationale de France, 1992.

Gifford, D. J. "Iconographical Notes towards a Definition of the Medieval Fool," *Journal of the Warburg and Courtauld Institutes* 37 (1974): 336–342.

Glatzer, Mordechai. "The Ashkenazi and Italian Haggadah and the Haggadot of Joel ben Simeon," in Weinstein, 137–169.

Glick, Thomas F. *Islamic and Christian Spain in the Early Middle Ages.* Princeton: Princeton University Press, 1979; rev. ed., Leiden: E. J. Brill, 2005.

Goldschmidt, Ernst Daniel. *The Passover Haggadah: Its Sources and History* (Hebrew). Jerusalem: Bialik Institute, 1969.

Goldstein, David. *The Ashkenazi Haggadah: A Hebrew Manuscript of the Mid-15th Century from the Collections of the British Library.* New York: Abradale Press and Harry N. Abrams, 1997.

Guggenheimer, Heinrich. *The Scholar's Haggadah.* Northvale, NJ: Jason Aronson, 1995.

Gutmann, Joseph. "The Illuminated Medieval Passover Haggadah: Investigations and Research Problems," *Studies in Bibliography and Booklore* 7 (1965): 3–25.

———. "When the Kingdom Comes: Messianic Themes in Medieval Jewish Art," *Art Journal* 27 (1967–1968): 168–175.

———. "Thirteen Manuscripts in Search of an Author: Joel ben Simeon, 15th-

Century Scribe-Artist," *Studies in Bibliography and Booklore* 9 (1969–1971): 76–95.

———. *Hebrew Manuscript Painting*. New York: Braziller, 1978.

Hamburg, Doris A. "The Washington Haggadah—A Conservator's Perspective," in Weinstein, 170–195.

Kasher, Menahem. *Haggadah Shlemah*. Jerusalem: Torah Shlemah Institute, 1967.

Kogman-Appel, Katrin. *Die Zweite Nürnberger und die Jehuda Haggada. Jüdische Illustratoren zwischen Tradition und Fortschritt*. Frankfurt/Main: Peter Lang—Europäischer Verlag der Wissenschaften, 1999.

———. *Illuminated Haggadot from Medieval Spain*. University Park, PA: Pennsylvania State University Press, 2006.

Landsberger, Franz. "The Washington Haggadah and Its Illuminator," *Hebrew Union College Annual* 21 (1948): 73–103.

Marcus, Ivan. *Rituals of Childhood: Jewish Acculturation in Medieval Europe*. New Haven: Yale University Press, 1996.

Merke, Franz. *History and Iconography of Endemic Goiter and Cretinism*. Lancaster: MTP Press, 1984.

Metzger, Mendel. *La Haggada enluminée. Étude iconographique et stilistique des manuscripts enluminés et decorés de la Haggada du XIIIe au XVIe siècle*. Leiden: E. J. Brill, 1973.

Metzger, Mendel, and Thérèse Metzger. *Jewish Life in the Middle Ages*. New York: Alpine Fine Arts Collection, 1982.

Narkiss, Bezalel. "The Art of the Washington Haggadah," in Weinstein, 27–101.

———. *Hebrew Illuminated Manuscripts*. Jerusalem and New York: Encyclopedia Judaica, 1969; rev. ed. (in Hebrew), Jerusalem: Keter, 1984.

Offenberg, Sara. "Expressions of Meeting the Challenges of the Christian Milieu in Medieval Jewish Art and Literature," Ph.D. thesis. Beer Sheva: Ben-Gurion University of the Negev, 2008.

Otto, Beatrice K. *Fools Are Everywhere: The Court Jester around the World*. Chicago: University of Chicago Press, 2001.

Raphael, Chaim. *A Feast of History: The Drama of Passover through the Ages: With a New Translation of the Haggadah for Use at the Seder*. New York: Simon and Schuster, 1972.

Reed-Blank, Debra. "*Sh'fokh hamatkha* and Eliyahu in the Haggadah: Ideology and Liturgy," *Conservative Judaism* 40/2 (1987): 73–86.

Richler, Benjamin, ed. *Hebrew Manuscripts in the Bibliotheca Palatina*. Jerusalem: Jewish National and University Library [National Library of Israel], 2001.

Ruß, Hubert, ed. *Der Bußprediger Capestrano auf dem Domplatz in Bamberg: Eine Bamberger Tafel um 1470/75*, exh. cat. Bamberg: Historisches Museum, 1989.

Safrai, Shmuel, and Zev Safrai. *Haggadah of the Sages* (Hebrew). Jerusalem: Carta, 1998.

Schmelzer, Menahem, and Evelyn M. Cohen. *The Rothschild Mahzor*. New York: Jewish Theological Seminary of America, 1983.

Segal, J. B. *The Hebrew Passover: From the Earliest Times to* A.D. *70*. London and Oxford: Oxford University Press, 1963.

Shoham-Steiner, Ephraim. *Involuntary Marginals: Marginal Individuals in Medieval Northern European Jewish Society* (Hebrew). Jerusalem: Zalman Shazar Center for Jewish History, 2008.

Spitzter, Moshe, ed. *The Bird's Head Haggada of the Bezalel National Art Museum in Jerusalem*. Jerusalem: Tarshish Books, 1965–1967.

Tabory, Joseph. *The Passover Ritual throughout the Generations* (Hebrew). Tel Aviv: Hakibbutz Hameuhad, 1996.

———. "Towards a History of the Passover Meal," in *Passover and Easter: Origin and History in Modern Times*, ed. Paul F. Bradshaw and Lawrence A. Hoffman. Notre Dame: Notre Dame University Press, 1999, 62–80.

———. *JPS Commentary on the Haggadah: Historical Introduction, Translation and Commentary*. Philadelphia: Jewish Publication Society, 2008.

Weinstein, Myron M., ed. *The Washington Haggadah: A Facsimile Edition of an Illuminated Fifteenth-Century Hebrew Manuscript at the Library of Congress Signed by Joel ben Simeon*. Washington, DC: Library of Congress, 1991.

Wolfson, Laurel, ed. *The First Cincinnati Haggadah: An Interactive CD Facsimile Edition*. Hebrew Union College—Jewish Institute of Religion, 2000.

Yerushalmi, Yosef Hayim. *Haggadah and History: A Panorama in Facsimile of Five Centuries of the Printed Haggadah, from the Collections of Harvard University and the Jewish Theological Seminary of America*. Philadelphia: Jewish Publication Society, 1975.

Yudlov, Isaac. *The Haggadah Thesaurus: Bibliography of Passover Haggadot from the Beginning of Hebrew Printing until 1960* (Hebrew). Jerusalem: Magnes Press, 1997.

Yuval, Israel J. *Two Nations in Your Womb: Perceptions of Jews and Christians in Late*

Antiquity and the Middle Ages, trans. Barbara Harshav and Jonathan Chipman. Berkeley: University of California Press, 2006.

Zirlin, Yael. "The Early Works of Joel ben Simeon, a Jewish Scribe and Artist in the 15th Century," Ph.D. thesis. Jerusalem: Hebrew University of Jerusalem, 1995.

———. "Joel Meets Johannes: A Fifteenth-Century Jewish Christian Collaboration in Manuscript Illumination," *Viator* 26 (1995): 265–282.

———. "Celui qui se cache derrière l'image: Colophons des enlumineurs dans les manuscripts hébraïques," *Revue des Études Juives* 155/1–2 (1996): 33–53.

Zucker, Shlomo. *The Moskowitz Mahzor of Joel ben Simeon*. Jerusalem: Jewish National and University Library [National Library of Israel], 2005.

THE WASHINGTON HAGGADAH

A NOTE ON THE TEXT

This text is based on Joseph Tabory's translation of the haggadah in Joseph Tabory, *The JPS Commentary on the Haggadah: Historical Introduction, Translation, and Commentary* (Philadelphia: Jewish Publication Society, 2008), with the permission of the Jewish Publication Society. I have extensively revised Tabory's text both for stylistic reasons and to accord with the text recorded in the Washington Haggadah.

Sections in italics refer to the directions in the haggadah, which Joel wrote in a smaller, semicursive script. The normal font indicates the larger, square script reserved for the haggadah's text itself. In my transcription I have not tried to replicate the larger initial letters or words, although a few unusual instances or deviations are cited in the notes. The biblical sources in parentheses have been provided for the present reader's convenience; they are not in the haggadah's text.

The marginal notes by later hands are all translated in the footnotes. Endnotes annotate all sources and special remarks.

[FOL. 1R] [In scroll at very top of page] *With good luck I shall write the order of the Passover [seder]. For Your honor, God.*[1]

On the eve of the fourteenth [of Nisan], one searches [the house] for leaven by the light of a candle. Any place in which leaven is not brought need not be searched.

In order to nullify the leaven, [one recites the following blessing]:

Blessed are You, God, our Lord, King of the universe, who has sanctified us by His commandments and commanded us about removing the leaven.

All leaven that is in my possession, that I have seen and not seen, that I have beheld and not beheld, that I have removed and not removed—let it be nullified and like the dust of the earth.[2]

Another order[3] *for [the rituals of] the Passover [seder]:*

Recite the benediction over wine, and wash the hands. Eat a green vegetable [*karpas*]. Break the middle *matsah*. Recite the haggadah. Wash ritually. Bring out the unleavened bread. The bitter herb. Eat the bitter herb and *matsah* together. Set the table for the meal. The hidden thing. Make the blessing of grace after the meal. Recite the *halel* (praise of God). It is accepted.[a]

a. The left margin contains the following note:

It is necessary to search in every corner in every room.

[An alternative version to the formula "All leaven":] All leaven that is in this house, that I have not seen and that I have not removed—let it be nullified and like dust.

[FOL. IV] *In the evening, after they return from the synagogue, they wash out the glasses [for wine] and bring to the table a large plate on which there are three* matsot *that have been guarded for the purpose of fulfilling the commandment.*[4] *[They also bring] a second plate on which there are vegetables—lettuce and parsley—and two cooked dishes, either meat or an egg or fish, one in remembrance of the [Passover sacrifice that was offered in] the Temple and the other in remembrance of the special holiday sacrifice* (hagigah); *and a dish with* haroset *in it in remembrance of the muddy plaster [with which the Israelites worked in Egypt]. Then [the head of the household] pours the first cup of wine and recites the blessing beginning, "Blessed," etc.*

Blessed are You, O God, our Lord, King of the universe, who has created the fruit of the vine.

Blessed are You, O God, our Lord, King of the universe, who has chosen us among the nations, and exalted us among every tongue, and sanctified us by His commandments. And you have given us, O God, our Lord, in love, Appointed Days for joy, festivals and times for re-

---

It is necessary to guard the pieces [of leaven] from the mice, for if they take one of the pieces and a [member of the household] finds it during Passover he will transgress the prohibitions against not seeing [leaven] and not finding it [among his possessions]. On the next day . . . they eat [leaven] until the fourth hour of [the day].

[The next line is illegible.]

They burn [the leaven] at the beginning of the sixth hour [on the next day].

When he burns it, he recites thus:

All leaven that is in this house that I have seen and not seen, that I have removed and not removed—let it be nullified like the dust.

On the lower-left margin the following text is written in a different hand:

Why do we not make the blessing of "who has kept us alive, [sustained us and brought us to this time]" over the search for leaven? We only make the blessing of "who has kept us alive, etc.," over joyous acts, and this is not a joyous act.

joicing, this day of the festival of unleavened bread, the time of our freedom, in love, a holy convocation, a remembrance of the Exodus from Egypt. For it is us You have chosen, and us whom You have sanctified from all the nations. The Appointed Days of Your holiness in happiness and rejoicing You have bequeathed us. Blessed are You, O God, who sanctifies Israel and the [special] times.

Blessed are You, O God, our Lord, King of the universe, who has kept us alive, sustained us and brought us to this time.

Then they drink. He then washes his hands and makes the blessing over ritually washing hands.

[FOL. 2R] *If Passover falls on the Sabbath, he begins here:*

"The heaven and the earth were finished, and all their array. On the seventh day the Lord finished the work that He had been doing, and He ceased on the seventh day from all the work that He had done. And the Lord blessed the seventh day and declared it holy, because on it the Lord ceased from all the work of creation that He had done" (Gen. 2:1–3).

Blessed are You, O God, our Lord, King of the universe, who has created the fruit of the vine.

Blessed are You, O God, our Lord, King of the universe, who has chosen us among all the nations, and exalted us among every tongue, and sanctified us by His commandments. And You have given us, O God, our Lord, in love, Sabbaths for rest and Appointed Days for joy, festivals and times for rejoicing, this day of Sabbath, and this day of the festival of unleavened bread, the time of our freedom, in love, a holy convocation, a remembrance of the Exodus from Egypt. For it is us You have chosen, and us whom You have sanctified from the nations. And the Sabbath and the Appointed Days of Your holiness in love and favor, in joy and rejoicing, You have bequeathed us. Blessed are You, O God, who sanctifies the Sabbath, Israel, and the [special] times.

Blessed are You, O God, our Lord, King of the universe, who has kept us alive, sustained us and brought us to this time.

If Passover falls on a Saturday night, one says YaKNeHaZ, *[an anagram for]* Yayin *[the blessing over wine],* Kidush *[the blessing over the holiday],* Ner *[the blessing over light],* Havdalah *[the blessing that ends the Sabbath and separates it from the week],* Zeman *[the blessing for bringing us to this time].*

Blessed are You, O God, our Lord, King of the universe, who has created the fruit of the vine.

Blessed are You, O God, our Lord, King of the universe, who has chosen us among the nations and exalted us among every tongue, and sanctified us by His commandments. And You have given us, O God, our Lord, in love, Appointed Days for joy, festivals and times for rejoicing, this day of the festival of unleavened bread, the time of our freedom, a holy convocation, a remembrance of the Exodus from Egypt. For it is us You have chosen, and us whom You have sanctified from all the nations. And the Appointed Days of Your holiness in happiness and rejoicing you have bequeathed us. Blessed are You, O God, who sanctifies Israel and the [special] times.

[FOL. 3R] Blessed are You, O God, our Lord, King of the universe, creator of the lights of the fire.

Blessed are You, O God, our Lord, King of the universe, who separates holy from profane, light from darkness, Israel from the nations, and the seventh day from the six days of work. The sanctity of the Sabbath You have separated from the sanctity of the festival, and the seventh day from the six days of work You have sanctified. You have separated and sanctified Your people, Israel, with Your sanctity. Blessed are You, O God, who separates sanctity from sanctity.

Blessed are You, O God, our Lord, King of the universe, who has kept us alive, sustained us and brought us to this time.

They drink. Then he washes his hands ritually and makes the following blessing:

Blessed are You, O God, our Lord, King of the universe, who has sanctified us by His commandments and commanded us about ritually washing the hands.

Then he takes parsley[5] *and makes the following blessing:*

Blessed are You, O God, our Lord, King of the universe, creator of the fruit of the land.

He dips it in the haroset *and gives some to all the members of his household.*

Then he takes the topmost matsah *and breaks it in half, and places one half under the tablecloth,*[6] *on account of the verse, "[So the people took their dough before it was leavened,] their kneading bowls wrapped in their cloaks . . ." (Exod. 12:34); and the other half back between the two whole* matsot, *on account of the verse, "[. . . for seven days, you shall eat unleavened bread,] bread of poverty" (Deut. 16:3).*[7]

Just as it is the wont of a poor person to have only a piece, so here there is only a piece. After this he lifts up the large plate, but he first removes from it the meat and egg lest he appear to be lifting up consecrated food outside the precincts of the Temple.

He then recites the section beginning,

Here is the bread, etc.

[FOL. 3V] Here is the bread of distress which our ancestors ate in the land of Egypt. Let anyone who is hungry come and eat. Let anyone who wishes come and participate in the Passover. Today we are here; next year, in the Land of Israel. Today we are slaves; next year, we shall be free men.

Then they pour the second cup of wine.

[FOL. 4R] What is different[8] about this night from all other nights?

On all other nights we may eat both leavened and unleavened bread; on this night we eat only unleavened bread.

On all other nights, we eat all kinds of vegetables; on this night we eat bitter herbs.

On all other nights we are not obligated to dip even once; on this night we do it twice.

On all other nights, we eat either sitting or reclining; and on this night, we all recline.

We were slaves to Pharaoh in Egypt and God, our Lord, took us out [FOL. 4V] from there with a mighty hand,[9] and with an outstretched arm.[10] And if the Holy One, blessed be He, had not taken our ancestors out of Egypt, then we, our children, and our children's children would [still] be subjugated to Pharaoh in Egypt. And even if all of us are sages, all of us men of understanding, all of us elders, all of us experts in the Torah, it is incumbent upon us to tell the story of the Exodus from Egypt. For whoever relates the story of the Exodus from Egypt—that one is to be praised!

It actually happened that R. Eliezer, R. Joshua, R. Eliezer b. Azaryah, R. Akiva, and R. Tarfon were banqueting in Bnei Brak and were relating the story of [FOL. 5R] the Exodus from Egypt all that night, until their students came and said to them: "Our masters, it is time to recite the morning *shema'*."[11]

Said R. Eliezer ben Azaryah: Look! I am about seventy years old, and I never merited [understanding why] the Exodus should be mentioned in the evening until Ben Zoma interpreted the following verse, as it says: "so that you may remember the day of your departure from the land of

els; recent research shows that Jewish scribes and craftsmen were occasionally found in Christian workshops. See also Zucker, xxiii, note 32.

3. He similarly indicated his origin in the Bodmer Haggadah, as we will see.

4. Joel's biography has been reconstructed step-by-step in several publications since 1937: Fooner; Landsberger; Cahn; Gutmann, "Thirteen Manuscripts in Search of an Author"; Narkiss, *Hebrew Illuminated Manuscripts;* Beit-Arié, "Joel ben Simeon's Manuscripts"; Edmunds; Narkiss in Weinstein; Zirlin, "The Early Works of Joel ben Simeon," and "Joel Meets Johannes."

5. Scholars disagree as to the provenance of the Parma Siddur; Yael Zirlin attributes it on codicological and textual grounds to Germany and groups it with the First Nuremberg and the First JTS Haggadot (Zirlin, "The Early Works of Joel ben Simeon"); Narkiss pointed out that the scarce traces of illustrations on the trimmed margins reveal Italian influence (Narkiss in Weinstein). Also, the fact that Joel explicitly mentions his origin in Bonn indicates that he was residing elsewhere at the time he wrote the colophon.

6. For background on the history of Jews in early-modern Italy, see Bonfil.

7. Goldstein.

8. Schmelzer and Cohen; Zucker; http://jnul.huji.ac.il/dl/mss/heb1384/index_eng.html.

9. Beit-Arié in Weinstein.

10. For thoughts on the acculturation of minorities in Iberia, see Glick; on that of Ashkenazi Jews, see Marcus.

11. On the notion of "cultural agents" and the role they play in these processes, see Even-Zohar.

12. Several haggadot predate Joel ben Simeon's activity: the Bird Head Haggadah in the Israel Museum, MS 180/57, made around 1300 in the Middle or Upper Rhine region; an early fourteenth-century haggadah in Paris, Bibliothèque nationale de France, cod. hébr. 644; another one in Parma, Biblioteca Palatina, MS Parm 3518. The latter two are particularly rich in spared-ground motifs. Around 1430 the Hamburg Miscellany, containing among other texts a haggadah, was produced in Mainz, Hamburg, Staats- und Universitätsbibliothek, cod. hebr. 37.

13. Very little is known about Italian Jewish manuscript painting before the fifteenth century. In most cases basic data of dates and provenances are still not solved. In this group of Italian haggadot produced before 1450 we can count a manuscript of

Egypt all the days of your life" (Deut. 16:3). "The days of your life" [refers to] the days themselves; "*all* the days of your life" [includes] the evenings.

But the sages say: "the days of your life" [refers to] this world; "all the days of your life" includes the messianic period.

Blessed is the Omnipresent, blessed is He. Blessed is He who [FOL. 5V] gave the Torah to Israel, blessed is He.

About four sons the Torah spoke: one who is wise; one who is wicked; one who is simple; and one who does not know how to ask.

The wise one—what does he say? "What are the decrees, laws, and rules that God, our Lord, has enjoined upon you?" (Deut. 6:20). And so you should explain to him some of the laws of Passover, [such as] "After the Passover meal, one may not indulge in revelry."[12]

The wicked one—what does he say? "What does this rite mean to you?" (Exod. 12:26). "To you," and not to him. And since he excluded himself from the community, he has denied a fundamental [belief]. You should set [FOL. 6R] his teeth on edge[13] and say to him, "It is because of what God did for me when I went free from Egypt" (Exod. 13:8)—"for me," not for *him*. If he had been there, he would not have been redeemed.

The simple son—what does he say? "What does this mean?" (Exod. 13:14). And you shall say to him: "It was with a mighty hand that God, our Lord, brought us out from Egypt, from the house of bondage" (Exod. 13:14).

And the one who does not know how to ask—you begin for him, as it says, “And you shall explain to your son on that day, ‘It is because of what God did for me when I went free from Egypt’” (Exod. 13:8).

I might think that [the obligation to tell the story of the Exodus] begins on the first day of the month [of Nisan]. Therefore Scripture teaches: “on that day” (Exod. 13:8). Now I might think that [the obligation] begins during the daytime. Therefore Scripture teaches: “for this” (Exod. 13:8)—[as if to say,] it speaks [FOL. 6V] only of the time when the unleavened bread and bitter herbs are placed in front of you.

In the beginning, idol worshipers were our ancestors, but now the Omnipresent has drawn us to His worship. As it says: “Then Joshua said to all the people, ‘Thus said God, the Lord of Israel: In olden times, your forefathers, Terah, father of Abraham and father of Nahor, lived beyond the Euphrates and worshiped other gods. But I took your father Abraham from beyond the Euphrates and led him through the whole land of Canaan and multiplied his offspring. I gave him Isaac, and to Isaac I gave Jacob and Esau. To Esau I gave the hill country of Seir [as his possession][14] while Jacob and his children went down to Egypt’” (Joshua 24:2–4).

[FOL. 7R] Blessed is He who keeps His promise to[15] Israel, Blessed is He. For the Holy one, Blessed be He, calculated the end to do as He had promised Abraham our forefather at the time of the Covenant between the Sections (Gen. 15:8–21), as it is said, “And He said to Abram, ‘Know well that your offspring shall be strangers in a land not theirs, and they shall be enslaved and oppressed for four hundred years; but I will execute judgment on the nation they shall serve, and in the end they shall go free with great wealth'" (Gen. 15:13–14).

And it is this [promise] that has stood by our fathers and us. For not just a single person has arisen against us to destroy us, but in every generation people arise against us to destroy us. And the Holy one, blessed be He, saves us from their hands.

[FOL. 7V] Go forth and see what Laban the Aramean sought to do to our ancestor, Jacob. For Pharaoh's decree was only against the males while Laban sought to destroy everyone, as it is said: "An Aramean tried to destroy my father.[16] He went down to Egypt and sojourned there with meager numbers; but there he became a great and very populous nation" (Deut. 26:5).

"He went down to Egypt" (Deut. 26:5)—compelled by the word [of God]

"and sojourned there" (Deut. 26:5)—this teaches us that he intended not to settle down in Egypt but just to sojourn there [temporarily], as it is said, "They told Pharaoh, 'To sojourn in this land [FOL. 8R] we have come, for there is no pasture for your servants' flocks, the famine being severe in the land of Canaan. Pray, then, let your servants stay in the region of Goshen'" (Gen. 47:4).

"with meager numbers" (Deut. 26:5)—as it is said, "Your ancestors went down to Egypt seventy persons in all; and now God, your Lord, has made you as numerous as the stars of heaven" (Deut. 10:22).

"but there they became a . . . nation" (Deut. 26:5)—this teaches that the Israelites were distinguishable there.

"great and mighty" (Deut. 26:5)—as it is said, ". . . the Israelites were fertile and prolific; they multiplied and increased very greatly, so that the land was filled with them" (Exod. 1:7).

"and very populous" (Deut. 26:5)—as it is said, "I let you grow like the plants of the field; and you continued to grow up until you attained to womanhood, until your breasts became firm and your hair sprouted. [FOL. 8R] You were still naked and bare" (Ezek. 16:7).

"The Egyptians dealt harshly with us and oppressed us; they imposed heavy labor upon us" (Deut. 26:6).

"The Egyptians dealt harshly with us" (Deut. 26:6)—as it is said, "Let us deal shrewdly with them, so that they may not increase; otherwise in the event of war they may join our enemies in fighting against us and rise from the ground" (Exod. 1:10).

"and oppressed us" (Deut. 26:6)—as it is said, ". . . to oppress them with forced labor; and they built garrison cities for Pharaoh: Pithom and Raamses" (Exod. 1:11).

[FOL. 9R] "they imposed heavy labor upon us" (Deut. 26:6)—as it is said, "The Egyptians ruthlessly imposed upon the Israelites the various labors that they made them perform" (Exod. 1:13–14).

"We cried to God, the Lord of our fathers, and God heard our plea and saw our plight, our misery, and our oppression" (Deut. 26:7).

"We cried to God, the Lord of our fathers" (Deut. 26:7)—as it is said, "A long time after that, the king of Egypt died. The Israelites were groaning under the bondage and cried out; and their cry for help from the bondage rose up to the Lord" (Exod. 2:23).

"and God heard our plea" (Deut. 26:7)—as it is said, "The Lord heard [FOL. 9V] their moaning, and the Lord remembered His covenant with Abraham and Isaac and Jacob" (Exod. 2:24).

"and saw our plight" (Deut. 26:7)—this refers to the enforced separation [of husbands from having sexual relations with their wives], as it is said, "the Lord looked upon the Israelites, and the Lord took notice of them" (Exod. 2:25).

"our misery" (Deut. 26:7)—these are the sons, as it is said, "Every boy that is born you shall throw into the Nile, but let every girl live" (Exod. 1:22).

"and our oppression" (Deut. 26:7)—this is the persecution, as it is said, "Moreover, I have seen how the Egyptians oppress them" (Exod. 3:9).

"God, our Lord, took us out from Egypt by a mighty hand, by an arm [FOL. 10R] outstretched, and by awesome power, and by signs and portents" (Deut. 26:8).

"God, our Lord, took us out from Egypt" (Deut. 26:8)—not by means of an angel, not by means of a seraph, not by means of an agent, but the Holy one, blessed be He, in His glory and by Himself, as it says, "For that night I will go through the land of Egypt and I will strike down every first-born in the land of Egypt, both man and beast; and on all the gods of Egypt I will mete out punishments, I am God" (Exod. 12:12).

"For that night I will go through the land of Egypt" (Exod. 12:12): I—and not an angel.
". . . and I will strike down every first-born in the land of Egypt" (Exod. 12:12): I—and not a seraph.
". . . and on all the gods of Egypt [FOL. 10V] I will mete out punishments" (Exod. 12:12): I—and not an agent.

I am He, and no other.

"by a mighty hand" (Deut. 26:8)—this refers to the pestilence, as it says, "Then the hand of God will strike your livestock in the fields—the horses, the asses, the camels, the cattle, and the sheep—with a very severe pestilence" (Exod. 9:3).

"by an outstretched arm" (Deut. 26:8)—this refers to the sword, as it says, ". . . with a drawn sword in his hand directed against Jerusalem" (1 Chron. 21:16).

"and by awesome power" (Deut. 26:8)—this refers to the revelation of the Divine presence, as it says, "Or has any god ventured to go and take for himself one nation from the midst of another by prodigious acts, [FOL. 11R] by signs and portents,[17] by war, by a mighty hand and an outstretched arm and awesome power, as God your Lord did for you in Egypt before your very eyes?" (Deut. 4:34).

"and by signs" (Deut. 26:8)—this refers to the staff [of Moses], as it says, "And take this rod in your hand, with which you shall perform the signs" (Exod. 4:17).

"and portents" (Deut. 26:8)—this refers to the blood, as it says, "I will set portents in the sky and on earth: Blood and fire and pillars of smoke" (Joel 3:3).

[FOL. 11V] Another interpretation [of Deut. 26:8]: "by a mighty hand" refers to two [plagues]; "by an outstretched arm" refers to two; "awesome power" refers to two; "and by signs" to two; "and portents," two.

These are the ten plagues which the Holy one, blessed be He, brought upon the Egyptians in Egypt. And these are: Blood, frogs, lice, swarms of insects, pestilence, boils, hail, locusts, darkness, and the death of the first-born.

R. Judah referred to them by a mnemonic: *DeTsaKh*, *'ADaSH*, *Be'AHaB*.

[FOL. 12R] R. Yose ha-Galili said: How do you know that the Egyptians suffered ten plagues in Egypt and that they suffered fifty plagues at the [Red] Sea?

What does it say regarding Egypt? "And the magicians said to Pharaoh, 'This is the finger of God!'" (Exod. 8:15). But what does it say regarding the Sea? "And when Israel saw the powerful hand which God had wielded against the Egyptians, the people feared God; they had faith in God and in His servant Moses" (Exod. 14:31). How much did they suffer from a finger? Ten plagues! Say, therefore, [FOL. 12V] that in Egypt they suffered ten plagues and at the Sea they suffered fifty plagues.

R. Eliezer says: How do we know that each and every plague that the Holy One, blessed be He, brought upon the Egyptians in Egypt was composed of four plagues? As it says, "He inflicted His burning anger upon them, wrath, indignation, trouble, a band of deadly messengers" (Ps. 78:49–50). "Wrath"[18] is one; "indignation," two; "trouble," [three];[19] "a band of deadly messengers," four. Say, therefore, that in Egypt [FOL. 13R] they suffered forty plagues, and at the Sea, two hundred plagues.

R. Akiva says: How do we know that each and every plague that the Holy one, blessed be He, brought upon the Egyptians in Egypt was composed of five plagues? As it says, "He inflicted His burning anger upon them, wrath, indignation, trouble, a band of deadly messengers" (Ps. 78:49–50). "Burning anger" is one; "wrath," two; "indignation," three; "trouble," four; "a band of deadly messengers," five. Say, therefore, that in Egypt they suffered fifty plagues and at the Sea they suffered two hundred and fifty plagues.

[FOL. 13V] For how many unnecessary favors are we obligated to the Omnipresent!

If He had taken us out of Egypt but not punished the [Egyptians],
it would have been sufficient for us.

If He had punished them but not done in their gods,
it would have been sufficient for us.

If He had done in their gods but not killed their first-born,
it would have been sufficient for us.

If He had killed their first-born [FOL. 14R] but not given us their money,
it would have been sufficient for us.

If He had given us their money but not divided the Sea for us,
it would have been sufficient for us.

If He had divided the Sea for us but not brought us through it on dry land, it would have been sufficient for us.

If He had brought us through it on dry land but not drowned our enemies in it, it would have been sufficient for us.

If He had drowned our enemies in it but not provided our needs in the desert for forty years, it would have been sufficient for us.

If He had provided our needs in the desert for forty years but not fed us the manna, it would have been sufficient for us.

If He had fed us the manna but not given us the Sabbath,
it would have been sufficient for us.

[FOL. 14V] If He had given us the Sabbath and not brought us before Mount Sinai, it would have been sufficient for us.

If He had brought us before Mount Sinai and not given us the Torah,
it would have been sufficient for us.

If He had given us the Torah and not brought us to the Land of Israel,
it would have been sufficient for us.

If He had brought us to the Land of Israel but not built the Temple for us, it would have been sufficient for us.

How much more so are we obligated for the doubled and redoubled favors that the Omnipresent [did] for us!

For He took us out of Egypt, [FOL. 15R] and punished the Egyptians, and destroyed their gods, and killed their first-born, and gave us their money, and divided the sea for us, and brought us through it on dry land, and drowned our enemies in it, and provided our needs in the desert for forty years, and fed us the manna, and gave us the Sabbath, and brought us before Mount Sinai, and gave us the Torah, and brought us to the Land of Israel, and built the Temple for us to atone for all our sins.

Rabban Gamliel used to say: Whoever does not explain these three things on Passover has not fulfilled his obligation. They are: The Passover sacrifice, the unleavened bread, [FOL. 15V] and the bitter herbs.

The Passover sacrifice that our ancestors ate when the Temple existed—what was the reason? For the reason that the Omnipresent passed over the houses of our ancestors in Egypt. As it says, "You shall say, 'It is the Passover sacrifice to God, because He passed over the houses of the Israelites in Egypt when He smote the Egyptians, but saved our houses.' The people then bowed low in homage" (Exod. 12:27).

This unleavened bread that we eat—what was the reason? For the reason that the dough of our ancestors did not have time to become leavened before the King of Kings, [FOL. 16R] the Holy One, blessed be He, revealed Himself before them and redeemed them. As it says, "And they baked unleavened cakes of the dough that they had taken out of Egypt, for it was not leavened, since they had been driven out of Egypt and could not delay; nor had they prepared any provisions for themselves" (Exod. 12:39–40).

These bitter herbs that we eat—what was the reason? For the reason that the Egyptians embittered the lives of our ancestors in Egypt. As it says, "They made life bitter for them with harsh labor at mortar and bricks and with all sorts of tasks in the field, the various labors that they made them perform ruthlessly" (Exod. 1:14).

[FOL. 16V] In every generation a person is obligated to see himself as if he had gone out of Egypt. As it says, "It is because of what God did for me when I went free from Egypt" (Exod. 13:8).

Not our ancestors alone did the Holy One, blessed be He, redeem, but us too He redeemed with them. As it says, "And us He freed from there, that He might take us and give us the land that He had promised on oath to our fathers" (Deut. 6:23).

[FOL. 17R] Therefore, we are obligated to thank, acclaim, praise, laud, exalt, extol, bless, and applaud Him, the One who performed these miracles for our ancestors and for us, all these miracles: He took us from slavery to freedom, from suffering to joy, from mourning to festivity, from darkness to a great light, and from subjection to redemption. And so we say before Him, Hallelujah.

[FOL. 17V] Hallelujah. O servants of God, give praise; praise the name of God. Let the name of God be blessed now and forever. From east to west the name of God is praised. God is exalted above all nations; His glory is above the heavens. Who is like God our Lord, who, enthroned on high, sees what is below, in heaven and on earth? From the dust He raises the poor, from the refuse heap He lifts up [FOL. 18R] the needy to set them with the great, with the great men of His people. He sets the childless woman among her household as a happy mother of children. Hallelujah (Ps. 113:1–9).

When Israel went forth from Egypt, the house of Jacob from a people of strange speech, Judah became His holy one, Israel, His dominion. The sea saw them and fled, the Jordan ran backward, mountains skipped like rams, hills like sheep. What alarmed you, O sea, that you fled; O Jordan, that you ran backward; O mountains, that you skipped like rams; O hills, like sheep? Tremble, O earth, at the presence of GOD, at the presence of the God of Jacob, who turned the rock into a pool of water, the flinty rock into a fountain (Ps. 114:1–8).

[FOL. 18V] Blessed are You, O God, our Lord, King of the universe, who redeemed us and redeemed our ancestors from Egypt, and brought us to this night to eat unleavened bread and bitter herbs. So may God, our Lord and the Lord of our ancestors, bring us to other holidays and pilgrimage festivals that come toward us in peace, rejoicing in the building of Your city and delighting in Your worship. And we shall eat there from the Paschal lambs and the sacrifices whose blood will be sprinkled on Your altar according to Your wish, and we shall praise You with a new song about our redemption and the salvation of our souls. Blessed [FOL. 19R] are You, O God, redeemer of Israel.

Blessed are You, O God, our Lord, King of the universe, creator of the fruit of the vine.

They drink while reclining to the left, and after doing so, they do not make the concluding blessing "over the grapevine and the fruit of the grapevine."[20]

NETILAT:[21] *He then ritually washes his hands and recites the blessing.*

Blessed are You, O God, our Lord, King of the universe, who has sanctified us by His commandments and commanded us about the ritual washing of hands.

SHELEMAH:[22] *[The master of the household] takes the topmost*[23] *piece of unleavened bread.*

MOTZI:[24] *He recites the following blessing:*

"Blessed are You, O God, our Lord, King of the universe, who brings forth bread from the earth."[25] *But he does yet not eat.*

U-FEROS:[26] *He takes the half piece of [the middle]* matsah, *and blesses:*

AKHAL:[27] *"Blessed are You, O God, our Lord, King of the universe, who has sanctified us by His commandments and commanded us about eating unleavened bread."*

'IMAH:[28] *He joins the two pieces and eats them together, and distributes a portion to all the members of the household.*

MAROR:[29] *After this, he takes a piece of the bitter herbs that they call lettuce,*[30] *and he dips it into the* haroset *and recites the following blessing:*

"Blessed are You, O GOD, our Lord, King of the universe, who has sanctified us by His commandments and commanded us about eating the bitter herbs."

He eats it, and gives a portion to all the members of his household.

BAREKH:[31] *After this, he takes the bottom-most* matsah, *and breaks it in half, and takes from the bitter herbs that they call* meerrettich [horseradish],[32] *and he eats it with the* matsah *but without reciting a blessing or dipping it [in the* haroset*], in remembrance of [the practice performed during the period of] the Temple according to the custom of Hillel. And he gives [portions] to everyone.*

Then they all eat and drink as much as they wish. And after the banquet is completed, he takes the afikomen *that he had placed beneath the napkin, and eats a piece of it equivalent in size to an olive, and he gives a portion to everyone. After this, they are not permitted to eat anything more the entire night so that the taste of the* matsah *will remain in their mouths.*

Then he ritually washes his hands but does not recite a blessing over the ritual washing, because ritual washing of hands at the end of the meal is obligatory but it does not require a blessing. Then they pour the third cup of wine for the grace after the meal.

[At this point the grace after the meal is recited, and the third cup of wine is drunk at its conclusion with a blessing over the wine.][33]

Then they pour the fourth cup of wine and complete the recitation of the Hallelujah.

[FOL. 19V] "Pour out Your fury on the nations that do not know You, upon the kingdoms that do not invoke Your name" (Ps. 79:6).[a]

[FOL. 20R] Not to us, GOD, not to us but to Your name bring glory for the sake of Your love and Your faithfulness. Let the nations not say, "Where, now, is their God?" when our God is in heaven and all that He wills He accomplishes. Their idols are silver and gold, the work of

a. On the top margin, a later hand added the following verses to be recited along with "Pour out Your fury":

"Pour out Your wrath on them; may Your blazing anger overtake them" (Ps. 69:34). ". . . For they have devoured Jacob, have devoured and consumed him, and have laid desolate his homesteads" (Jer. 10:25). "Pay them according to their deeds, their malicious acts; according to their handiwork pay them, give them their deserts" (Ps. 28:4). "May they be erased from the book of life, and not be inscribed with the righteous" (Ps. 69:29). "Give them, O Lord, their deserts according to their deeds" (Lam. 3:64). "Add that to their guilt; let them have no share of Your beneficence" (Ps. 69:29). "Give them anguish of heart; Your curse be upon them!" (Lam. 3:65). "Give them, O Lord—give them what? Give them a womb that miscarries, and shriveled breasts!" (Hos. 9:14). "May their encampments be desolate; may their tents stand empty" (Ps. 69:26).

A second hand added still another verse: "O, pursue them in wrath and destroy them from under the heavens of the Lord" (Lam. 3:66). According to M. Kasher (*Haggadah Shelemah* [Jerusalem: Makhon Torah Shelemah, 1955], 178), the verses cited attest to the northern French rite.

men's hands. They have mouths, but cannot speak; eyes, but cannot see; they have ears, but cannot hear; noses, but cannot smell; they have hands, but cannot touch; feet, but cannot walk; they can make no sound in their throats. Those who fashion them, all who trust in them, shall become like them. O Israel, trust in God! He is their help and shield. O house of Aaron, trust in God! He is their help and shield. [FOL. 20V] O you who fear God, trust in God! He is their help and shield (Ps. 115:1–11).

God is mindful of us. He will bless us; He will bless the house of Israel; He will bless the house of Aaron; He will bless those who fear God, small and great alike. May God increase your numbers, yours and your children's also. May you be blessed by God, Maker of heaven and earth. The heavens belong to God, but the earth He gave over to man. The dead cannot praise God, nor any who go down into silence. But we will bless God now and forever. Hallelujah (Ps. 115:12–18).

I love God for He hears my voice, [FOL. 21R] my pleas; for He turns His ear to me whenever I call. The bonds of death encompassed me; the torments of Sheol overtook me. I came upon trouble and sorrow and I invoked the name of God, "God, save my life!" God is gracious and beneficent; our God is compassionate. God protects the simple; I was brought low and He saved me. Be at rest, once again, O my soul, for God has been good to you. You have delivered me from death, my eyes from tears, my feet from stumbling. I shall walk before God in the lands of the living. I trust [in God]; out of great suffering I spoke and said rashly, "All men are false" (Ps. 116:1–11).

[FOL. 21V] How can I repay God for all His bounties to me? I raise the cup of deliverance and invoke the name of God. I will pay my vows to

God in the presence of all His people. The death of His faithful ones is grievous in God's sight. God, I am Your servant; I am Your servant, the son of Your maidservant; You have undone the cords that bound me. I will sacrifice a thanksgiving offering to You and invoke the name of God. I will pay my vows to God in the presence of all His people, in the courts of the house of God, in the midst of Jerusalem. Hallelujah.

[FOL. 22R] Praise God, all you nations; extol Him, all you peoples, for great is His steadfast love toward us; the faithfulness of God endures forever. Hallelujah (Ps. 117).

Praise God, for He is good, His steadfast love is eternal.
Let Israel declare, "His steadfast love is eternal."
Let the house of Aaron declare, "His steadfast love is eternal."
Let those who fear God declare, "His steadfast love is eternal."
(Ps. 118:1–4)

In distress I called on God; God answered me and brought me relief. God is on my side, I have no fear; what can he do to me, [FOL. 22V] man? With God on my side as my helper, I will see the downfall of my foes. It is better to take refuge in God than to trust in mortals; it is better to take refuge in God than to trust in the great. All nations have beset me; by the name of God I will surely cut them down. They beset me, they surround me; by the name of God I will surely cut them down. They have beset me like bees; they shall be extinguished like burning thorns; by the name of God I will surely cut them down. You pressed me hard, I nearly fell; but God helped me. God is my strength and might; He has become my deliverance. The tents of the victorious resound with joyous shouts of deliverance, "The right hand of God is triumphant! The right hand of God is exalted! The right hand of God is triumphant!" I shall not die but live and proclaim the works of God. [FOL. 23R] God punished me severely but did not hand me over to death. Open the gates of victory for me that I may enter them and praise God. This is the gateway to God—the victorious shall enter through it (Ps. 118:5–20).

I praise You, for You have answered me, and have become my deliverance (Ps. 118:21).
I praise You . . .[34]

The stone that the builders rejected has become the chief [FOL. 27V] cornerstone (Ps. 118:2).
The stone . . .

Through God this came about; it is marvelous in our sight (Ps. 118:23).
Through God . . .

This is the day that God has made—let us exult and rejoice on it (Ps. 118:24).
This is . . .

O please God, deliver us! (Ps. 118:25).
O please God, deliver us!
O please God, let us prosper! (Ps. 118:25).
[FOL. 23V] O please God, let us prosper!

May he who enters be blessed in the name of God; we bless you from the House of God (Ps. 118:26).
May he who enters be blessed . . .

El is God; He has given us light; bind the festal offering with cords to [FOL. 28R] the horns of the altar (Ps. 118:27).

El . . .

My Lord You are and I will praise You; You are my Lord and I will praise You (Ps. 118:28).

My Lord . . .

Praise God for He is good, His steadfast love is eternal (Ps. 118:29).

May all Your creations praise You, God, our Lord, and Your pious ones, the righteous ones [FOL. 24R] who do Your will, and Your people, the house of Israel, with song will acknowledge and bless, praise and enthrone, exalt and fear, sanctify and declare the kingship of Your name, our King, for it is good to acknowledge You and to sing Your name supreme, for You are the Lord forever and ever.

Blessed are You, O God, the King who is extolled with words of praise.

And they begin Halel Ha-gadol *(the Great Praise), and* Nishmat *("The Soul of Every Living Thing"):*[35]

Praise GOD; for He is good,	His steadfast love is eternal;
Praise the Lord of lords,	His steadfast love is eternal;
Praise the Master of masters,	His steadfast love is eternal;
[FOL. 24V] Who works great marvels,	His steadfast love is eternal;
Who made the heavens with wisdom,	His steadfast love is eternal;
Who spread the earth over the water,	His steadfast love is eternal;
Who made the great lights,	His steadfast love is eternal;
The sun to dominate the day,	His steadfast love is eternal;
The moon and the stars to dominate the night,	His steadfast love is eternal;

Who struck Egypt through their first-born, His steadfast love is eternal;
And brought Israel out of their midst, His steadfast love is eternal;
With a strong hand and outstretched arm, His steadfast love is eternal;
Who split apart the Sea of Reeds, His steadfast love is eternal;
And made Israel pass through it, His steadfast love is eternal;
[FOL. 25R] Who hurled Pharaoh and his army into the Sea of Reeds, His steadfast love is eternal;
Who led His people through the wilderness, His steadfast love is eternal;
Who struck down great kings, His steadfast love is eternal;
And slew mighty kings— His steadfast love is eternal;
Sihon, king of the Amorites, His steadfast love is eternal;
Og, king of Bashan— His steadfast love is eternal;
And gave their land as a heritage, His steadfast love is eternal;
A heritage to His servant Israel, His steadfast love is eternal;
Who took note of us in our degradation, His steadfast love is eternal;
And rescued us from our enemies, His steadfast love is eternal;
Who gives food to all flesh, His steadfast love is eternal;
Praise the Lord of heaven, His steadfast love is eternal.
(Ps. 136:1–26)

Sing forth, O you righteous, to God, it is fit that the upright acclaim Him (Ps. 33:1).[36]

[FOL. 25V] The soul of every living thing will bless Your name, God our Lord, and the spirit of all flesh will glorify Your fame, our King, constantly. Eternally, You are the Lord, and other than You we have no king, redeemer and saviour, ransomer and rescuer, supporting and compassionate in all times of trouble and distress. We have no king other than You. [FOL. 26R] Lord of the first and the last, Lord of all creatures, Lord of all generations, extolled with a multiplicity of praises, who conducts His world with mercy and His creatures with compassion. And God neither sleeps nor slumbers[37]—He who awakes sleepers and arouses slumberers, who gives speech to the dumb and frees the fettered and braces the fallen and supports the bowed. To you only we give thanks. If our mouths were full of song as the sea, and our tongues [music][38] as the multitude of the waves, and our lips [praise] as the expanse of the firmament, our eyes [shining] like the sun and the moon, our hands [outstretched] like those of the eagles of the heaven, our legs [nimble] as antelope, we would still not be adequately capable of thanking [FOL. 26V] You, God, our Lord and the Lord of our fathers, or to bless Your name for one thousand of the thousand thousands and the myriad of myriads of good deeds that You did for our ancestors and for us. From Egypt You redeemed us, O God our Lord; from the house of slavery, You ransomed us; in times of famine, You nourished us; and in times of prosperity, You supported us; from the sword, You saved us; and from plague, You rescued us; and from wicked, numerous, and serious illnesses, You delivered us. Until now, Your compassion has succored us and Your mercy has not abandoned us, God our Lord. And do not abandon us, God our Lord, not ever. Therefore, the limbs [FOL. 27R] You have distributed in us, the spirit and the breath You have breathed into us and the tongue You have placed in our mouth—let them acknowlege, bless, praise and glorify, exalt and revere, sanctify and declare the kingship of Your name, our King. For every mouth will acknowledge You, and every tongue will swear to You, every knee will bend to You, and all that stands will prostrate before You, and all the hearts will fear You, and every inward part and organ will sing to Your name, as the word is written, "All my bones shall say, God, who is like You? You save the poor from one stronger than he, the poor and needy from his despoiler" (Ps. 35:10). Who can compare to You? And who [FOL. 27V] can equal you? And who can match You, the Lord, great, mighty and awesome (Deut. 10:17), supreme Lord, Creator of heaven and earth through His mercy? Let us praise You, let us laud You, and bless the name of Your holiness, as it says, "Of David. Bless God, O my soul, all my being, His holy name" (Ps.103:1).

"The Lord" (Deut. 10:17)—in the might of Your power; "great" (Deut. 10:17)—in the glory of your name; "mighty" (Deut. 10:17)—forever; "and awesome" (Deut. 10:17)—in your awe-inspiring acts.[39] The King who sits on a high and exalted throne! The One who dwells forever, on high! Holy is His name! And it is written, "Sing forth, O you righteous, to God, it is fit that the upright acclaim Him" (Ps. 33:1).

[FOL. 28R] In the mouths of the upright, You shall be praised;
In the words of the righteous, You shall be blessed;
In the tongue of the pious, You shall be exalted;
In the midst of the holy, You shall be sanctified.

In the choirs of the myriads of Your people, the house of Israel, in song will be glorified Your name, our King, in every generation. For it is the obligation of all creatures, O God, our Lord, and the God of our ancestors, to acknowledge, to laud, praise, glorify, exalt, beautify, bless, applaud, and acclaim You beyond all the songs of praise of David, the son of Jesse, Your servant, Your anointed one.

[FOL. 28V] May Your name be praised forever, the Lord, the great and holy King in heaven and on earth, for to You, O God, our Lord, and the Lord of our ancestors, are appropriate song and praise, laud and hymn, might and sovereignty, eternity, greatness and power, fame and glory, holiness and kingship, blessings and gratitude from now and forever. Blessed are You, God, Lord King, great in praise, Lord of acknowledgments, Master of wonders,[a] the One who chooses melodious song, King Lord, life of the universe.

[FOL. 29R] *And they say the following on the first night:*

Then you performed many miracles at night.
At the beginning of the watch of this night,
A righteous convert You caused to be victorious as the night was divided.[40]
And it came to pass in the middle of the night.

You judged the king of Gerar in a dream at night.[41]
You frightened the Aramean [FOL. 29V] at night.[42]
Israel struggled with the angel and defeated him at night.[43]
And it came to pass in the middle of the night.

The seed of the first-born of Patros you crushed at midnight.[44]
The [Egyptians] did not find their forces when they rose in the night.
The flight of the prince of Haroshet you crushed with the stars of the night.[45]
And it came to pass in the middle of the night.

The blasphemer threatened to stretch his hand over the desired place [Jerusalem], and you dried his corpses at night.[46]

a. In a tiny hand in black ink between the lines, a later hand inserted, "Creator of all souls, Master of all Creatures."

[FOL. 30R] Bel and his founder collapsed at night.[47]
To the beloved man was revealed the secret of the vision at night.[48]
And it came to pass in the middle of the night.

The one who got drunk from the holy vessels was killed at night.[49]
The one who was saved from the lion's den solved the frights of night.[50]
Agagi bided his hate and wrote letters at night.[51]
And it came to pass in the middle of the night.

You aroused your victory over him by disturbing the sleep of the night.
[FOL. 30V] You will trod the vintage for the watchman who calls, "What of the night?"[52]
He called like the watchman and said, "Day has come, and also night."
And it came to pass in the middle of the night.

The day is coming which will be neither day nor night.
O Supreme One, announce it for the day is Yours and also the night.
Appoint watchmen over your city all day and all night.
Enlighten as the light of the day the darkness of the night.
And it came to pass in the middle of the night.

[FOL. 31R] *[On the second night,] the following is recited:*
You wondrously showed your might on Passover.[53]
First of all festivals you celebrated the Passover.[54]
You disclosed to the citizen at midnight on Passover.[55]
And you shall say, "It is the sacrifice for Passover."

You knocked at his door, at the heat of the day, on Passover.[56]

He fed the shining ones cakes of unleavened bread on Passover.

He ran to the cattle, as a reminder to "The Ox," the reading of Passover.

And you shall say, "It is the sacrifice for Passover."

The Sodomites were angry and burned with fire on Passover.[57]

[FOL. 31V] Lot was saved from them and he baked unleavened bread at the time of Passover.

You swept away the land of Moph and Noph when you passed by on Passover.[58]

And you shall say, "It is the sacrifice for Passover."

God, the first seed you crushed on the night of vigil on Passover.

Mighty one, You passed over the first-born son on account of the blood of Passover,

To prevent the destroyer from entering my doors on Passover.

And you shall say, "It is the sacrifice for Passover."

The besieged one fell at the time of Passover.[59]

Midian was destroyed by a loaf of barley bread of [FOL. 32R] the *ʿomer* on Passover.[60]

The fat of Pul and Lud was burned in the burning of the fire on Passover.[61]

And you shall say, "It is the sacrifice for Passover."

This same day at Nob He shall stand (Is. 10:32) until the arrival of the time of Passover.[62]

A palm of the hand wrote to destroy Babylon on Passover.[63]

"Light the candle," "Set the table!" (cf. Is. 21:5) on Passover.[64]

And you shall say, "It is the sacrifice for Passover."

Hadassah gathered the community for a three-day fast on Passover.[65]

The head of the house of evil you destroyed by a fifty-cubit tree on Passover.

These two things you shall suddenly bring upon Uzit on Passover.[66]

[FOL. 32V] Let your hand be strong; Your right hand, exalted as on the night of the hallowing of the festival of Passover.[67]

[And you shall say, "It is the sacrifice for Passover."][68]

For to Him, [praise] is fitting; for to Him, it is proper.

All-powerful[69] in sovereignty, selected as is right, His legions say to Him:

For You, and for You; Yours, for it is Yours; For You, Even for You; To You, God, is the kingship.

For Him, [praise] is fitting; for Him, it is proper.

Distinguished in sovereignty; glorified as is right; His faithful say to Him:

For You, and for You; Yours, for it is Yours; For You, Even for You; To You, God, is the sovereignty.

For Him, [praise] is fitting; for Him, it is proper.

[FOL. 33R] Pure in sovereignty, mighty as is right, His dignitaries say to Him:

For You, and for You; Yours, for it is Yours; For You, Even for You; To You, God, is the sovereignty.

For Him, [praise] is fitting; for Him, it is proper.

Singular in sovereignty, powerful as is right, His disciples say to Him:

For You, and for You; Yours, for it is Yours; For You, Even for You; To You, God, is the sovereignty.

For Him, [praise] is fitting; for Him, it is proper.

Sovereign in sovereignty, awesome as is right, those surrounding him say to Him:

For You, and for You; Yours, for it is Yours; For You, Even for You; To You, God, is the sovereignty.

[FOL. 33V] For Him, [praise] is fitting; for Him, it is proper.

Majestic in sovereignty, crowned as is right, His hosts say to Him:

For You, and for You; Yours, for it is Yours; For You, Even for You; To You, God, is the sovereignty.

For Him, [praise] is fitting; for Him, it is proper.

Holy in sovereignty, compassionate as is right, His angels say to Him:

For You, and for You; Yours, for it is Yours; For You, Even for You; To You, God, is the sovereignty.

For Him, [praise] is fitting; for Him, it is proper.

Potent in sovereignty, perfect as is right, His upright ones say to Him:

For You, and for You; Yours, for it is Yours; For You, Even for You; To You, God, is the sovereignty.

[FOL. 34R] NEXT YEAR IN JERUSALEM.

Blessed are You, God, creator of the fruit of the vine.

All-powerful[70] is He! *May He build His house very soon, speedily, speedily, in our times, very soon. O Lord, build! O Lord, build! May He build His house soon.*

Blessed is He! May He build, etc.

Great! Distinguished! Handsome!
Venerable! Pure! Pious! Good! Unique! Mighty!
His disciples![71] King! Awesome! Those who surround Him!
Majestic! Redeemer! His hosts! Holy! Merciful!
Shaddai! Potent!

[FOL. 34V] The work was completed, and it is sufficient.[72] And today is the twenty-fifth day of the month of Shevat in the year 238 according to the short enumeration. The word of the least of the scribes, Joel, the son of Simeon of blessed memory.

[FOL. 35R] FOR ONE WHO WISHES TO LINK COURTYARDS:[73]

He gathers flour from every household, makes out of it whatever he wishes with the intention that all be included in it, and recites the blessing for the commandment of the common courtyard ('eruv).

Blessed are You, O God, our Lord, King of the universe, who has sanctified us by His commandments and commanded us about the commandment of the common courtyard.[74]

By virtue of this [object created from dough], it is permissible for us tomorrow on the Sabbath to carry from this house to the next house, and from the courtyard to a house, and from a house to the courtyard—for us, and for all who dwell in this city from the Sabbath on this year's Passover to the Passover in the coming year.

AND FOR ONE WHO WISHES TO CREATE A LINKING [OF THE HOLIDAY AND SABBATH] FOR COOKING:[75]

He should take some fish or cooked meat or an egg, and place it in a dish, and recite the following blessing:

Blessed are You, O God, our Lord, King of the universe, who has sanctified us by His commandments and commanded us about the commandment of the dispensation.[76] By virtue of this [food], it is permissible for us tomorrow to use this dispensation [FOL. 35V] to bake, to cook, to carry, to take out and to take in,[77] and to do whatever is necessary—for us, and for all Israelites who dwell in this city, on the holiday for the Sabbath, and on the Sabbath for the holiday.[78]

NOTES

1. On this formula, see Beit-Arié, 134–135, note 39.

2. This formulaic recitation is in Aramaic, not Hebrew.

3. See Glatzer, 150.

4. The Hebrew is very faint: *shemurim lesheim mitzvah.*

5. Hebrew: *Afyya;* Old French: *apje,* from the Latin *apium,* parsley or celery. See Weinstein, 12.

6. Hebrew: *bein hamapah.*

7. Hebrew: *lehem 'oni,* JPS: "bread of distress."

8. For my translation of this passage, see Richard C. Steiner, "On the Original Structure and Meaning of *Mah Nishtanah* and the History of Its Reinterpretation," *Jewish Studies Internet Journal* 7 (2008): 1–41. The article is available at http://www.biu.ac.il/JS/SIJ/7-2008/Steiner.pdf. As Steiner shows, this translation was the native Ashkenazic understanding of the passage's question, as well as its original meaning in the Mishnah.

9. Deut. 6:21.

10. Deut. 5:15.

11. The daily prayer that includes the recitation of Deut. 6:4, "Hear O Israel" *(shema' yisrael)*—hence the prayer's name.

12. "Revelry" is the translation of the Hebrew *afikomen* (from the Greek *epikomion,* an after-dinner procession from one banquet or symposium to another). This line is the last statement of the laws of the Passover meal in Mishnah Pesahim 10, and effectively means, one should teach him all the laws of Passover concluding with, "After the Passover meal, one may not go off on a procession to another drinking party." Only later did the word *afikomen* come to mean all after-dinner revelry, then dessert, and finally, the last sad piece of unleavened bread eaten as a kind of poor substitute for dessert.

13. Hebrew: *hakhei et shinav.* This phrase appears twice in the Bible, in Jer. 31:29 and Ezek. 18:1, in both cases where the parents are said "to eat sour grapes and their children's teeth are set on edge" or "blunted." The colloquial meaning here seems to be that the father is asked to refute the wicked son's statement.

14. These last three bracketed words were initially omitted by the scribe and later added to the margin.

15. Hebrew: *shel,* "of." Most other texts have *le,* "to."

16. The English translation here reflects the haggadah's midrashic interpretation of the Hebrew verse. JPS and most translations have "A wandering Aramaean was my father."

17. Even though this is the continuation of Deut. 4:34, Joel ben Simeon put the remainder of the verse in a separate paragraph in order to preserve the symmetry of the layout. "By war" is in rubrics.

18. Joel mistakenly added the word *veza'am,* "and indignation," to the text here.

19. Joel mistakenly left out the bracketed word *shalosh* ("three"), and a later hand added it in the margin.

20. This refers to a special short version of the grace after the meal specifically tailored to those who have eaten only the seven species of grain and wine.

21. Literally, "Washing." The Hebrew words here and in the following lines, all written in a larger square hand, are short-hand terms for the various ritual acts described immediately after them in a smaller, semicursive script.

22. Lit., "the whole piece [of *matsah*]."

23. Hebrew: *rishonah,* lit., "first."

24. Lit., "who brings forth," a reference to the blessing over bread, as it follows in the next line.

25. This blessing and the others on the page are written in a square script but in the same small size as the instructions, which are written in a semicursive hand.

26. Lit., "and he divides."

27. Lit., "he eats," after blessing.

28. Lit., "with it," that is, together.

29. Lit., "the bitter herb."

30. Hebrew: *lituga,* Old French, *laitugue,* from the Latin *lactuca.* See Weinstein, 12.

31. Lit., "he blesses." As Glatzer (p. 150) notes, however, this word was written in error and should be *karekh,* "he joins together," as the following lines indicate.

32. See Weinstein, 12.

33. Somewhat oddly, Joel ben Simeon did not include the blessing for the third cup of wine.

34. The remainder of the verse is to be repeated.

35. Which immediately follows the *Halel Ha-gadol* on p. 147.

36. On this last verse, see Glatzer, 155.

37. In the left margin a later hand added the word *hinei*, "behold," which presumably should preface the statement, though it is not found in most texts.

38. In the Washington Haggadah, this word and the others in brackets have all been omitted; it is unclear whether this was the scribe's error or whether he was working from a slightly different version of the text.

39. This small litany of praise is couched as an exegesis of Deut. 10:17, quoted several lines earlier.

40. This refers to the battle of Abraham against the five kings, with special reference to Genesis 14:15.

41. Avimelech was warned, in a dream, to return Sarah to Abraham (Gen. 20:6).

42. Laban was warned, in a dream, not to harm Jacob (Gen. 31:24).

43. Gen. 32:26–30.

44. Ezek. 29:14 refers to Patros as the homeland of the Egyptians.

45. Sisera's base was Harosheth-goyim (Judges 4:2). The stars in their paths fought against Sisera (Judges 5:20).

46. Senacharib was a blasphemer (2 Kings 18:4) who threatened to destroy Jerusalem. His forces were devastated at night (2 Kings 19:35).

47. This is a reference to the apocryphal story of Bel, which appears in the Septuagint as an appendix to the Book of Daniel, according to which Daniel sets a trap by which he proves that the so-called actions of Bel are really the nocturnal activities of the priests.

48. This line, and the first two lines of the next stanza, refer to events in Daniel, according to which Daniel, the beloved man (Daniel 9:23, 10:11), was granted the secret of Nebuchadnezzar's dream in Daniel's own nightly vision (Daniel 2:19).

49. Belshazzar drank from the vessels of the Jerusalem Temple and was killed that same night (Daniel 5).

50. This line refers to the solution of Nebuchadnezzar's dream (Daniel 2:1, 4:2) by Daniel, who was saved from the lion's den; the first one agitated his spirit while the second one frightened him.

51. This line and the first line of the next stanza refer to Haman, the Agagite, and to the turning point in the Book of Esther when King Ahasueros is unable to sleep (Esther 6:1ff.). According to Rabbinic legend, the latter occurred on either the first or second night of Passover.

52. See Isaiah 21:11.

53. This begins a list of events which occurred on Passover.

54. Passover is the first of the festivals given to the Israelites, and it is the first festival mentioned in the biblical lists of festivals.

55. Etan Ha-ezrahi (which may be translated as "Etan the citizen"), mentioned as the author of Psalm 89, was identified by the rabbis with Abraham. The event referred to here is the Covenant between the Sections (Gen. 15), in which God first revealed to Abraham that his children would be slaves in Egypt and would be redeemed.

56. This stanza refers to the visit of the angels to Abraham (Gen. 18), which according to Rabbinic tradition happened on Passover. "The ox, the reading of Passover," refers to the passage of the Torah beginning with Lev. 22:27 read on Passover.

57. These two lines refer to Gen. 19, and the angel's visit to Lot (Gen. 19).

58. This line and the next stanza refer to the death of the first-born of Egypt on Passover. Moph (Memphis) is mentioned as a major city of Egypt, while Noph is apparently a variant name for the same place.

59. Jericho fell on Passover.

60. This refers to Gideon's victory over Midian (Judges 7). The victory was foretold by one of the Midianites who saw that a "loaf of barley bread was whirling through the Midianite camp. It came to a tent and struck it, and it fell; it turned it upside down, and the tent collapsed." Some sages understood the loaf of barley to be a reference to the *'omer* sacrifice of barley, brought on the second day of Passover.

61. Pul was the name of a king of Assyria (2 Kings 15:19), but the poet calls Assyria by the name. Pul is also the name of another nation near a nation known as Lud, but their location is unknown (Isaiah 66:19). The poet uses Pul and Lud as appellations for Assyria and its king, Senaharib. The reference is to the destruction of the latter's armies as he camped before the city of Jerusalem (2 Kings 19/Isaiah 37).

62. This is a continuation of the last line of the previous stanza. It refers to Senaharib's camping at Nob, on the way to Jerusalem. Senaharib did not realize that his camping there was ordained so that he would arrive at Jerusalem on Passover, the time meant for salvation and redemption.

63. This was the handwriting on the wall which was explained by Daniel (5) as announcing the destruction of Babylon.

64. The modern JPS translation for the first expression is "Let the watchman watch!" (Isaiah 21:5). However, the sages understood it to mean "Light the candle." This line is the fulfillment of the prophecy in the prior line about the destruction of Babylon.

65. This line and the next refer to the story of Purim as told in the scroll of Esther. Hadassah is the Hebrew name of the scroll's heroine, Esther (see Esther 2:7); when she learns that the wicked Haman has convinced King Ahasueros to execute all the Jews of Persia, she calls upon the Jews to fast for three days and nights (Esther 4:16). "The head of the house of evil" refers to Haman, who with his ten sons is hung from the gallows he built for Mordehai, Esther's uncle.

66. "These two things" is a reference to Isaiah 47:9, which voices the hope that God will bring the punishments of widowhood and loss of children on Edom. Uzit is an appellation for Edom (which is, in turn, an appellation for Rome), based on Lam. 4:21.

67. Based on Psalm 89:14, this is an appeal to God to show His strong hand and redeem His people, as He did on the first Passover celebration.

68. Probably as an oversight, Joel failed to write the refrain for this last stanza of the hymn.

69. The first line of each stanza in this hymn follows an alphabetical acrostic, with the first letter of each phrase beginning with the next letter of the alphabet. Thus, *a*dir bimelukhah, *b*ahur ke-halakhah, *g*edudav yomru lo, and so on. Alas, it has been impossible to translate the acrostic into English.

70. This hymn again follows an alphabetical acrostic, with all the predicates modifying God following the letters of the Hebrew alphabet. Where I have been able to, I have supplied synonyms in English; unfortunately, it has not been possible to do this in all cases.

71. Hebrew: *limudav.* This is possibly an error for *lamud,* "learned," a transposition of the text from the earlier hymn, which has *limudav,* "his disciples." Equally awkward, out-of-place constructions are repeated three words later with *sevivav* and in the next line with *tseva'av.*

72. Cf. Exod. 36:17, and the Talmudic expression *u-deyo* (for example, in Sotah 14b). For a full exposition of the phrase, see Beit-Arié, 130, note 1, where he also discusses the pun on *udeyo,* "and its ink was also completed."

73. On the Sabbath it is normally forbidden to carry objects outside of one's home into public property. In the case of persons living in separate houses around a common courtyard, however, Rabbinic law permits the various properties involved to create a legal fiction called in Hebrew *'eruv hatserot*, which effectively permits them to consider the courtyard and all the houses surrounding it a single spatial property within which all parties can carry objects between houses and through the courtyard on the Sabbath. The following passage describes the ritual act and blessing to create this legal fiction.

74. Hebrew: *'eruvei hatserot.*

75. It is permissible to cook food on a festival like Passover, but only for use on the festival day itself, not afterward. If Passover falls on a Friday (with the first seder on Thursday night), and it is necessary to cook in preparation for the Sabbath (on which it is forbidden to cook at all), Rabbinic law permits a person to create a special dispensation that effectively allows him or her to prepare food on the holiday for the Sabbath. The following passage describes the ritual act and blessing required to create this special dispensation.

76. Hebrew: *'eruvei tavshilin.*

77. On the last two phrases, which were written in error in this prayer, see Glatzer, 156–157.

78. This last phrase was also written in error; see Glatzer, 157.

FOL. 38 V

FOL. 38 R

FOL. 37 V

FOL. 37 R

FOL. 36 V

FOL. 36 R

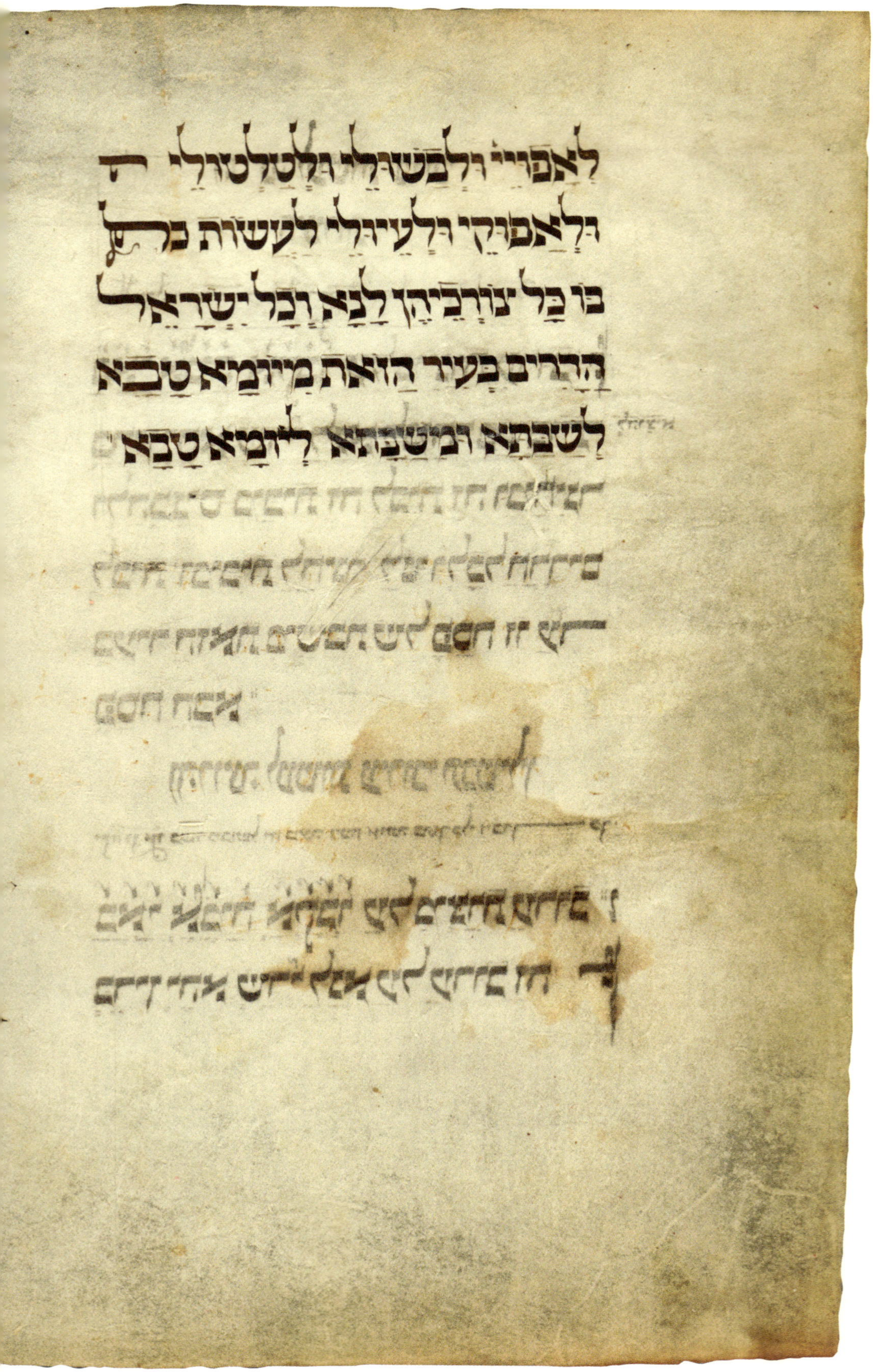
לאפויי ולבשולי ולטלטולי
ולאפוקי ולעיולי לעשות כרצ
נו כל צורכיהן לנא ולכל ישראל
הדרים בעיר הזאת מיומא טבא
לשבתא ומשבתא ליומא טבא

FOL. 35 V

הרוצה לעשות עירובי

חצרות

ובוטל מכל בית קליה ויעשה לפי רצונו ויניח בכלי ומברך על מצות ערוב ואומר

בא״י אמ״ה אקב״ו על מצות ערוב

להוציא בדין יהא שרי לנא למחר בשבת

ולהכניס מבית זה לבית זה ומחצר

לבית ומבית לחצר לנו ולכל הדרים

בעיר הזאת משבת של פסח זו עד

פסח הבא

והרוצה לעשות עירובי תבשילין

יקח יין בשר מבושל או ביצה ויניח אותה בתוך כלי ויברך כך

בא״י אמ״ה אקב״ו על מצות ערוב

בדין יהא שרי לנא על ערוב זה

35

FOL. 35 R

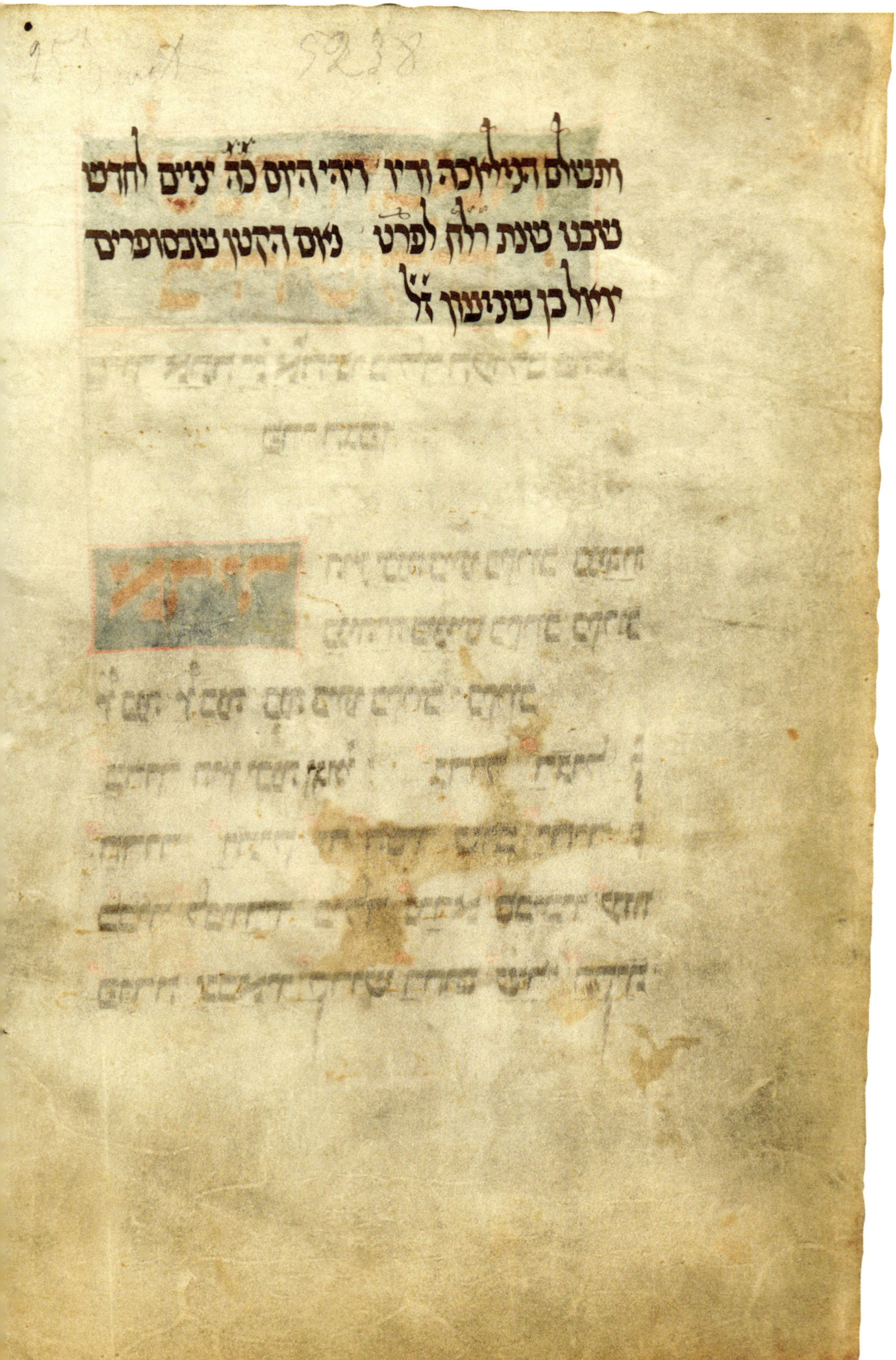

FOL. 34 V

לשנה הבאה בירושלים

ברוך אתה יי אלהינו מלך העולם בורא

פרי הגפן

אדיר הוא יבנה ביתו בקרוב במהרה

במהרה בימינו בקרוב בקרוב

אל בנה אל בנה בנה ביתו בקרוב בקרוב

ברוך הוא יבנה וגומ' גדול דגול

הדור ותיק זך חסיד טהור יחיד

כביר למודיו מלך נורא סביביו עזוז

פודה צבאיו קדוש רחום שדי תקיף

FOL. 34 R

כי לו נאה כי לו יאה ׳

עזוז במלוכה ׳ פודה

כהלכה ׳ צבאיו יאמרו לו ׳ לך ולך

לך אף לך ׳ לך כי לך ׳ לך ייי המלוכה ׳׳

כי לו נאה כי לו יאה ׳

קדוש במלוכה ׳

רחום כהלכה ׳ שנאניו יאמרו לו ׳

לך ולך לך אף לך ׳ לך כי לך ׳ לך ייי

המלוכה ׳׳

כי לו נאה כי לו יאה ׳

תקיף במלוכה ׳ תומך

כהלכה ׳ תמימיו יאמרו לו ׳ לך ולך ׳

לך כי לך ׳ לך אף לך ׳ לך ייי המלוכה ׳׳

זך במלוכה חסין בהלכה טפסריו
יאמרו לו לך ולך לך אף לך לך כי
לך לך יי׳ הממלכה

כי לו נאה כי לו יאה יחיד
במלוכה כביר בהלכה
למודיו יאמרו לו לך
ולך לך אף לך לך כי לך לך יי׳
הממלכה

כי לו נאה כי לו יאה מלך
במלוכה נורא בהלכה
סביביו יאמרו לו לך
ולך לך אף לך לך כי לך לך יי׳
הממלכה

FOL. 33 R

תעוז ידך ותרום ימינך כליל

התקדש חג פסח

כי לו נאה כי לו יאה

אדיר במלוכה

בחור כהלכה גדודיו

יאמרו לו לך ולך לך אף לך לך

כי לך לך יי הממלכה

כי לו נאה כי לו יאה

דגול במלוכה הדור

כהלכה ותיקיו

יאמרו לו לך ולך לך אף לך לך כי

לך לך יי הממלכה

כי לו נאה כי לו יאה

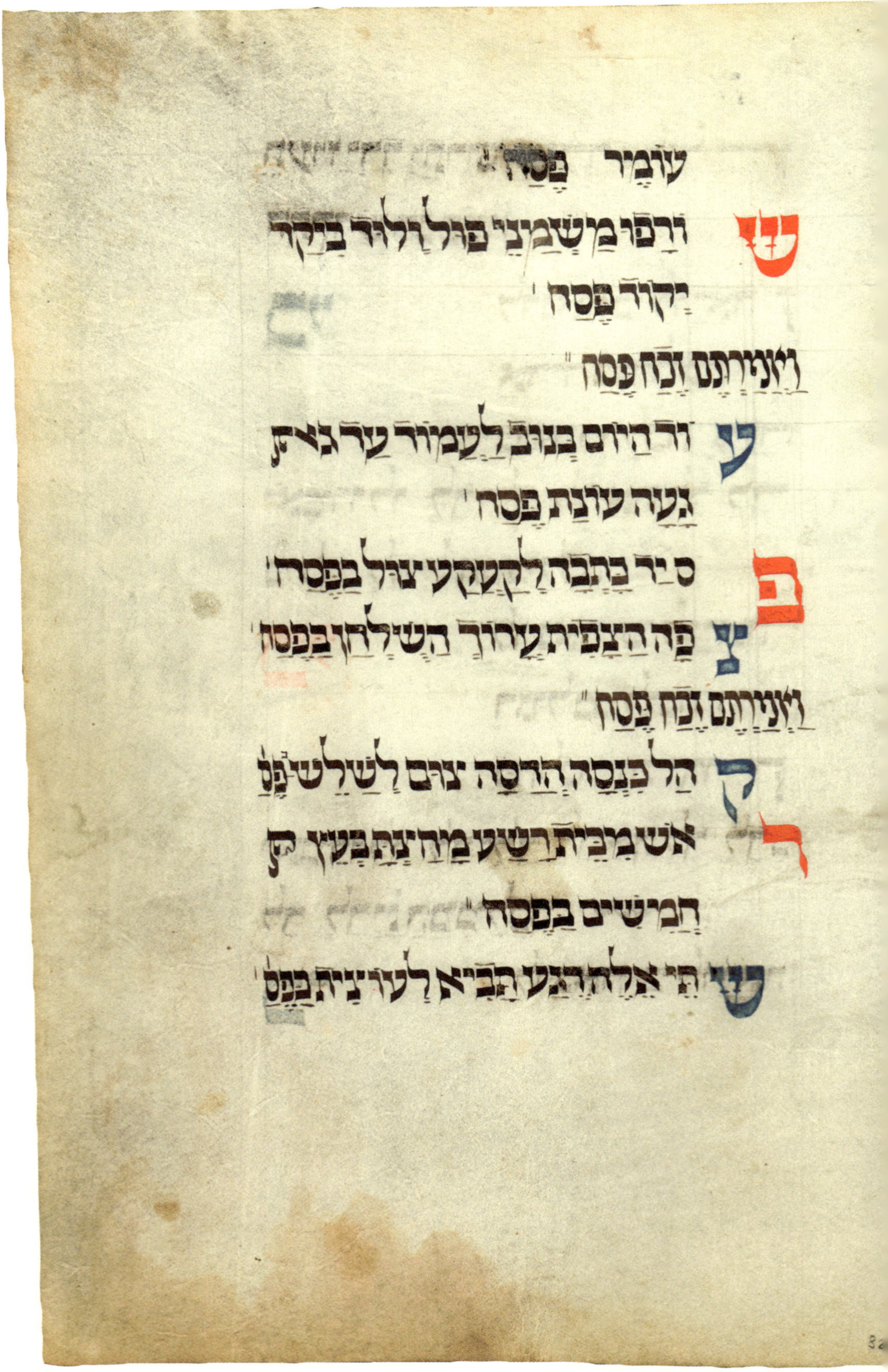

עומר בפסח

שורפו משמני פול ולוד ביקד
יקוד בפסח

ואמרתם זבח פסח

עוד היום בנוב לעמוד עד גאת
געה עונת בפסח

פס יד כתבה לקעקע צול בפסח

צפה הצפית ערוך השלחן בפסח

ואמרתם זבח פסח

קהל כנסה הדסה צום לשלש בפס

ראש מבית רשע מחצת בעץ
חמשים בפסח

שתי אלה רגע תביא לעוצית בפס

FOL. 32 R

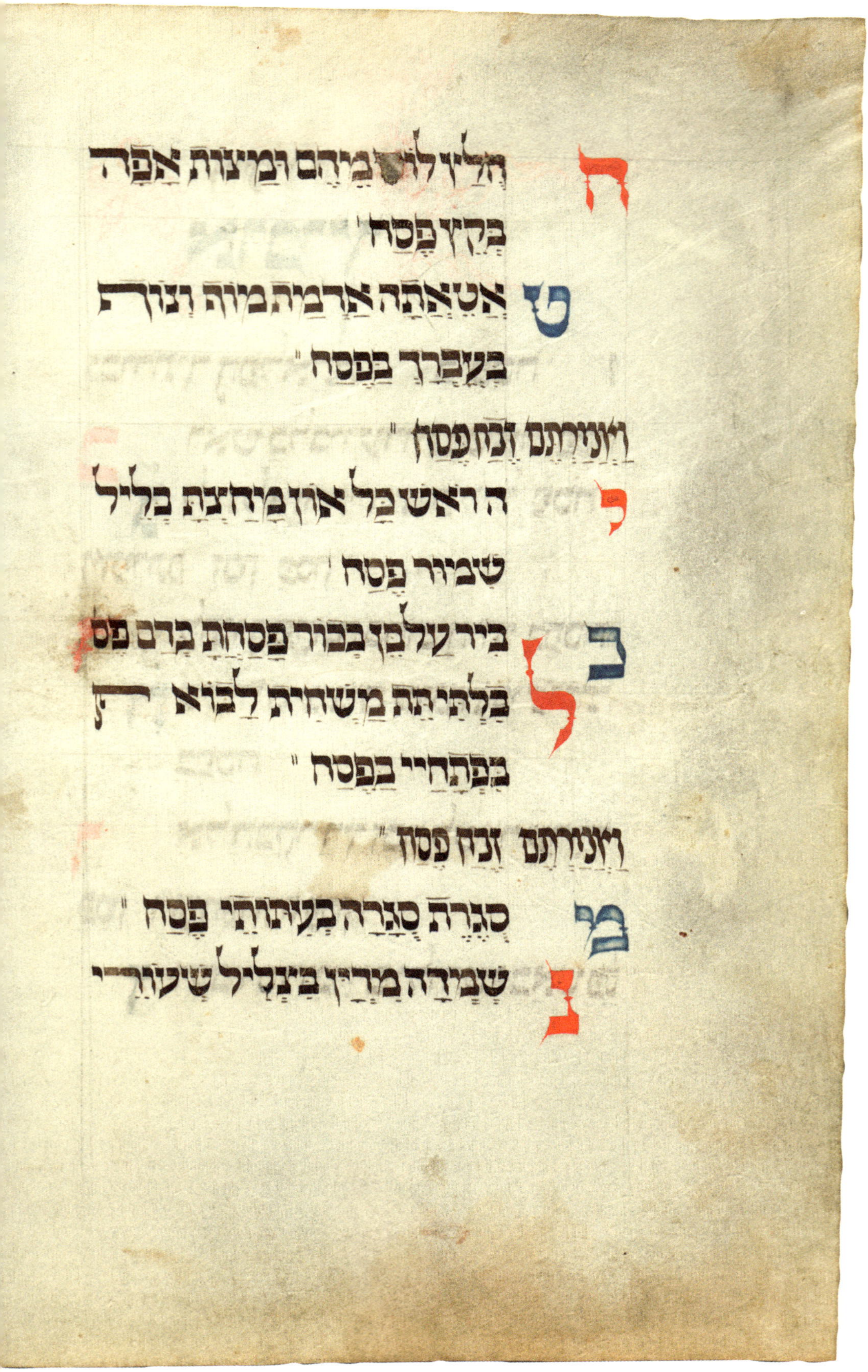

חלץ לוט מהם ומצות אפה
בקץ פסח
טאטאת אדמת מוף ונוף
בעברך בפסח
ואמרתם זבח פסח
יה ראש כל און מחצת בליל
שימור פסח
כביר על בן בכור פסחת בדם פס
לבלתי תת משחית לבוא
בפתחיי בפסח
ואמרתם זבח פסח
מסגרת סגרה בעיתותי פסח
נשמדה מדין בצליל שעורי

FOL. 31 V

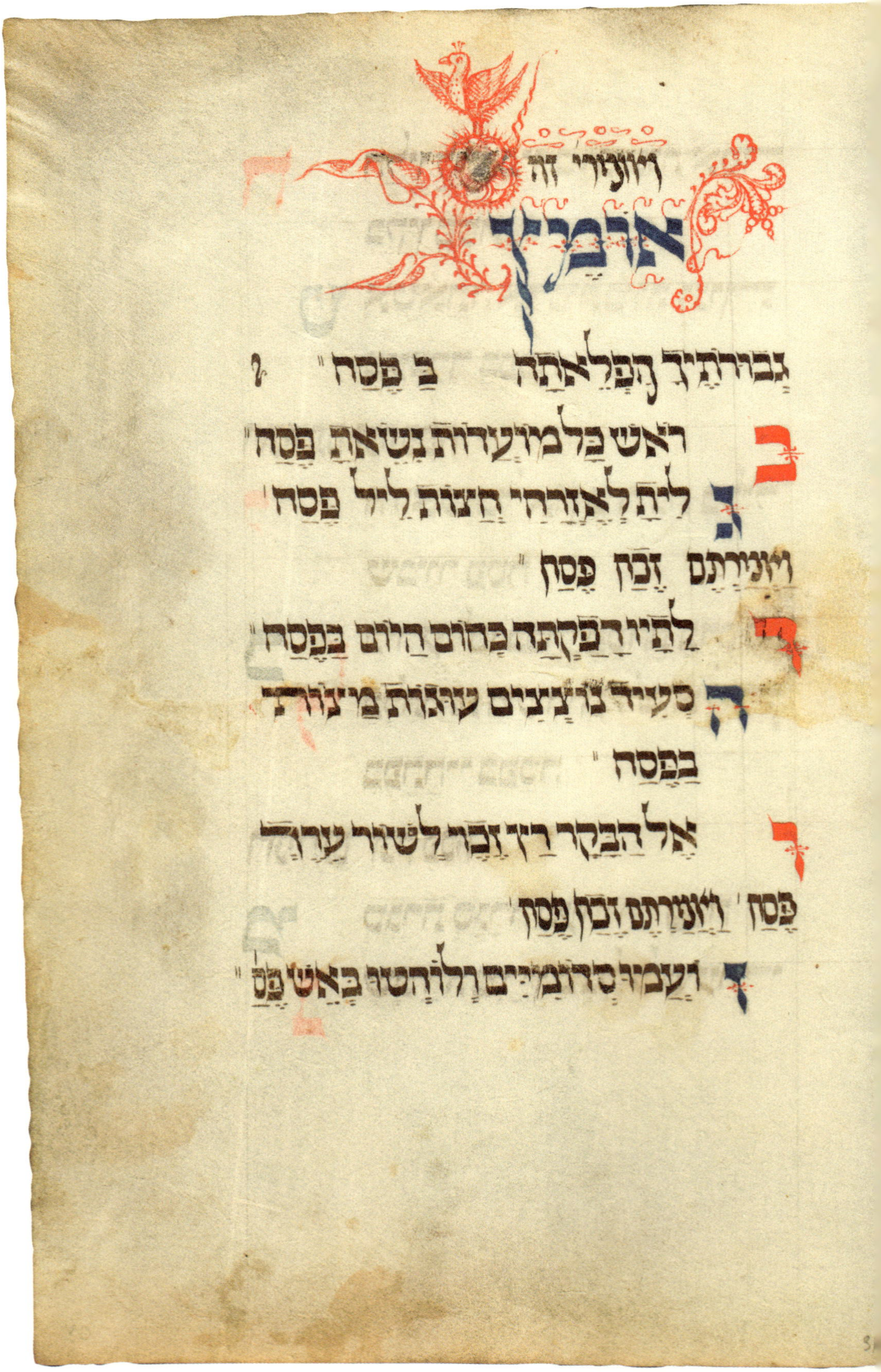

ואמרי זה

אומץ

גבורותיך הפלאתה בפסח

ב ראש כל מועדות נשאת פסח

ג לית לאזרחי חצות ליל פסח

ואמרתם זבח פסח

ד לתיו דפקתה כחום היום בפסח

ה סעיד נוצצים עוגות מצות

בפסח

ו אל הבקר רץ זכר לשור ערך

פסח ואמרתם זבח פסח

ז ועמו סדומיים ולוהטו באש פס

FOL. 31 R

פורה תדרוך לשומר מה מלילה

צרח כשומר ושח אתא

בוקר וגם לילה

ויהי בחצי הלילה

קרב יום אשר הוא לא

יום ולא לילה

רם הודיע כי לך יום

ואף לך לילה

שומרים הפקד לעירך

כל היום וכל הלילה

תאיר כאור יום

חשכת לילה

ויהי בחצי הלילה

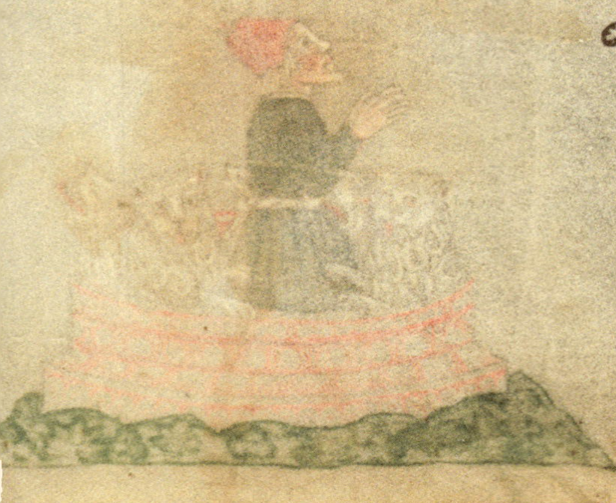

FOL. 30 V

כ רע בל ומצבו באישון לילה

ל איש חמודות נגלה

רז חזות לילה

ויהי בחצי הלילה

מ שתכר בכלי קודש

נהרג בו בלילה

נ ושע מבור אריות

פותר בעתותי לילה

ש נאה נטר אגגי

וכתב ספרים בלילה

ויהי בחצי הלילה

ע וררת נצחך עליו

בנדד שנת לילה

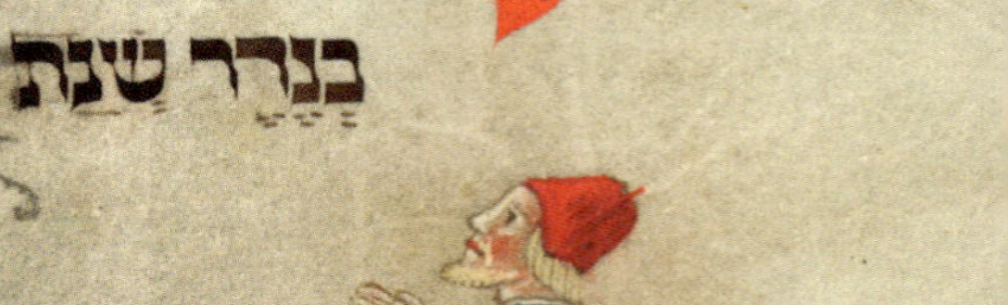

30

FOL. 30 R

באמש לילה

ו ישראל ישר לא׳

ויוכל לו לילה

ויהי בחצי הלילה

זרע בכורי פתרוס

מחצת בחצי הלילה

חילם לא מצאו

בקומם בלילה

טיסת נגיד חרושת

סלית בכוכבי לילה

ויהי בחצי הלילה

יעץ מחרף לנופף

אווי הובשת פגריו בלילה

FOL. 29 V

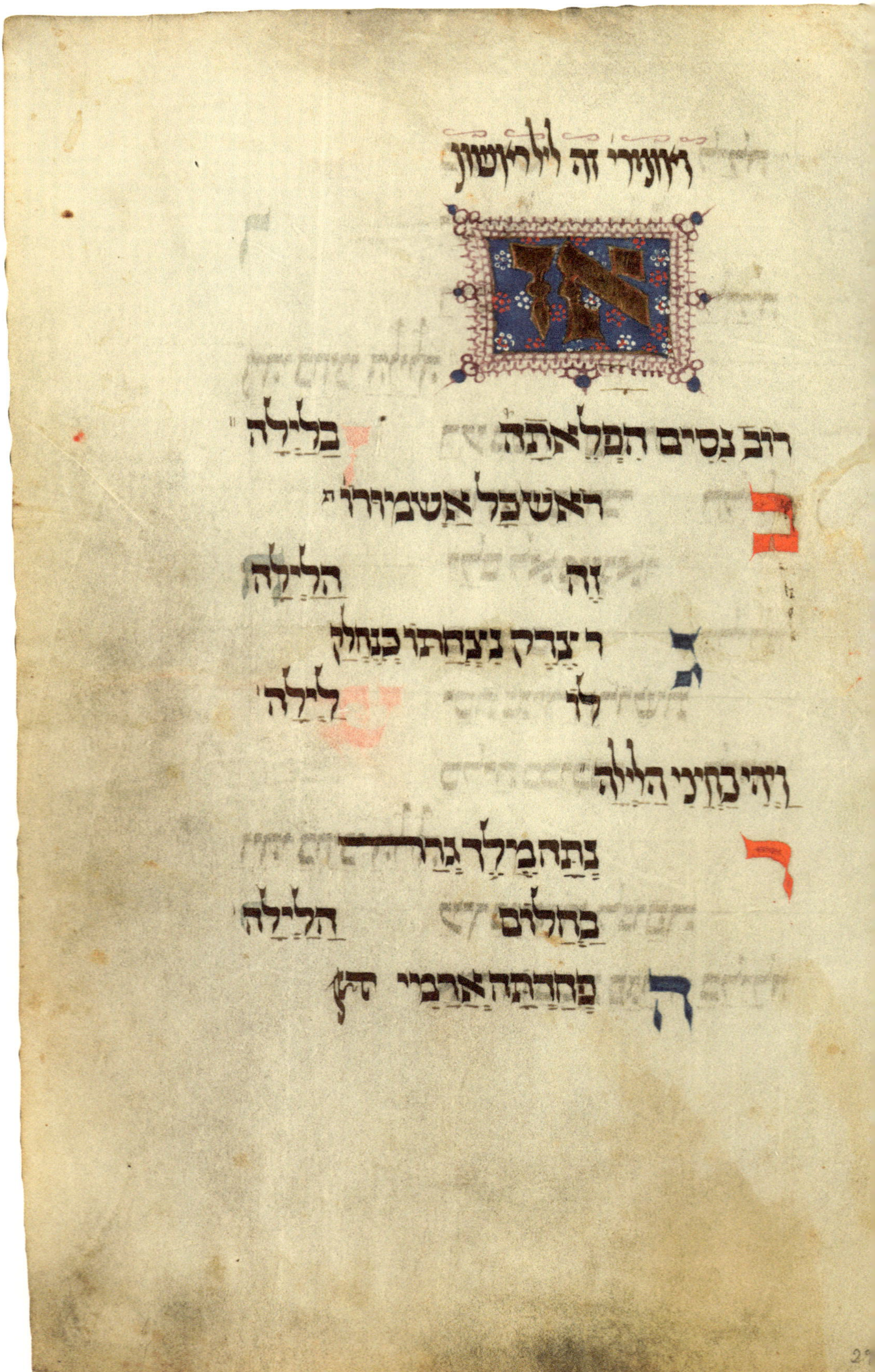
אז רוב נסים הפלאת בלילה
בראש אשמורות
זה הלילה
גר צדק נצחתו כנחלק
לו לילה
ויהי בחצי הלילה
דנת מלך גרר
בחלום הלילה
הפחדת ארמי

FOL. 29 R

בפי ישרים תתהלל
ובדברי צדיקים תתברך
ובלשון חסידים תתרומם
ובקרב קדושים תתקדש

ובמקהלות

רבבות עמך בית ישראל ברינה יתפאר שמך
מלכינו בכל דור ודור שכן חובת כל היצורים לפניך
יי' אלהינו ואלהי אבותינו להודות להלל לשבח לפאר
לרומם להדר לברך לעלה ולקלס על כל דברי שירות
ותושבחות דוד בן ישי עבדך
משיחך

28

FOL. 28 R

ישוה לך ומי יערוך לך האל הגדול
הגבור והנורא אל עליון קונה ברחמיו
שמים וארץ: נהללך ונשבחך ונברך
את שם קדשך: כאמור לדוד ברכי
נפשי את יי וכל קרבי את שם קדשו:

האל בתעצומות עזך
הגדול בכבוד שמך
הגבור לנצח והנורא
בנוראותיך: המלך היושב על כסא
רם ונשא: שוכן עד מרום וקדוש שמו
וכתוב רננו צדיקים ביי לישרים
נאוה תהילה:

FOL. 27 V

שפלגת בנו ורוח ונשמה שנפחת
באפינו ולשון אשר שמת בפינו
הן הם יודו ויברכו וישבחו
ויפארו וירוממו ויעריצו ויקדישו
וימליכו את שמך מלכינו כי כל פה
לך יודה וכל לשון לך תשבע וכל
ברך לך תכרע וכל קומה לפניך
תשתחוה וכל לבבות ייראוך
וכל קרב וכליות יזמרו לשמך כדבר
שכתוב כל עצמותי תאמרנה יי מי
כמוך מציל עני מחזק
ממנו עני ואביון מגזלו
מי ידמה לך ומי

27

FOL. 27 R

לך יי אלהינו ואלהי אבותינו ולברך את
שמך ״ על אחת מאלף אלף
אלפי אלפים ורבי רבבות פעמים
הטובות שעשית עם אבותינו ועמנו ׳
ממצרים גאלתנו יי אלהינו ומבית
עבדים פדיתנו ״ ברעב זנתנו
ובשובע גדול כלכלתנו ומחרב
הצלתנו ׳ ומדבר מלטתנו ומחלאים
רעים רבים ונאמנים דליתנו ״
עד הנה עזרונו
רחמיך ולא עזבונו חסדיך יי אלהינו
ואל תטשינו יי אלהינו לנצח ״
על כן אברים

אלהי הראשונים והאחרוני'
אלוה כל בריות אדון כל תולדות המהולל
ברוב בהשבחות המנהג עולמו בחסד
ובריותיו ברחמים ויי' לא ינום ולא הנה
ישן המעורר ישנים והמקיץ רדומים
והמשיח אלמים והמתיר אסורים
והסומך נופלים והזוקף כפופים לך לבד ך
אנחנו מודים
אילו פינו מלא שירה כים ולשונינו
כהמון גליו ושפתותינו כמרחבי רקיע
ועינינו כשמש וירח וידינו כנשרי
שמים ורגלינו כאילות
אין אנו מספיקין להודו'

26

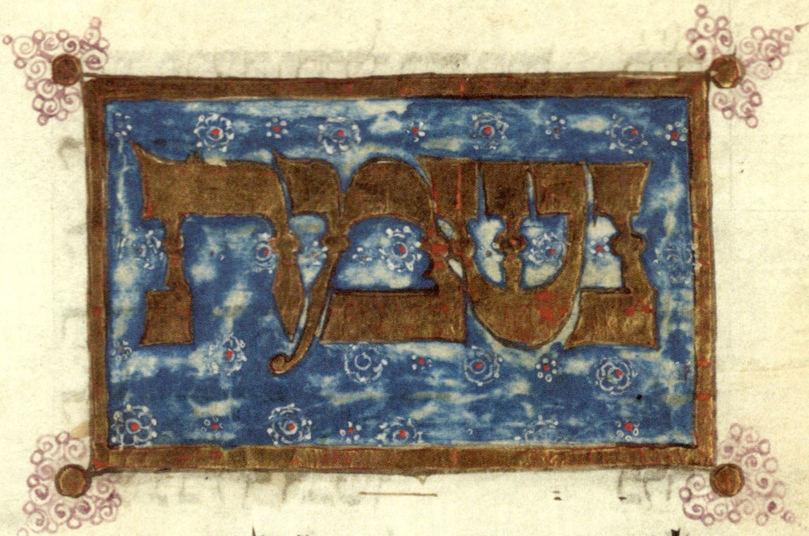

כל חי תברך את שמך יי אלהינו ורוח
כל בשר תפאר ותרומם זכרך מלכנו ת
תמיד מן העולם ועד העולם אתה אל
ומבלעדיך אין לנו מלך גואל
ומושיע פודה ומציל ומפרנס
ומרחם בכל עת צרה וצוקה אין לנו
מלך אלא אתה

וינער פרעה וחילו בים סוף כל״ח

למוליך עמו במדבר כל״ח

למכה מלכים גדולים כל״ח

ויהרוג מלכים אדירים כל״ח

לסיחון מלך האמורי כל״ח

ולעוג מלך הבשן כל״ח

ונתן ארצם לנחלה כל״ח

נחלה לישראל עבדו כל״ח

שבשפלינו זכר לנו כל״ח

ויפרקנו מצרינו כל״ח

נותן לחם לכל בשר כל״ח

הודו לאל השמים כל״ח

רננו צדיקים בי״י לישרים נאוה תהלה

לעושה נפלאות גדולות כי לעולם
חסדו
לעושה השמים בתבונה כל״ח
לרוקע הארץ על המים כל״ח
לעושה אורים גדולים כל״ח
את השמש לממשלת ביום כל״ח
ואת הירח וכוכבים לממשלות בלילה
כל״ח
למכה מצרים בבכוריהם כל״ח
ויוצא ישראל מתוכם כל״ח
ביד חזקה ובזרוע נטויה כל״ח
לגוזר ים סוף לגזרים כל״ח
והעביר ישראל בתוכו כל״ח

FOL. 24 V

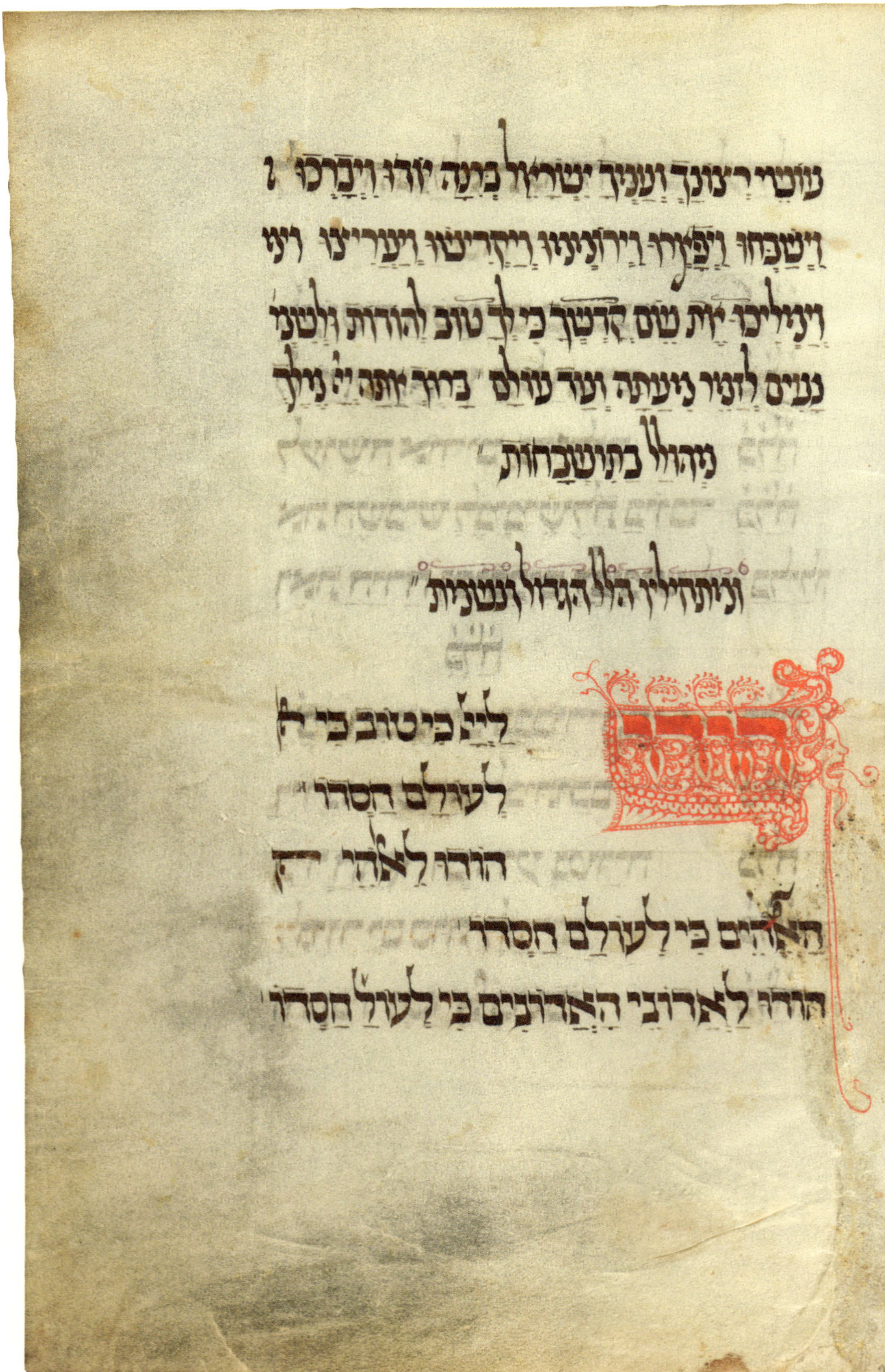
עושי רצונך ועמך ישראל ברנה יודו ויברכו
וישבחו ויפארו וירוממו ויקדישו ויעריצו וי
וימליכו את שם קדשך כי לך טוב להודות ולשמך
נעים לזמר מעתה ועד עולם ברוך אתה יי מלך
מהולל בתשבחות
ומתחילין הלל הגדול
הודו
ליי כי טוב כי
לעולם חסדו
הודו לאלהי
האלהים כי לעולם חסדו
הודו לאדוני האדונים כי לעול׳ חסדו

FOL. 24 R

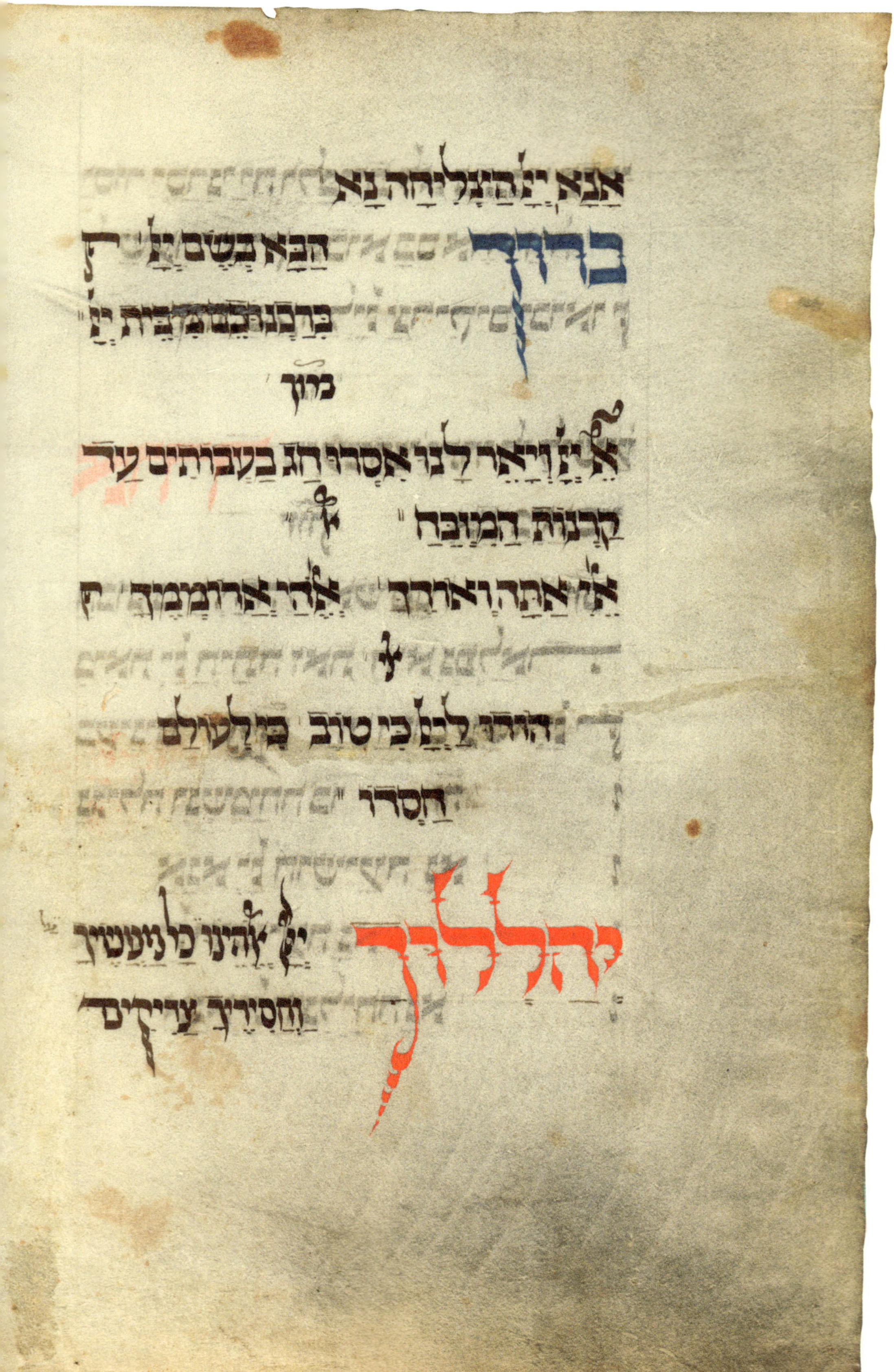

אנא יי הצליחה נא
ברוך הבא בשם יי
ברכנוכם מבית יי
ברוך
אל יי ויאר לנו אסרו חג בעבותים עד
קרנות המזבח
אלי אתה ואודך אלהי ארוממך
הודו ליי כי טוב כי לעולם
חסדו
יהללוך יי אלהינו כל מעשיך
וחסידיך צדיקים

FOL. 23 V

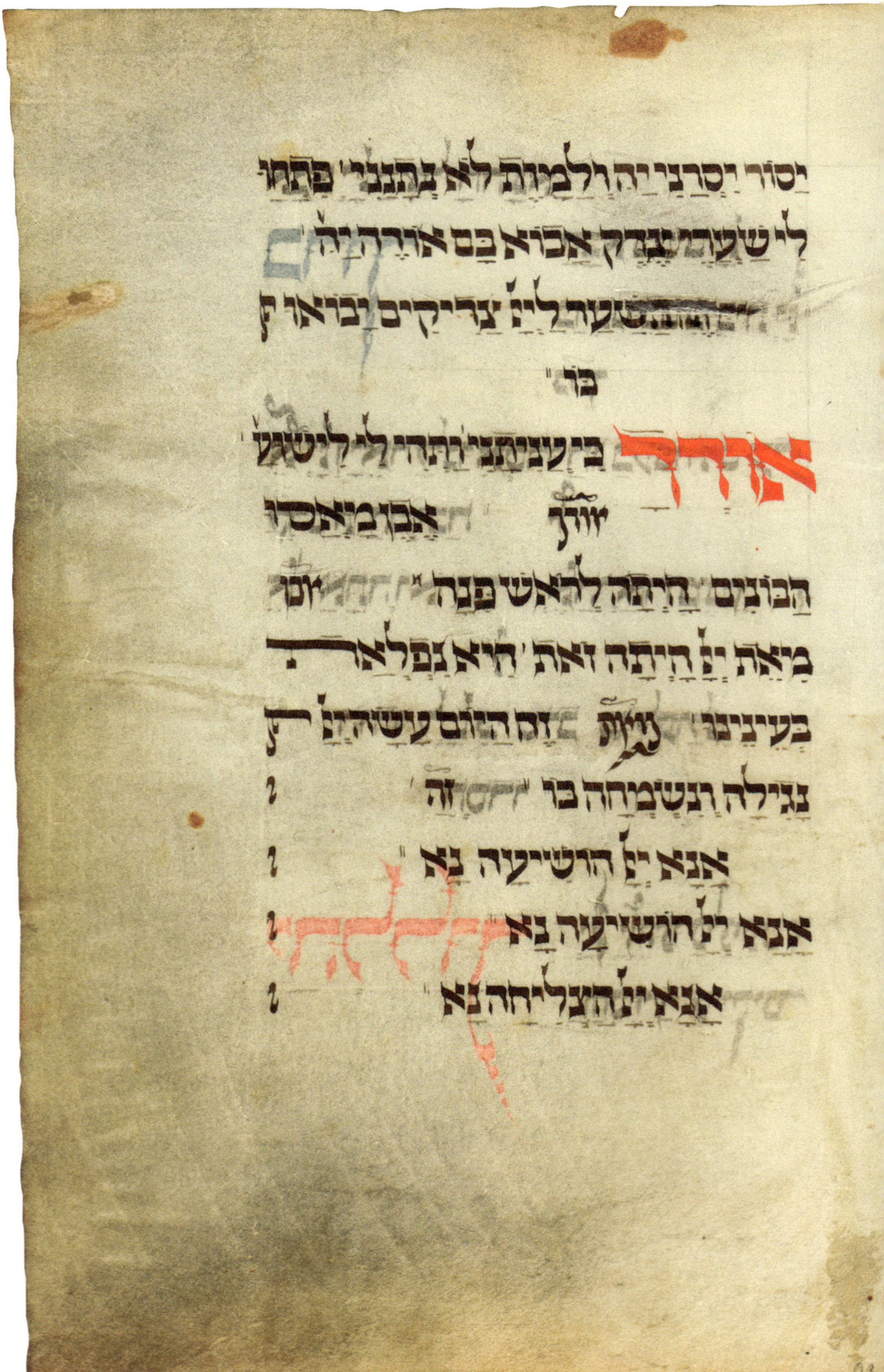
יסור יסרני יה ולמות לא נתנני פתחו
לי שערי צדק אבא בם אודה יה
זה השער ליי צדיקים יבואו בו
כו'
אודך כי עניתני ותהי לי לישועה
אבן מאסו
הבונים היתה לראש פנה
מאת יי היתה זאת היא נפלאת
בעינינו זה היום עשה יי
נגילה ונשמחה בו זה
אנא יי הושיעה נא
אנא יי הושיעה נא
אנא יי הצליחה נא

FOL. 23 R

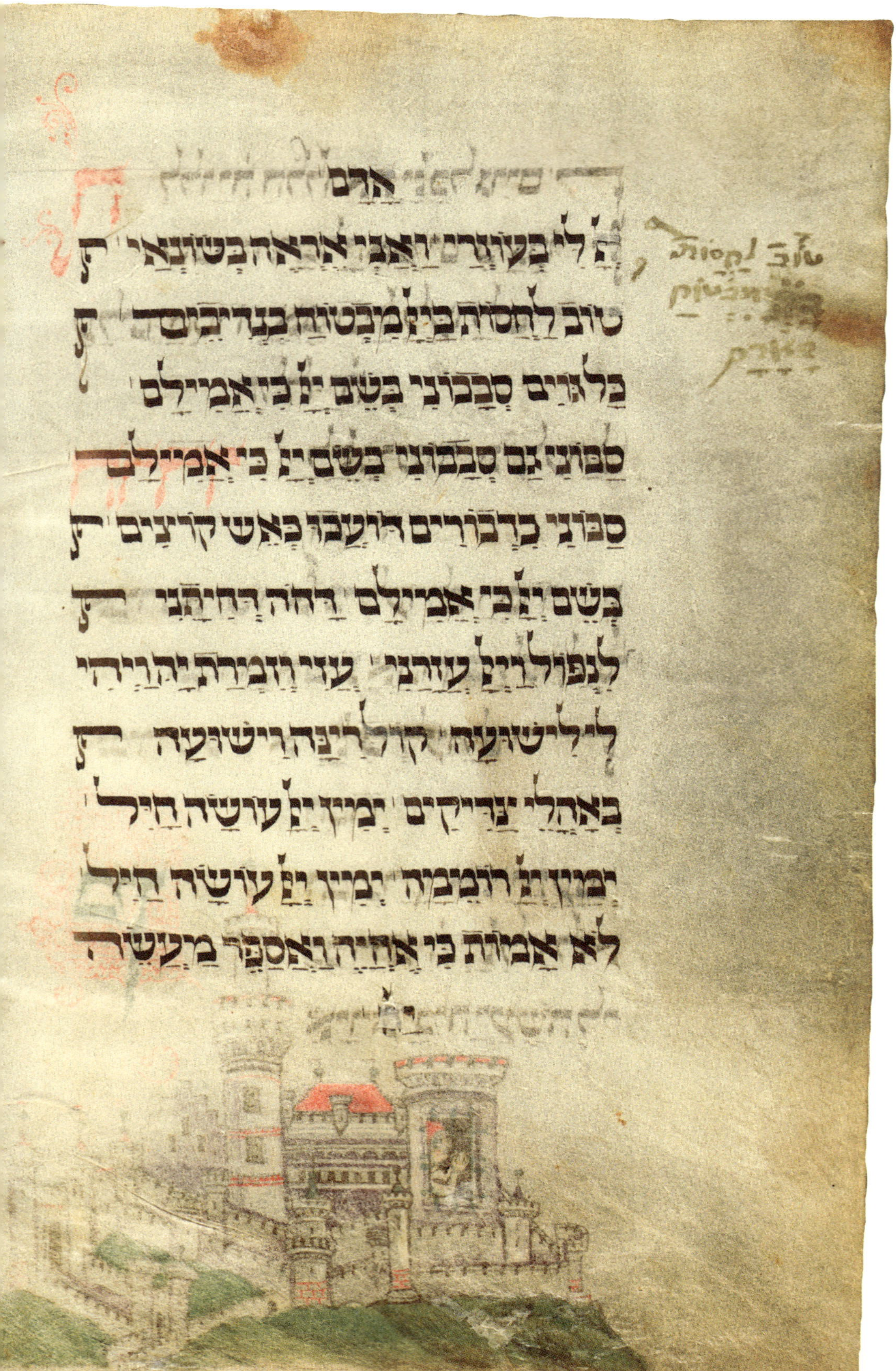
הרם
יי' לי בעוזרי ואני אראה בשונאי
טוב לחסות ביי' מבטוח בנדיבים
כל גוים סבבוני בשם יי' כי אמילם
סבוני גם סבבוני בשם יי' כי אמילם
סבוני כדבורים דועכו כאש קוצים
בשם יי' כי אמילם דחה דחיתני
לנפול ויי' עזרני עזי וזמרת יה ויהי
לי לישועה קול רנה וישועה
באהלי צדיקים ימין יי' עושה חיל
ימין יי' רוממה ימין יי' עושה חיל
לא אמות כי אחיה ואספר מעשי

FOL. 22 V

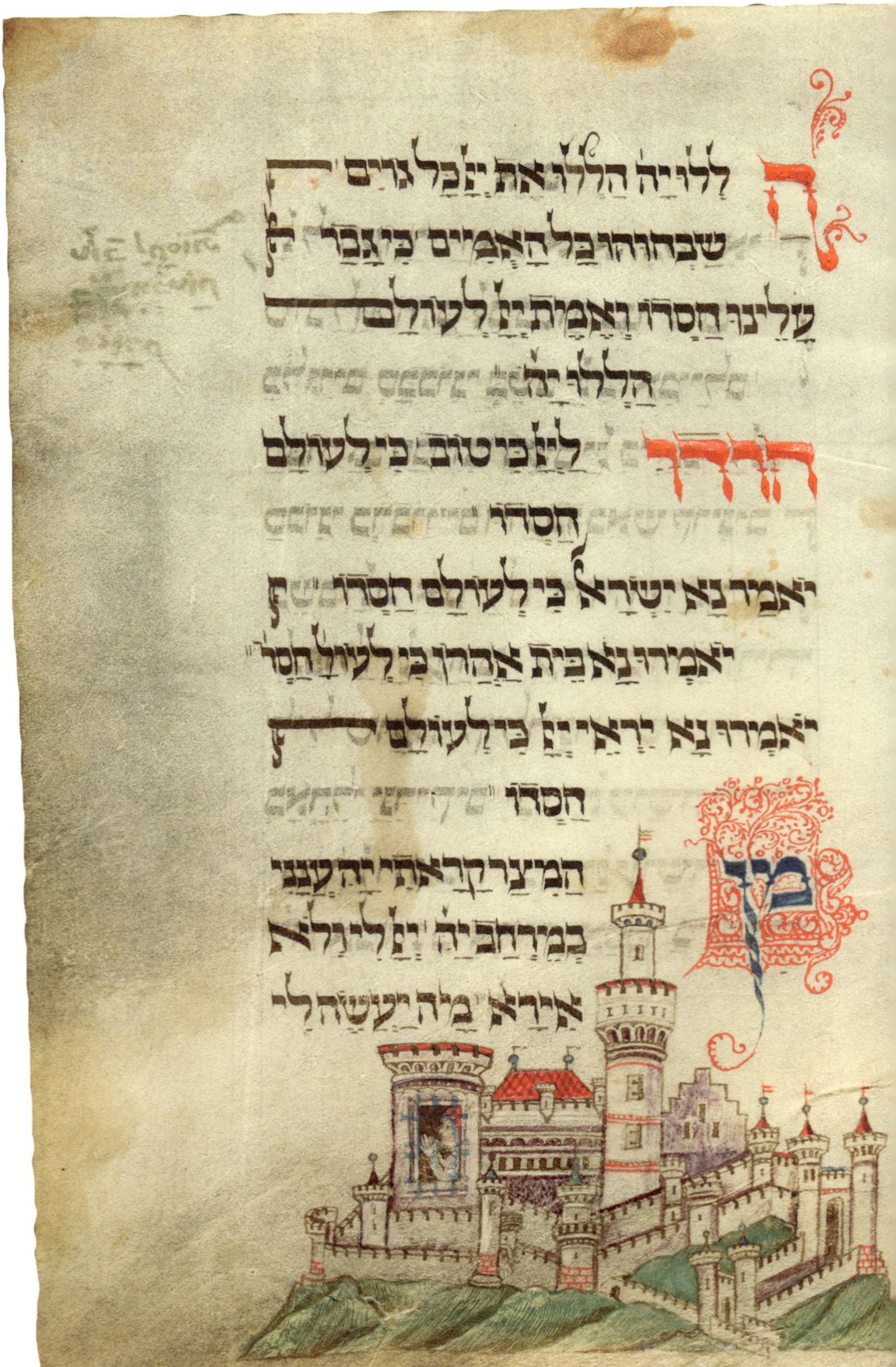
הללויה הללו את יי כל גוים
שבחוהו כל האמים כי גבר
עלינו חסדו ואמת יי לעולם
הללו יה
הודו ליי כי טוב כי לעולם
חסדו
יאמר נא ישראל כי לעולם חסדו
יאמרו נא בית אהרן כי לעול' חסד'
יאמרו נא יראי יי כי לעולם
חסדו
מן המצר קראתי יה ענני
במרחב יה יי לי לא
אירא מה יעשה לי

FOL. 22 R

מה אשיב ליי כל תג

תגמולוהי עלי:

כוס ישועות אשא

ובשם יי אקרא נדרי ליי אשלם

נגדה נא לכל עמו יקר בעיני יי

המותה לחסידיו אנא יי כי אני

עבדך אני עבדך בן אמתך פתחת

למוסירי לך אזבח זבח תודה ובשם

יי אקרא נדרי ליי אשלם נגדה נא

לכל עמו בחצרות בית יי בתוככי

ירושלים

הללויה

תחנוני כי הטה אזנו לי ובימי אקרא
אפפוני חבלי מות מיצרי שאול
ומצאוני צרה ויגון אמצא ובשם
יי אקרא אנא יי מלטה נפשי חנון
יי וצדיק ואלהינו מרחם שומר פתאים
יי דלותי ולי יהושיע שובי נפשי
למנוחיכי כי יי גמל עליכי כי חלצת
נפשי ממות את עיני מן דמעה את
רגלי מדחי אתהלך לפני יי בארצות
החיים האמנתי כי אדבר אני עניתי
מאד אני עניתי מאד אני אמרתי
בחפזי כל האדם
כוזב

21

FOL. 21 R

יראי יי׳ בטחו ביי׳ עזרם ומגינם הוא
יי׳ זכרנו יברך יברך את בית
ישראל יברך את בית
אהרן יברך יראי יי׳
הקטנים עם הגדולים יוסף יי׳
עליכם ועל בניכם ברוכים
אתם ליי׳ עושה שמים וארץ
השמים שמים ליי׳ והארץ נתן לבני
אדם לא המתים יה ולא כל יורדי יהללו
דומה ואנחנו נברך יה מעתה ועד
עולם הללו יה

אהבתי כי ישמע
יי׳ את קולי

FOL. 20 V

לא לנו יי׳ לא לנו כי לשמך

תן כבוד על חסדך

ועל אמתך למה

יאמרו הגוים איה נא אלהיהם ואלהינו

בשמים כל אשר חפץ עשה עצביהם

כסף וזהב מעשה ידי אדם פה להם

ולא ידברו עינים להם לא יראו

אזנים להם לא ישמעו אף להם לא

יריחון ידיהם ולא ימישון רגליהם

ולא יהלכון ולא יהגו בגרונם כמוהם

יהיו עושיהם וכל אשר בוטח בהם

ישראל בטח ביי׳ עזרם ומגנם הוא בית

אהרן בטחו ביי׳ עזרם ומגנם הוא

ישתבח

שמך לעד מלכנו האל המלך הגדול והקדוש ב
בשמים ובארץ כי לך נאה יי אלהינו ואלהי אבותינו
שיר ושבחה הלל וזמרה עוז וממשלה נצח גדולה
וגבורה תהלה ותפארת קדושה ומלכות ברכות
והודאות מעתה ועד עולם ברוך אתה יי אל מלך
גדול בתושבחות אל
ההודאות אדון הנפלאות
בורא כל הנשמות אדון כל המעשים
הבוחר בשירי זמרה
מלך אל חי העו
למים אמן

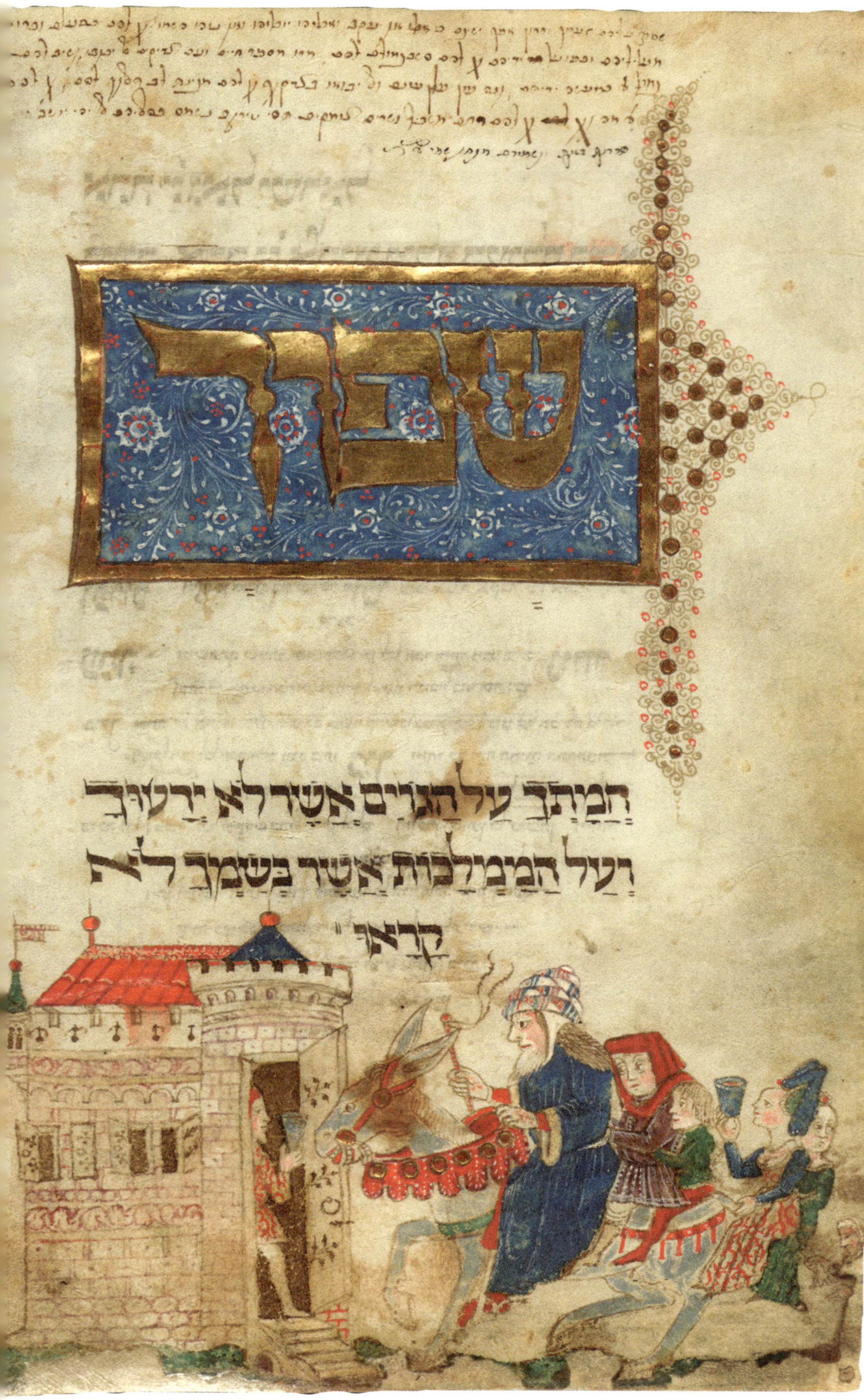

FOL. 19 V

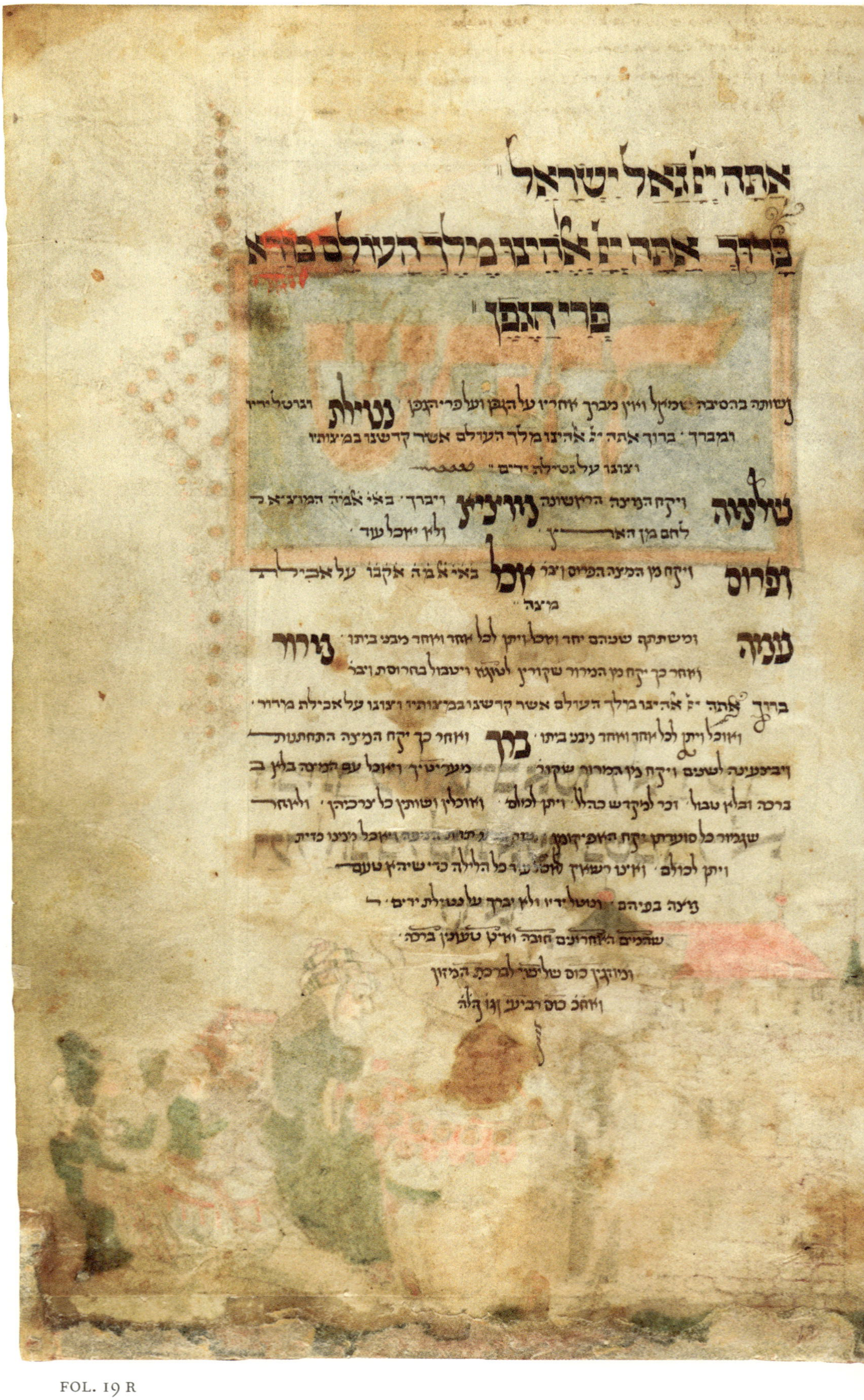

אתה יי גאל ישראל

ברוך אתה יי אלהינו מלך העולם בורא

פרי הגפן

ושותה בהסיבה שמאל ואין מברך אחריו על הגפן ועל פרי הגפן **נטילת** ונוטל ידיו
ומברך ברוך אתה יי אלהינו מלך העולם אשר קדשנו במצותיו
וצונו על נטילת ידים

[illegible] ויקח המצה הראשונה **מוציא** ויברך באי אמ"ה המוציא
לחם מן הארץ ולא יאכל עד

ופרוס ויקח מן המצה הפרוס ויב' **אכל** באי אמ"ה אקבו על אכילת
מצה

[illegible] ומשתתף שניהם יחד ואוכל ויתן לכל אחד ואחד מבני ביתו **מרור**
ואחר כך יקח מן המרור שקורין [illegible] ויטבול בחרוסת ויבר'
ברוך אתה יי אלהינו מלך העולם אשר קדשנו במצותיו וצונו על אכילת מרור
ואוכל ויתן לכל אחד ואחד מבני ביתו **כורך** ואחר כך יקח המצה התחתונה
ויבצענה לשנים ויקח מן המרור שקורין מעריטיך ויאכל עם המצה בלא ב
ברכה ובלא טבול זכר למקדש כהלל ויתן לכולם ואוכלין ושותין כל צרכיהן ואחר
שגמרו כל סעודתן יקח האפיקומן [illegible] ויאכל ממנו כזית
ויתן לכולם ואינו רשאי לאכול עד כל הלילה כדי שיהא טעם
מצה בפיהם ונוטל ידיו ולא יברך על נטילת ידים
שהמים האחרונים חובה ואינו טעונין ברכה
ומוזגין כוס שלישי לברכת המזון
ואחכ כוס רביעי וגו' הלה

FOL. 19 R

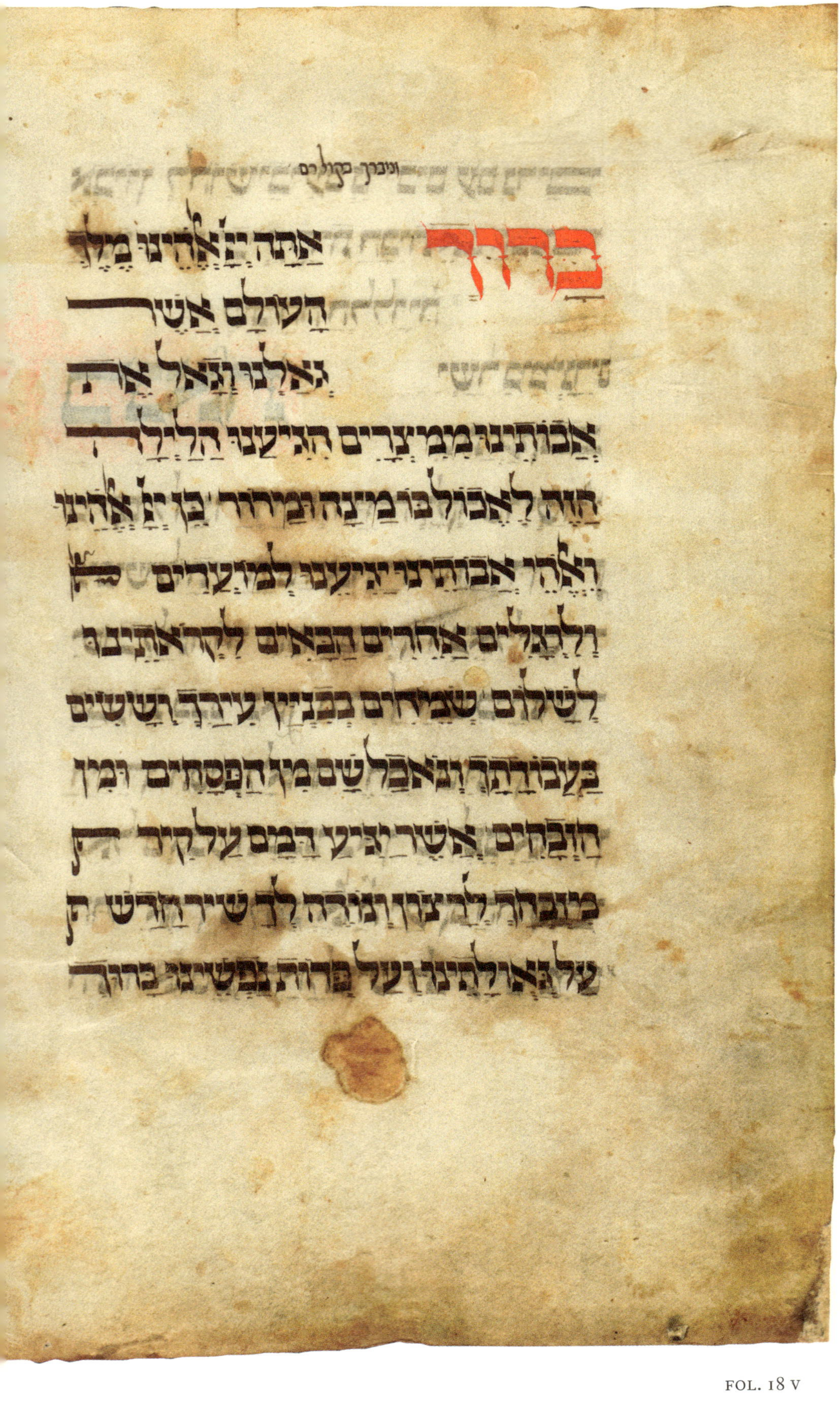
ומברך בקול רם

ברוך אתה יי אלהינו מלך
העולם אשר
גאלנו וגאל את
אבותינו ממצרים והגיענו הלילה
הזה לאכול בו מצה ומרור כן יי אלהינו
ואלהי אבותינו יגיענו למועדים
ולרגלים אחרים הבאים לקראתינו
לשלום שמחים בבנין עירך וששים
בעבודתך ונאכל שם מן הפסחים ומן
הזבחים אשר יגיע דמם על קיר
מזבחך לרצון ונודה לך שיר חדש
על גאולתינו ועל פדות נפשינו ברוך

FOL. 18 V

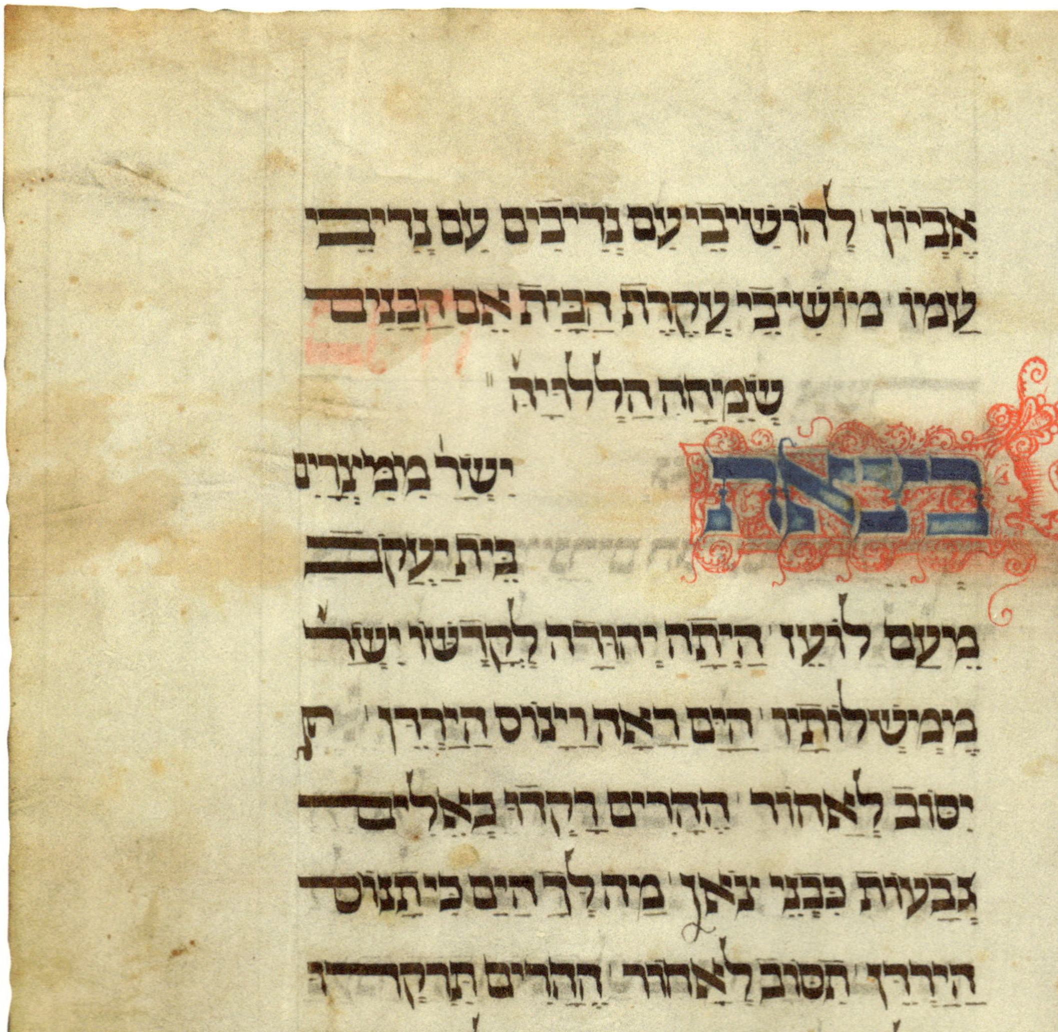

אביון להושיבי עם נדיבים עם נדיבי
עמו מושיבי עקרת הבית אם הבנים
שמחה הללויה
בצאת ישראל ממצרים
בית יעקב
מעם לועז היתה יהודה לקדשו ישראל
ממשלותיו הים ראה וינוס הירדן
יסוב לאחור ההרים רקדו באלים
גבעות כבני צאן מה לך הים כי תנוס
הירדן תסוב לאחור ההרים תרקדו
כאלים גבעות כבני צאן מלפני אדון
חולי ארץ מלפני אלוה יעקב ההפכי
הצור אגם מים חלמיש למעינו מים

FOL. 18 R

הללויה

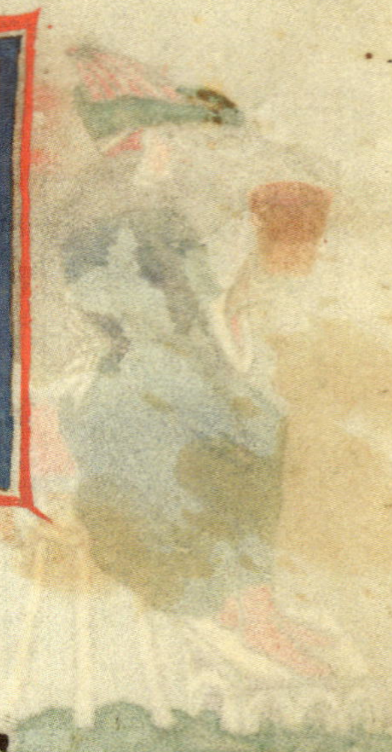

הללו עבדי יי הללו את שם יי יהי
שם יי מבורך מעתה ועד עולם
ממזרח שמש עד מבואו מהולל שם
יי רם על כל גוים יי על השמים
כבודו מי כיי אלהינו המגביהי לשבת
המשפילי לראות בשמים ובארץ
מקימי מעפר דל מאשפות ירים

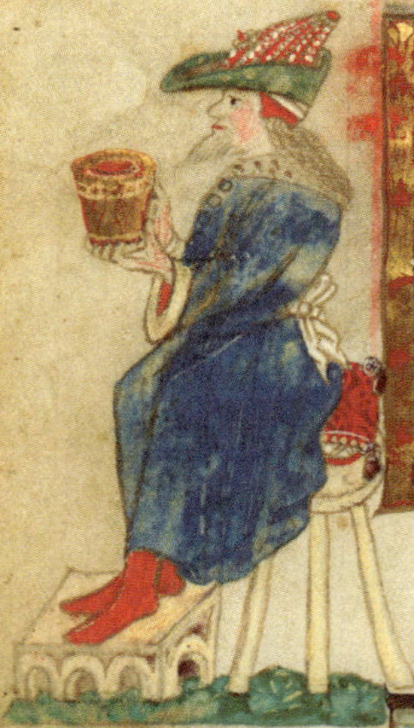

לפיכך

אנחנו חייבין להודות להלל לשבח
לפאר לרומם להדר לברך לעלה ולקלס
למי שעשה נסים לאבותינו ולנו את
כל הנסים האילו הוציאנו מעבדות
לחירות מיגון לשמחה ומאבל ליום
טוב ומאפילה לאור גדול ומשעבוד
לגאולה ונאמר לפניו הללויה

FOL. 17 R

בכל דור ודור חייב
אדם לראות את
עצמו כאילו הוא יצא ממצרים
שנ' והגדת לבנך ביום ההוא בעבור
זה עשה יי' לי בצאתי ממצרים

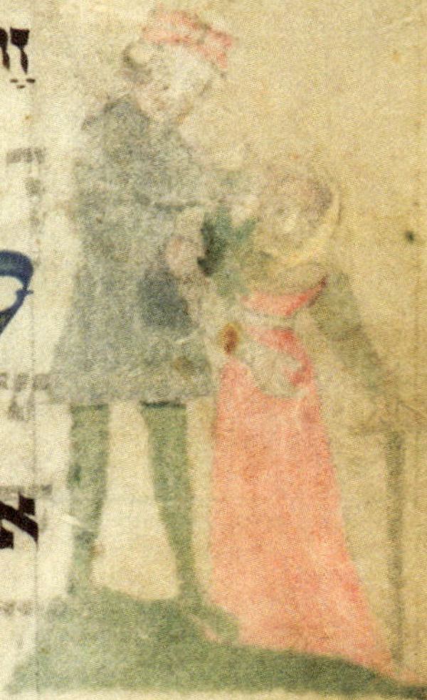

לא את אבותינו גאל
הקב"ה בלבד אלא אף
אותנו גאל עמהם שנ' ואותנו הוציא
משם למען הביא
אותנו לתת לנו את
הארץ
אשר נשבע לאבותינו

הקב״ה וגאלם שנ׳ ויאפו את הבצק
אשר הוציאו ממצרים עגות מצות
כי לא חמץ כי גורשו ממצרים ולא
יכלו להתמהמה וגם צדה לא עשו
להם

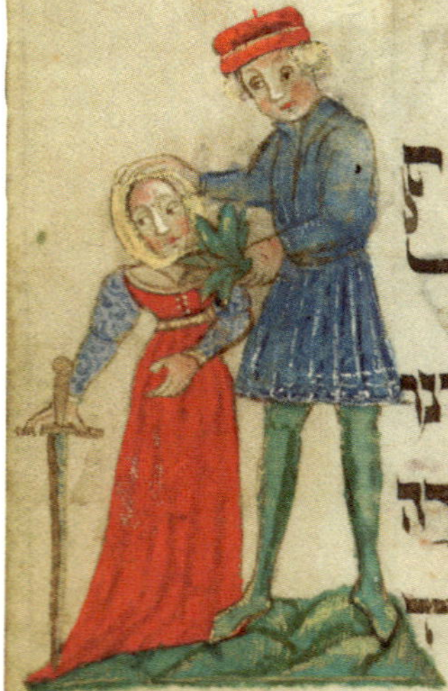

מרור

זה שאנו אוכלין
על שום מה על
שום שמררו המצרים את חיי אבותינו
במצרים שנ׳ וימררו את חייהם בעבודה
קשה בחומר ובלבנים ובכל עבודה
בשדה את כל עבודתם אשר עבדו
בהם בפרך

FOL. 16 R

ומיר׳ פסח שהיו אבותינו אוכלין
בזמן שבית המקדש קיים על שום
מה על שום שפסח המקום על בתי
אבותינו במצרים שנ׳ ואמרתם זבח
פסח הוא ליי׳ אשר פסח על בתי בני
ישראל בנגפו את מצרים ואת בתינו
הציל ויקד העם
וישתחוו :

מצה

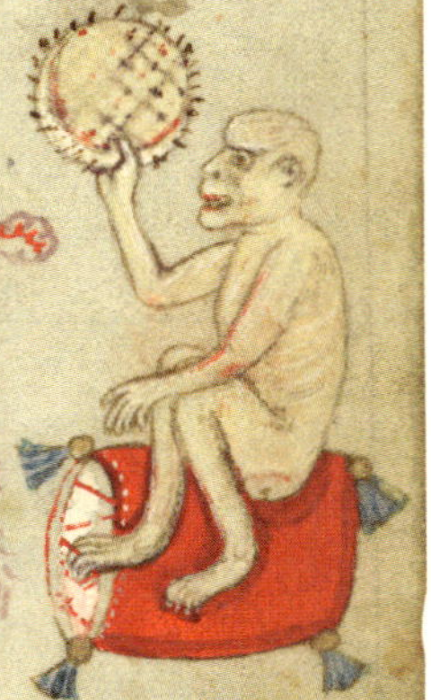

זו שאנו אוכלין
על שום מה על
שום שלא הספיק
בצקת אבותינו להחמיץ עד שנגלה
עליהם מלך מלכי המלכים

של

FOL. 15 V

ועשה בהם שפטים ועשה באלהיהם

והרג בכוריהם ונתן לנו את ממונם

וקרע לנו את הים והעבירנו בתוכו ד

בחרבה ושקע צרינו בתוכו וספק ד

צרכינו במדבר ארבעים שנה והאכילנו

את המן ונתן לנו את השבת וקרבנו

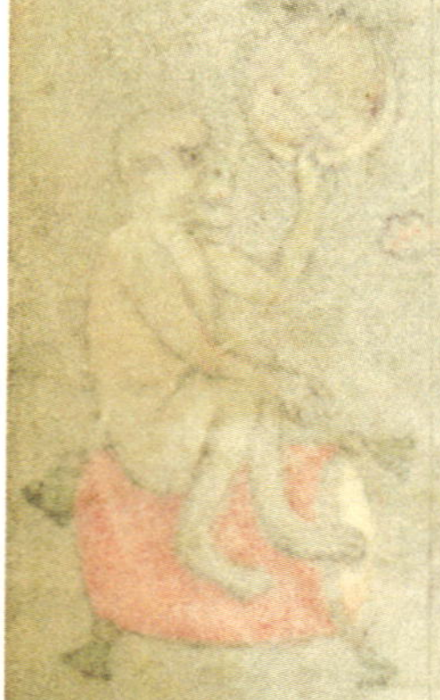

לפני הר סיני ונתן לנו את התורה ד

והכניסנו לארץ ישראל ובנה לנו את

בית הבחירה לכפר על כל עונותינו

רבן גמליאל היה אומר

כל שלא אומ׳ שלשה

דברים הללו בפסח

לא יצא ידי חובתו אילו הן פסח מצה

15

FOL. 15 R

אילו נתן לנו את השבת

ולא קרבנו לפני הר סיני דיינו

אילו קרבנו לפני הר סיני

ולא נתן לנו את התורה דיינו

אילו נתן לנו את התורה

ולא הכניסנו לארץ ישר׳ דיינו

אילו הכניסנו לארץ ישר׳

ולא בנה לנו את בית הבחירה

דיינו

על אחת כמה וכמה טובה

כפולה ומכופלת

למקום עלינו שהוציאנו ממצרים

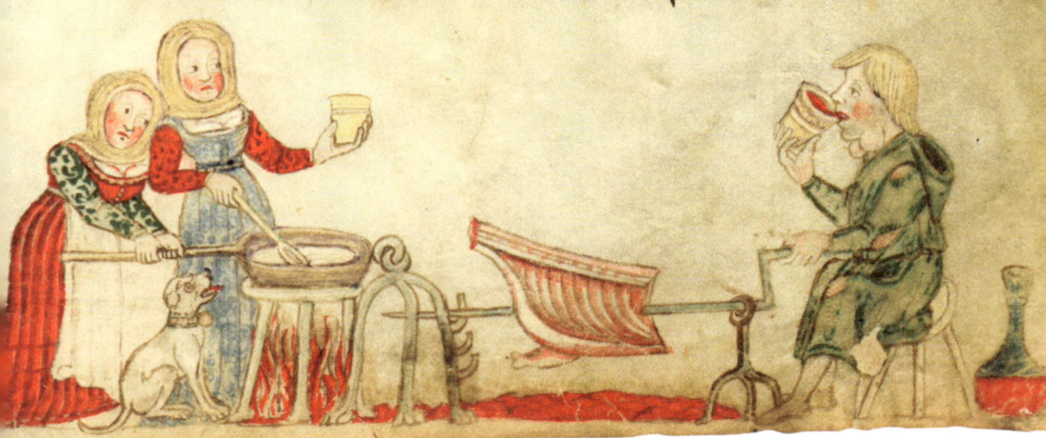

ולא נתן לנו את ממונם דיינו

אילו נתן לנו את ממונם

ולא קרע לנו את הים דיינו

אילו קרע לנו את הים

ולא העבירנו בתוכו בחרב דיינו

אילו העבירנו בתוכו בחרבה

ולא שקע צרינו בתוכה דיינו

אילו שקע צרינו בתוכה

ולא ספק צרכי' במד' ארבעי' שנ' דיינו

אילו ספק צרכי' במדב' ארבעי' שנה

ולא האכילנו את המן דיינו

אילו האכילנו את המן

ולא נתן לנו את השבת דיינו

FOL. 14 R

כמה

מעלות טובות למקום עלינו

אילו הוציאנו ממצרים

ולא עשה בהם שפטים דיינו

אילו עשה בהם שפטים

ולא עשה באלהיהם דיינו

אילו עשה באלהיהם

ולא הרג את בכוריהם דיינו

אילו הרג את בכוריהם

FOL. 13 V

לקו ארבעים מכות ועל הים לקו

מאתים מכות

רבי עקיבא אומר מנין שכל

מכה ומכה שהביא

הקב״ה על המצרים במצרים היתה

של חמש מכות שנ׳ ישלח בם חרון

אפו עברה וזעם וצרה משלחת חר

מלאכי רעים אפו אחת עברה

שתים וזעם שלוש וצרה ארבע

משלחת מלאכי רעים חמש אמור

מעתה במצרים לקו

חמשים מכות ועל הים

לקו מאתים וחמשים מכות

FOL. 13 R

במצרים לקו עשר מכות ועל הים

לקו חמשים מכות

רבי אליעזר אומ'

מניין שכל

מכה ומכה

שהביא הקב"ה על המצריים במ

במצרים היתה של ארבע מכות

שנ' ישלח בם חרון אפו עברה

וזעם וצרה משלחת מלאכי

רעים עברה אחת וזעם

שתים וצרה משלחת מלאכי שלוש

רעים ארבע אמור מעתה

במצרים

FOL. 12 V

ר׳ יוסי הגלילי אומר מנין

אתה אומר שלקו

המצריים במצרים עשר מכות ועל

הים לקו חמשים מכות

במצרים מה הוא אומ׳

ויאמרו

החרטמים אל פרעה אצבע אלהים

היא ועל הים מה הוא אומר וירא

ישרא׳ את היד הגדולה אשר עשה

יי׳ במצרים וייראו העם את יי׳

ויאמינו ביי׳ ובמשה עבדו

במה לקו באצבע עשר

מכות אמור מעתה

FOL. 12 R

דבר אחר ביד חזקה שתים

ובזרוע נטויה שתים

ובמורא גדול שתים ובאותות שתים

ובמופתים שתים

אילו עשר מכות שהביא

הקב״ה על המצרים

במצרים אילו הן׳ דם׳ צפרדע׳

כנים׳ ערוב׳ דבר׳ שחין׳ ברד׳

ארבה׳ חשך׳ מכת בכורות

ר׳ יהודה היה נותן

בהם סימנים

דצ״ך עד״ש

באח״ב״

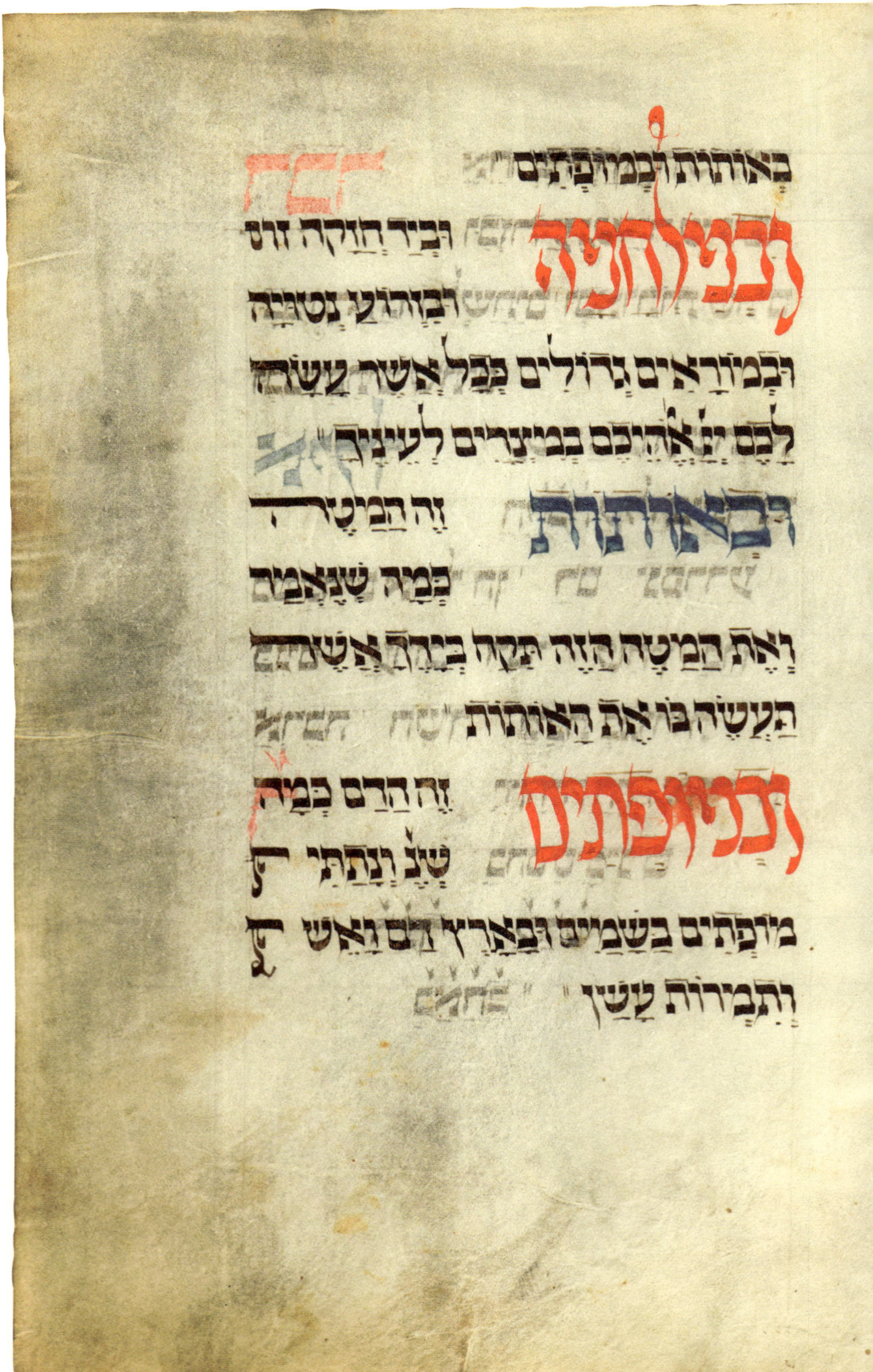
באותות ובמופתים
ובמלחמה וביד חזקה זרו
ובזרוע נטויה
ובמוראים גדולים ככל אשר עשה
לכם יי' אלהיכם במצרים לעיניך
ובאותות זה המטה
כמה שנאמר
ואת המטה הזה תקח בידך אשר
תעשה בו את האותות
ובמופתים זה הדם כמה
שנ' ונתתי
מופתים בשמים ובארץ דם ואש
ותמרות עשן

FOL. 11 R

אלהי מצרים אעשה שפטים אני יי׳ א
אני ולא השליח אני הוא ולא אחר

ביד חזקה זו הדבר כמה
שנ׳ הנה יד יי׳ הויה
במקנך אשר בשדה בסוסים
בחמורים בגמלים בבקר ובצאן דבר
כבד מאד

ובזרוע נטויה זו החרב
כמה שנ׳ וחרבו
שלופה בידו נטויה על ירושלים

ובמורא גדול זו גילוי שכינה
שנ׳ או הנסה אלהים
לבא לקחת לו גוי מקרב גוי במסות

FOL. 10 V

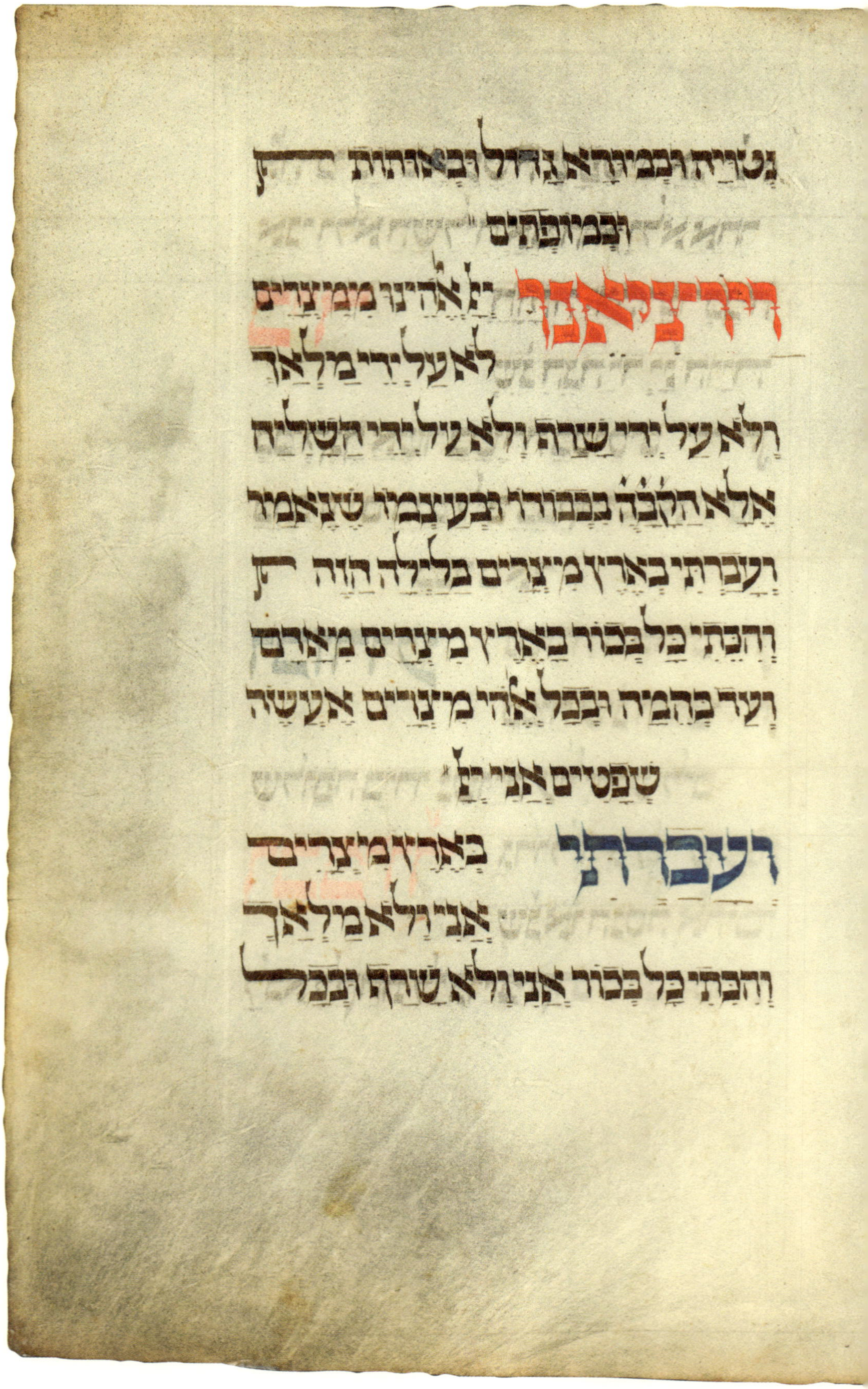
נטויה ובמורא גדול ובאותות
ובמופתים
ויוציאנו יי׳ אלהינו ממצרים
לא על ידי מלאך
ולא על ידי שרף ולא על ידי השליח
אלא הקב״ה בכבודו ובעצמו שנאמר
ועברתי בארץ מצרים בלילה הזה
והכתי כל בכור בארץ מצרים מאדם
ועד בהמה ובכל אלהי מצרים אעשה
שפטים אני יי׳
ועברתי בארץ מצרים
אני ולא מלאך
והכתי כל בכור אני ולא שרף ובכל

FOL. 10 R

נאקתם ויזכר אלהים את בריתו את
אברהם את יצחק ואת יעקב

וירא את ענינו זו פרישות
דרך ארץ כמה שנ'
וירא אלהים את בני ישראל וידע אלהים

ואת עמלינו אילו הבנים
כמה שנ' כל הבן הילוד
היאורה תשליכהו וכל הבת תחיון

ואת לחצינו זו הדחק כמה
שנ' וגם ראיתי את
הלחץ אשר מצרים לוחצים אותם

ויוציאנו יי' אלהינו ממצרים
ביד חזקה ובזרוע

FOL. 9 V

ויתנו עלינו עבודה קשה כמ'
שנ' ויעבידו מצרים את
בני ישרא' בפרך
ונצעק אל יי' אלהי אבותינו
וישמע יי' את קולינו
וירא את ענינו ואת עמלינו ואת לחצנו
ונצעק אל יי' אלהי אבותינו
כמה שנ' ויהי בימים
הרבים ההם וימת מלך מצרים
ויאנחו בני ישרא' מן העבודה ויזעקו
ותעל שועתם אל האלהים מן העבודה
וישמע יי' את קולינו כמה שנ'
וישמע אלהים את

FOL. 9 R

ואת ערום ועריה

וירעו אותנו המצרים

ויענונו ויתנו עלינו

עבודה קשה

וירעו אותנו המצרים כמה

שנ' הבה נתחכמה לו

פן ירבה והיה כי תקראנה מלחמה

ונוסף גם הוא על שונאינו ונלחם

בנו ועלה מן הארץ

ויענונו כמה שנ' למען

ענותו בסבלותם

ויבן ערי

מסכנות לפרעה את פיתום ואת רעמסס

באנו כי אין מרעה לצאן אשר לעבדיך
כי כבד הרעב בארץ כנען ועתה ישבו נא
עבדיך בארץ גושן
במתי מעט כמה שנ' בשבעי'
נפש ירדו אבותיך
מצרימה ועתה שמך יי' אלהיך ככוכבי
השמים לרוב ויהי שם לגוי
מלמד שהיו ישר' מצויינין שם גדול
ועצום שנ' ובני ישר' פרו וישרצו וירבו
ויעצמו במאד מאד ותמלא הארץ
אתם ורב כמה שנ' רבבה כצמ'
השדה נתתיך ותרבי ותגדלי ותבואי
בעדי עדיים שדים נכונו ושערך צמח

צא ולמד מה בקש לבן הארמי
לעשות ליעקב אבינו
שפרעה לא גזר אלא על הזכרים ולבן
בקש לעקור את הכל שנ׳ ארמי אובד
אבי וירד מצרימה ויגר שם במתי
מעט ויהי שם לגוי גדול עצום
ורב׳

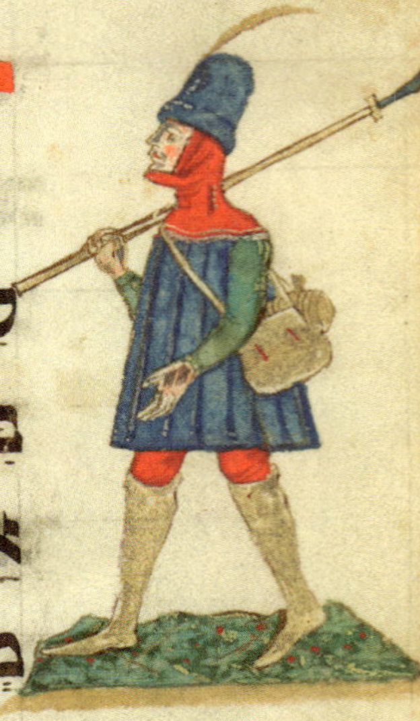

וירד מצרימה אנוס
על פי הדבור
ויגר שם מלמד
שלא ירד להשתקע אלא
לגור שם שנאמר ויאמרו אל
פרעה לגור בארץ

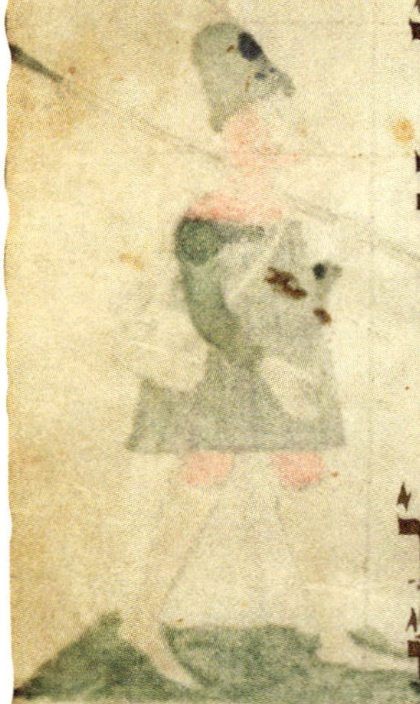

ברוך שומר הבטחתו לישר'
ברוך הוא שהקב"ה חשב
את הקץ לעשות כמה שאמר לאברהם
אבינו בברית בין הבתרים שנ' ויאמר
לאברם ידוע תדע כי גר יהיה זרעך בא'
לא להם ועבדום וענו אותם ארבע מא'
שנה וגם את הגוי אשר יעבודו
דן אנכי ואחרי כן יצאו ברכוש גדול
והיא שעמדה לאבותינו ולנו
שלא אחד בלבד עומד
עלינו לכלותינו אלא שבכל דור ודור
עומדים עלינו לכלותינו והקב"ה
מצילנו מידם

FOL. 7 R

אלא בשעה שיש מצה ומרור מונחים
לפניך ׃ מתחלה עובדי עז היו
אבותינו ועכשיו קרבנו המקום לעבוד תו
שנ' ויאמר יהושע אל כל העם כה אמ'
יי' אלהי ישראל בעבר הנהר ישבו אבותיכ'
מעולם תרח אבי אברהם ואבי נחור
ויעבדו אלהים אחרים ׃
ם ואקח את אביכם את אברה
מעבר הנהר ואולך אותו בכל ארץ כנען
וארבה את זרעו ואתן לו את יצחק
ואתן ליצחק את יעקב ואת עשו ואתן
לעשו את הר שעיר ויעקב ובניו ירדו לרשת אותו
מצרימה ׃

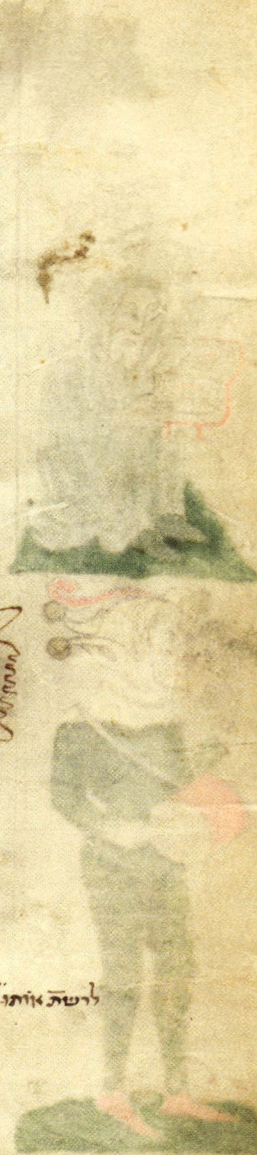

את שניו ואמור לו בעבור זה עשה יי׳ לי
בצאתי ממצרים לי ולא לו אילו היה
שם לא היה נגאל

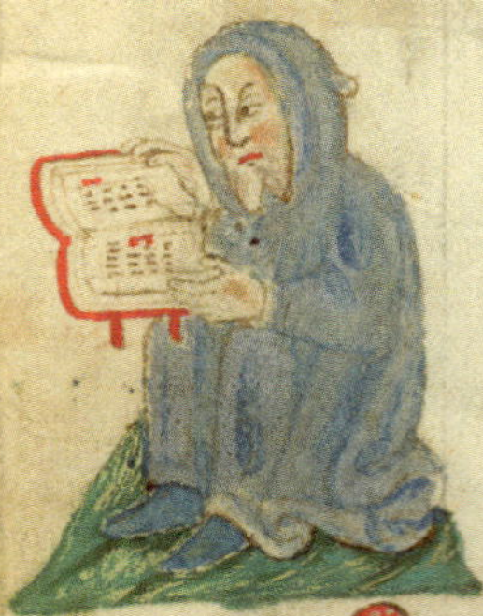

תם מה הוא אומ׳ מה זאת
ואמרת אליו בחוזק יד
הוציאנו יי׳ ממצרים מבית עבדים

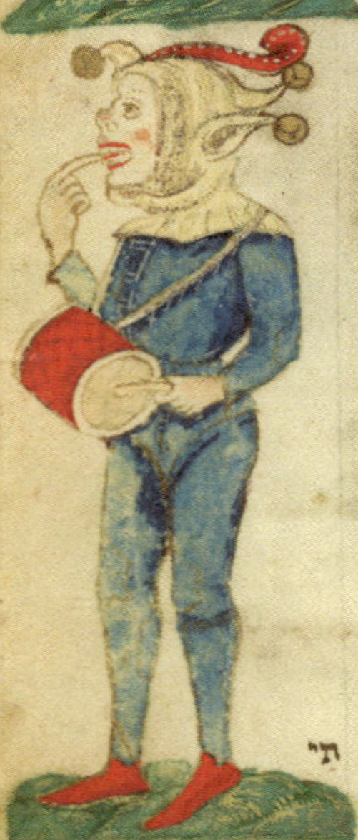

ושאינו יודע לשאול את פת׳
לו שנ׳ והגדת לבנך
ביום ההוא לאמר בעבור זה עשה יי׳
לי בצאתי ממצרים

יכול מראש חודש ת״ל ביום
ההוא אי ביום ההוא
יכול מבעוד יום ת״ל בעבור זה לא אמר

FOL. 6 R

שנתן תורה לעמו ישראל ברוך הוא
כנגד ארבעה בנים דברה תורה אחד
חכם ואחד רשע ואחד תם ואחד שאינו
יודע לשאל

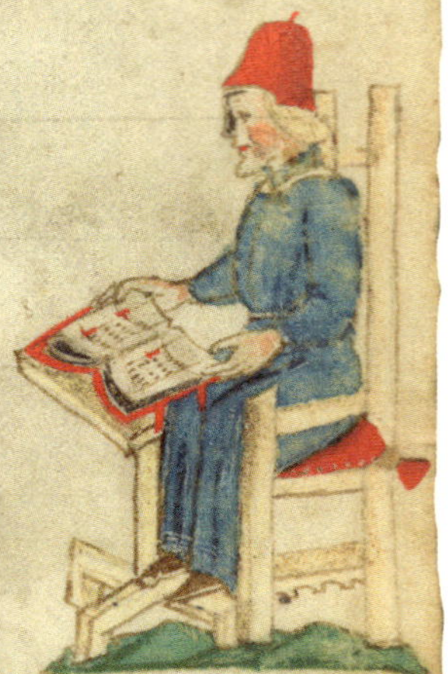

חכם מה הוא אומר מה
העדות והחקים והמשפטי'
אשר צוה יי' אלהינו אתכם ואף אתה
אמור לו כהלכות הפסח אין מפטירין
אחר הפסח אפיקומן

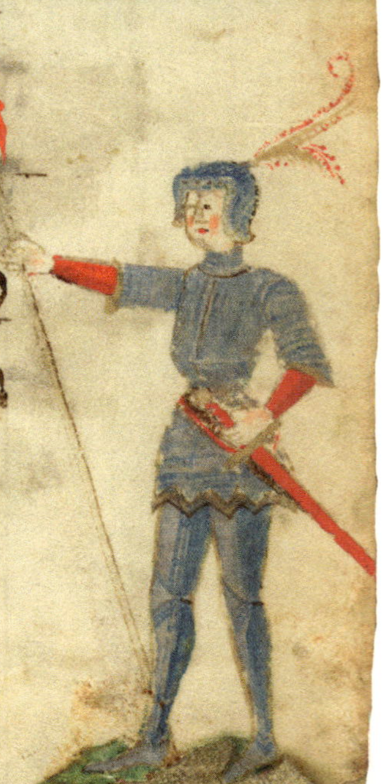

רשע מה הוא אומר מה
העבודה הזאת לכם
לכם ולא לו ולפי שהוציא את עצמו
מן הכלל כפר בעקר ואף אתה הקהה

FOL. 5 V

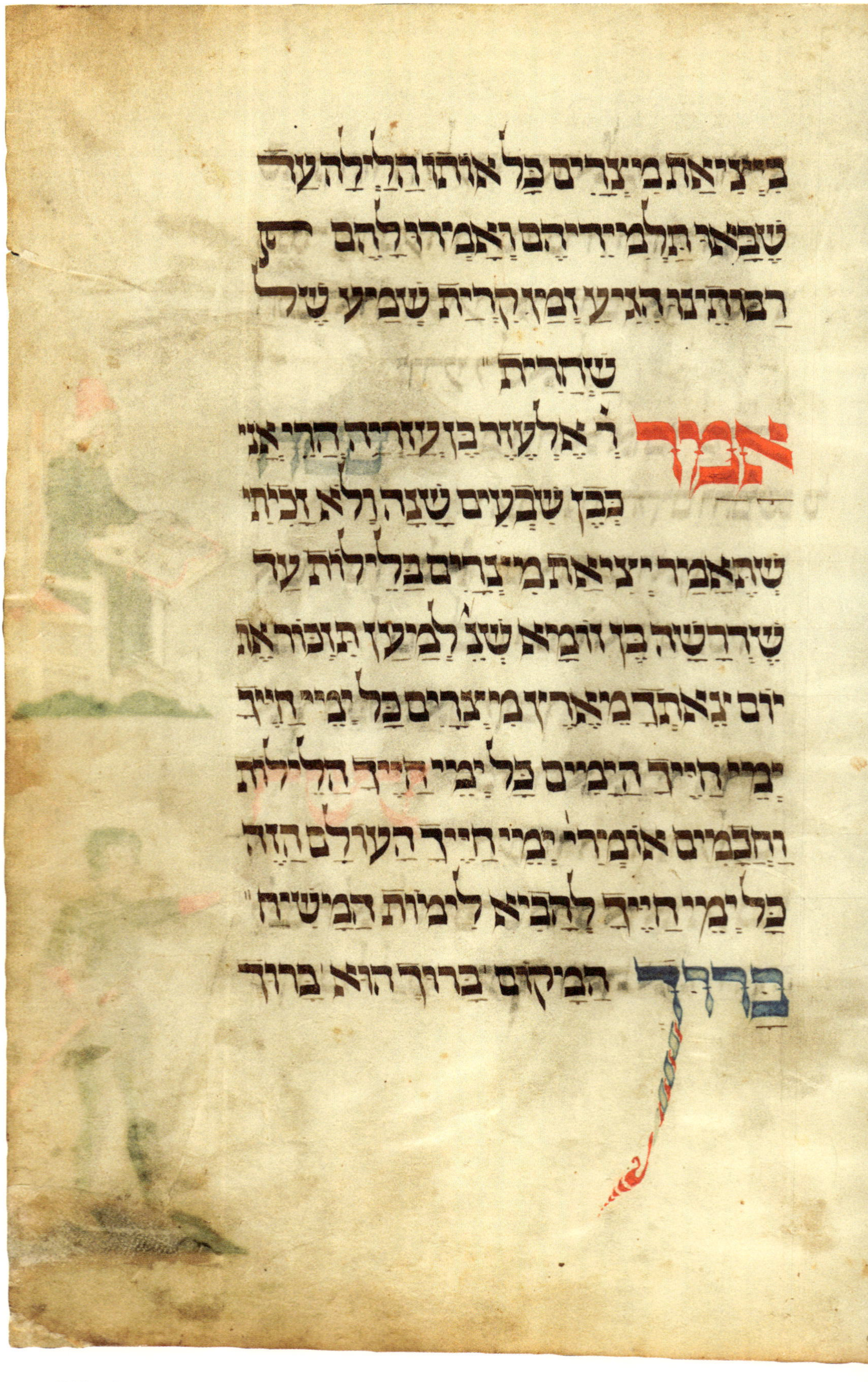

ביציאת מצרים כל אותו הלילה עד
שבאו תלמידיהם ואמרו להם
רבותינו הגיע זמן קרית שמע של
שחרית
אמר ר' אלעזר בן עזריה הרי אני
כבן שבעים שנה ולא זכיתי
שתאמר יציאת מצרים בלילות עד
שדרשה בן זומא שנ' למען תזכור את
יום צאתך מארץ מצרים כל ימי חייך
ימי חייך הימים כל ימי חייך הלילות
וחכמים אומרי' ימי חייך העולם הזה
כל ימי חייך להביא לימות המשיח
ברוך המקום ברוך הוא ברוך

FOL. 5 R

יי׳ אלהינו משם ביד חזקה ובזרוע נטוי׳
ואלו לא הוציא הקב״ה את אבותינו
ממיצרים הרי אנו ובנינו ובני בנינו
מישועבדים היינו לפרעה במיצרים
ואפילו כלנו חכמים כלנו נבונים
כלנו זקנים כלנו יודעים את התורה
מיצוה עלינו לספר ביציאת מיצרים
שכל המספר ביציאת מיצרים הרי זה
משובח

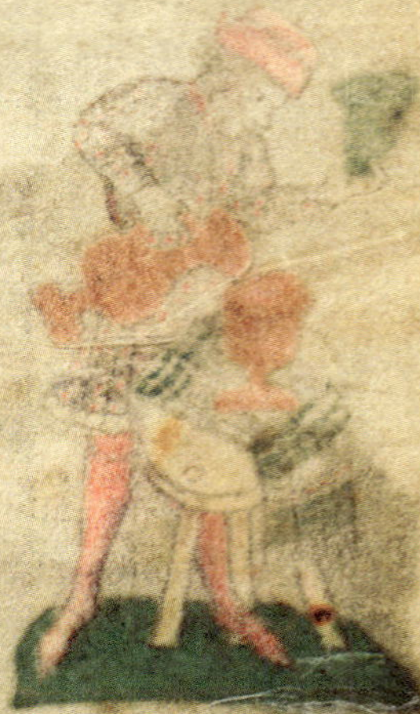

מעשה בר׳ אליעזר ור׳
יהושע ור׳ אלעזר
בן עזריה ור׳ עקיבא ור׳ טרפון שהיו
מסובין בבני ברק והיו מספרין

FOL. 4 V

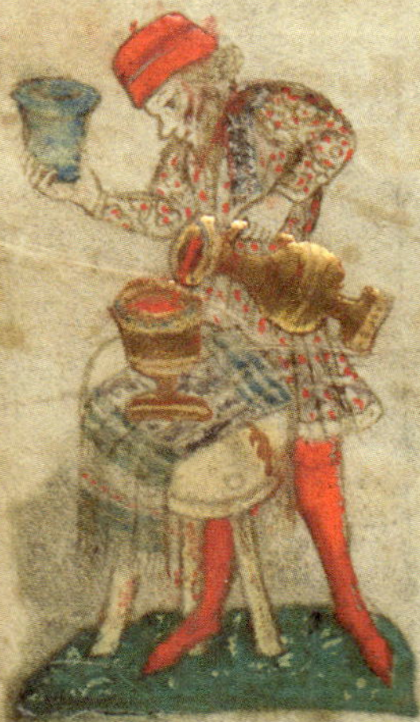

מה נשתנה הליל
הזה מכל
הלילות שבכ
הלילות אנו אוכלין חמץ ומצה
הלילה הזה כלו מצה שבכל הלילות
אנו אוכלין שאר ירקות הלילה הזה
מרור שבכל הלילות אין אנו חייבין
לטבל אפילו פעם אחת הלילה הזה
שתי פעמים שבכל הלילות אנו אוכלי
בין יושבין ובין מסובין הלילה הזה
כלנו מסובין

עבדים היינו לפרעה
במצרים ויוצי

FOL. 4 R

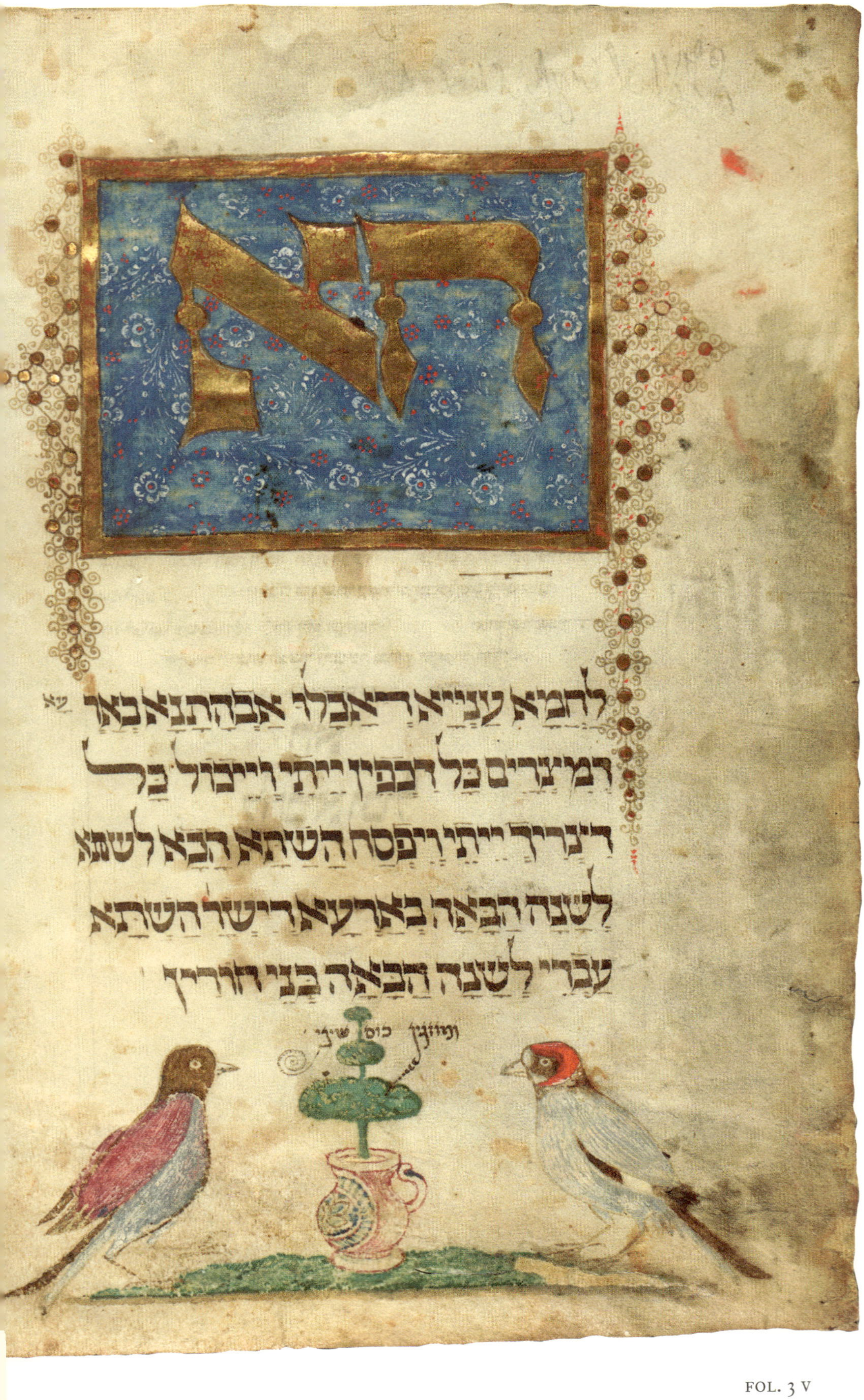
הא

לחמא עניא דאכלו אבהתנא באר עא

דמצרים כל דכפין ייתי וייכול כל

דצריך ייתי ויפסח השתא הכא לשתא

לשנה הבאה בארעא דישראל השתא

עבדי לשנה הבאה בני חורין

FOL. 3 V

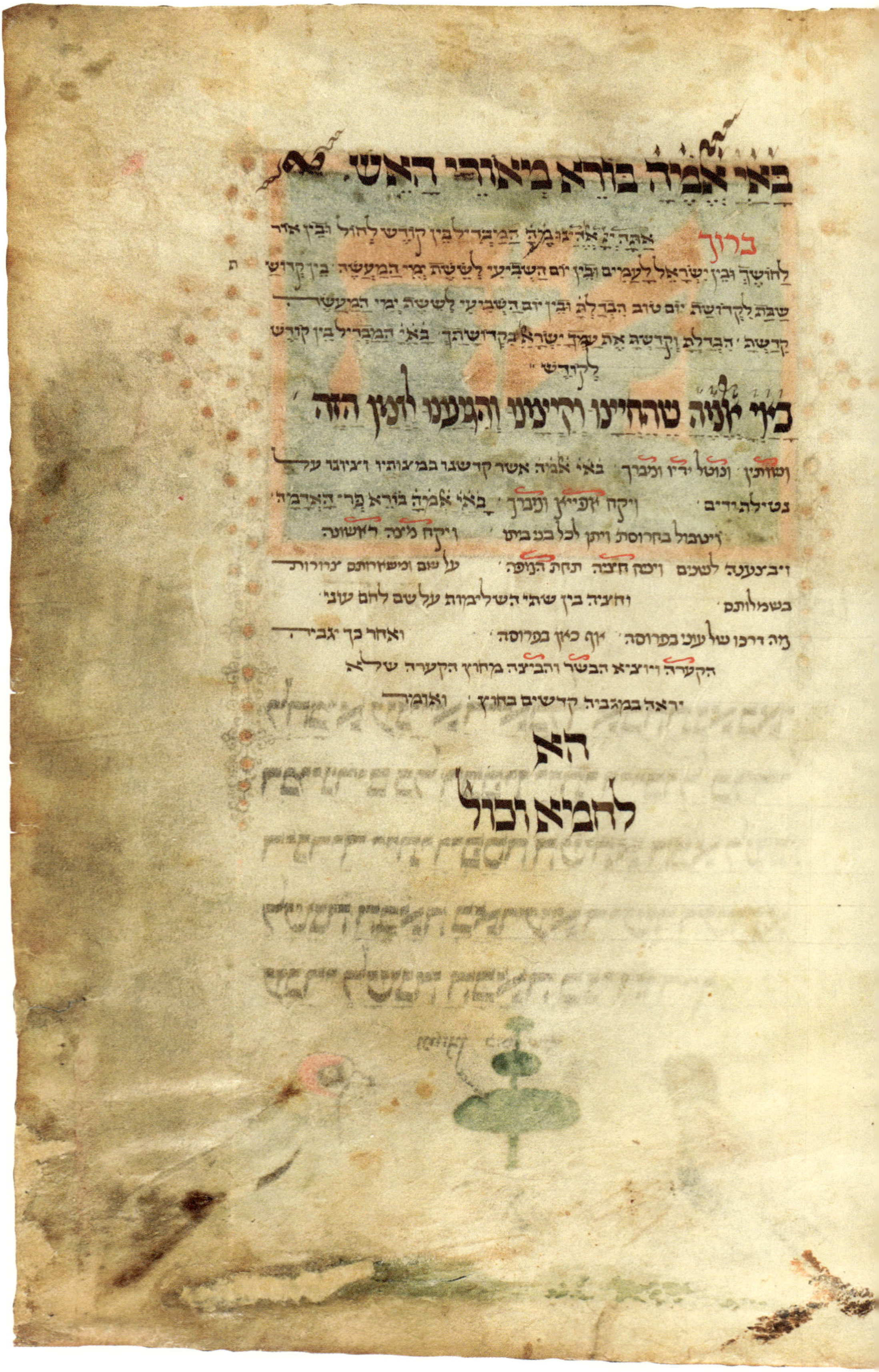
באי אמיה בורא מאורי האש׳
ברוך אתה יי אלהינו מלך המבדיל בין קודש לחול ובין אור
לחושך ובין ישראל לעמים ובין יום השביעי לששת ימי המעשה בין קדוש
שבת לקדושת יום טוב הבדלת ובין יום השביעי לששת ימי המעשה
קדשת הבדלת וקדשת את עמך ישראל בקדושתך באי המבדיל בין קודש
לקודש׳
באי אמיה שהחיינו וקימנו והגיענו לזמן הזה׳
ושותין ונוטל ידיו ומברך באי אמיה אשר קדשנו במצותיו וצונו על
נטילת ידים ויקח אפייא ומברך באי אמיה בורא פרי האדמה׳
ויטבול בחרוסת ויתן לכל בני ביתו ויקח מצה ראשונה
ויבצענה לשנים ויתן חצה תחת המפה׳ על שם ומשארותם צרורות
בשמלותם וחציה בין שתי השלימות על שם לחם עוני
מה דרכו של עני בפרוסה אף כאן בפרוסה ואחר כך יגביה
הקערה ויוציא הבשר והביצה מחוץ הקערה שלא
יראה במגביה קדשים בחוץ ואומר
הא
לחמא עניא

FOL. 3 R

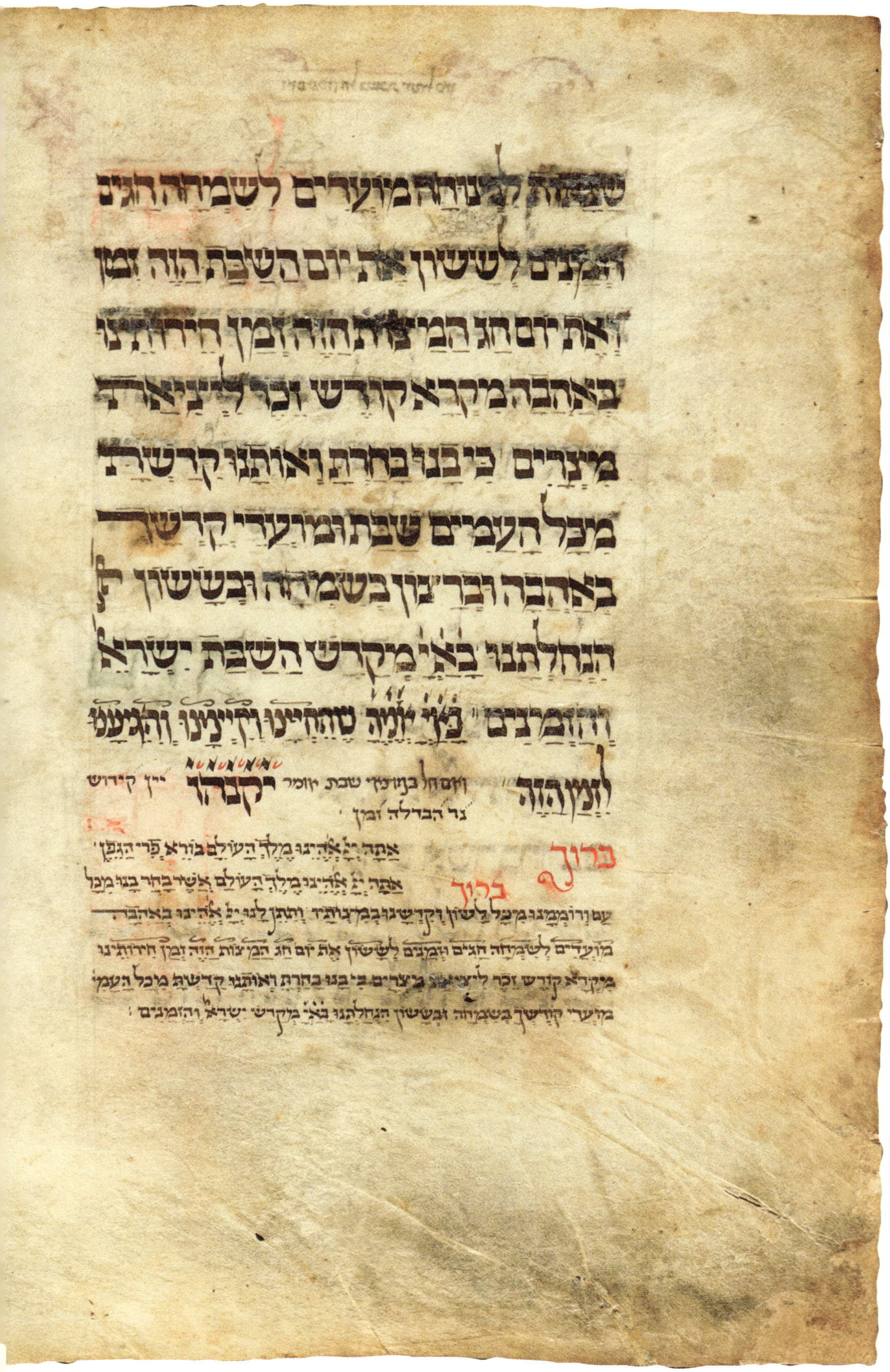
שבתות למנוחה מועדים לשמחה חגים
וזמנים לששון את יום השבת הזה וזמן
ואת יום חג המצות הזה זמן חירותנו
באהבה מקרא קודש זכר ליציאת
מצרים כי בנו בחרת ואותנו קדשת
מכל העמים שבת ומועדי קדשך
באהבה וברצון בשמחה ובששון יי
הנחלתנו בא״י מקדש השבת ישרא׳
והזמנים ׃ בא״י אמ״ה שהחיינו וקיימנו והגיענו
לזמן הזה ׃ ואם חל במוצאי שבת יומר יקנה״ז יין קידוש
נר הבדלה זמן ׃
ברוך אתה יי׳ אלהינו מלך העולם בורא פרי הגפן ׃
ברוך אתה יי׳ אלהינו מלך העולם אשר בחר בנו מכל
עם ורוממנו מכל לשון וקדשנו במצותיו ותתן לנו יי׳ אלהינו באהבה
מועדים לשמחה חגים וזמנים לששון את יום חג המצות הזה זמן חירותינו
מקרא קודש זכר ליציאת מצרים כי בנו בחרת ואותנו קדשת מכל העמי׳
מועדי קודשך בשמחה ובששון הנחלתנו בא״י מקדש ישרא׳ והזמנים ׃

FOL. 2 V

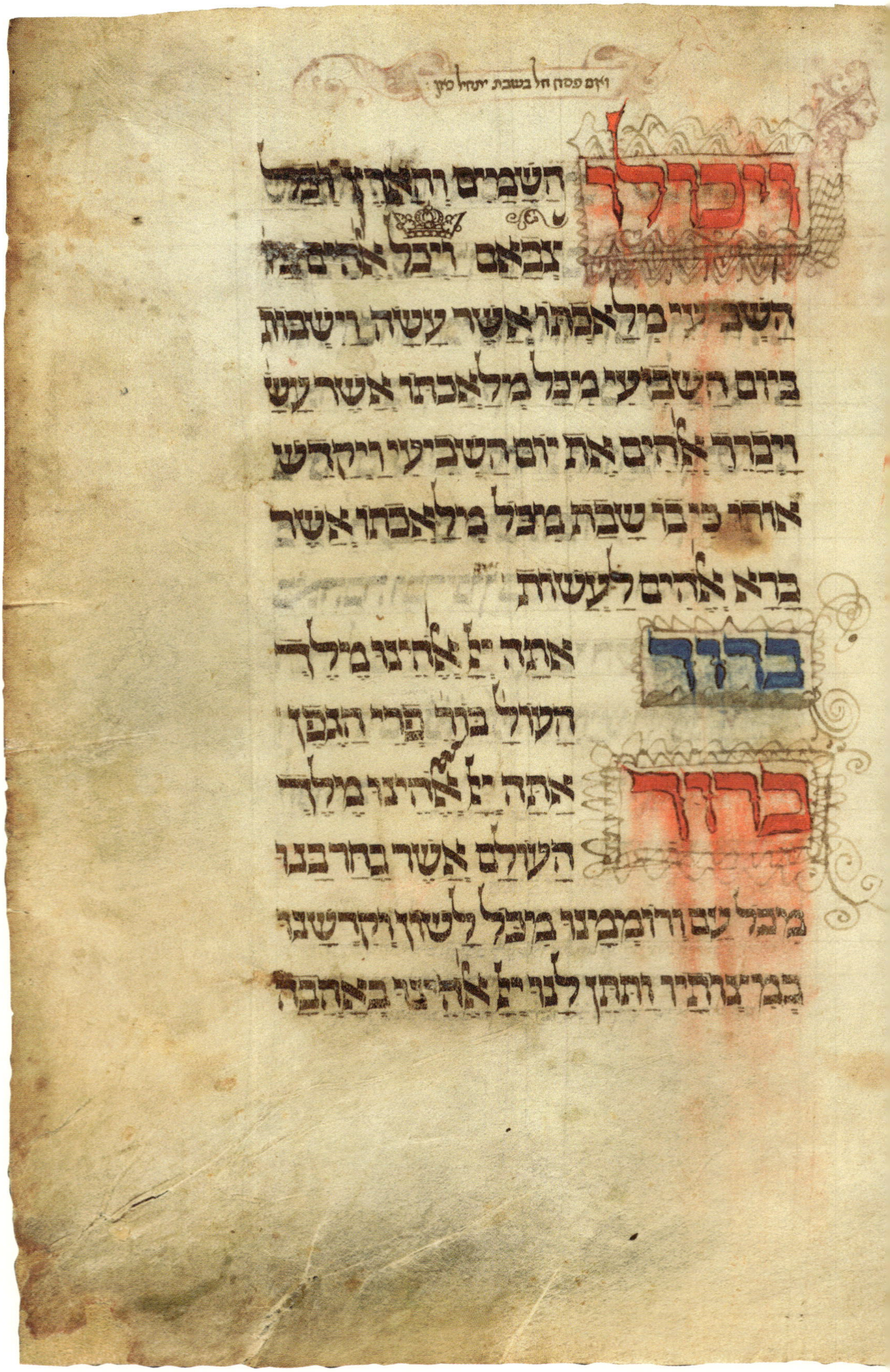
ויום פסח חל בשבת יתחיל כאן:
ויכלו השמים והארץ וכל
צבאם ויכל אלהים ביו
השביעי מלאכתו אשר עשה וישבות
ביום השביעי מכל מלאכתו אשר עש
ויברך אלהים את יום השביעי ויקדש
אותו כי בו שבת מכל מלאכתו אשר
ברא אלהים לעשות
ברוך אתה יי אלהינו מלך
העולם בורא פרי הגפן
ברוך אתה יי אלהינו מלך
העולם אשר בחר בנו
מכל עם ורוממנו מכל לשון וקדשנו
במצותיו ותתן לנו יי אלהינו באהבה

FOL. 2 R

במערב כשבאין מבית הכנסת שוטפין את הכוסות ומביאין על
השולחן קערה ובה שלש מצות שמורות [illegible] וקערה
אחרת ובה מיני ירקות לטיבול ואיפיא ושני [illegible] בשר וביצ
או רג׳ אחד לזכר למקד׳ ואחר לחגיגה׳ וכלי שבו חרוסת זכר לטיט׳ ומוזג כוס
ראשון ומברך ברוך וכול׳

ברוך אי׳ אמ״ה בורא פרי הגפן
אי׳ אמ״ה אשר בחר בנו מכל
עם ורוממנו מכל לשון יי׳
וקדשנו במצותיו ותתן לנו יי׳ אלהינו יי׳
באהבה מועדים לשמחה חגים וזמנים
לששון את יום חג המצות הזה זמן ח
חרותנו באהבה מקרא קודש זכר ליציא
מצרים כי בנו בחרת ואותנו קדשת מכל
העמים מועדי קודשך בשמחה ובששון
הנחלתנו בא״י מקדש ישר׳ והזמנים

בא״י אמ״ה שהחיינו וקיימנו והגיענו לזמן הזה ושותין ונוטל ידיו ומברך בה״ל

עג׳

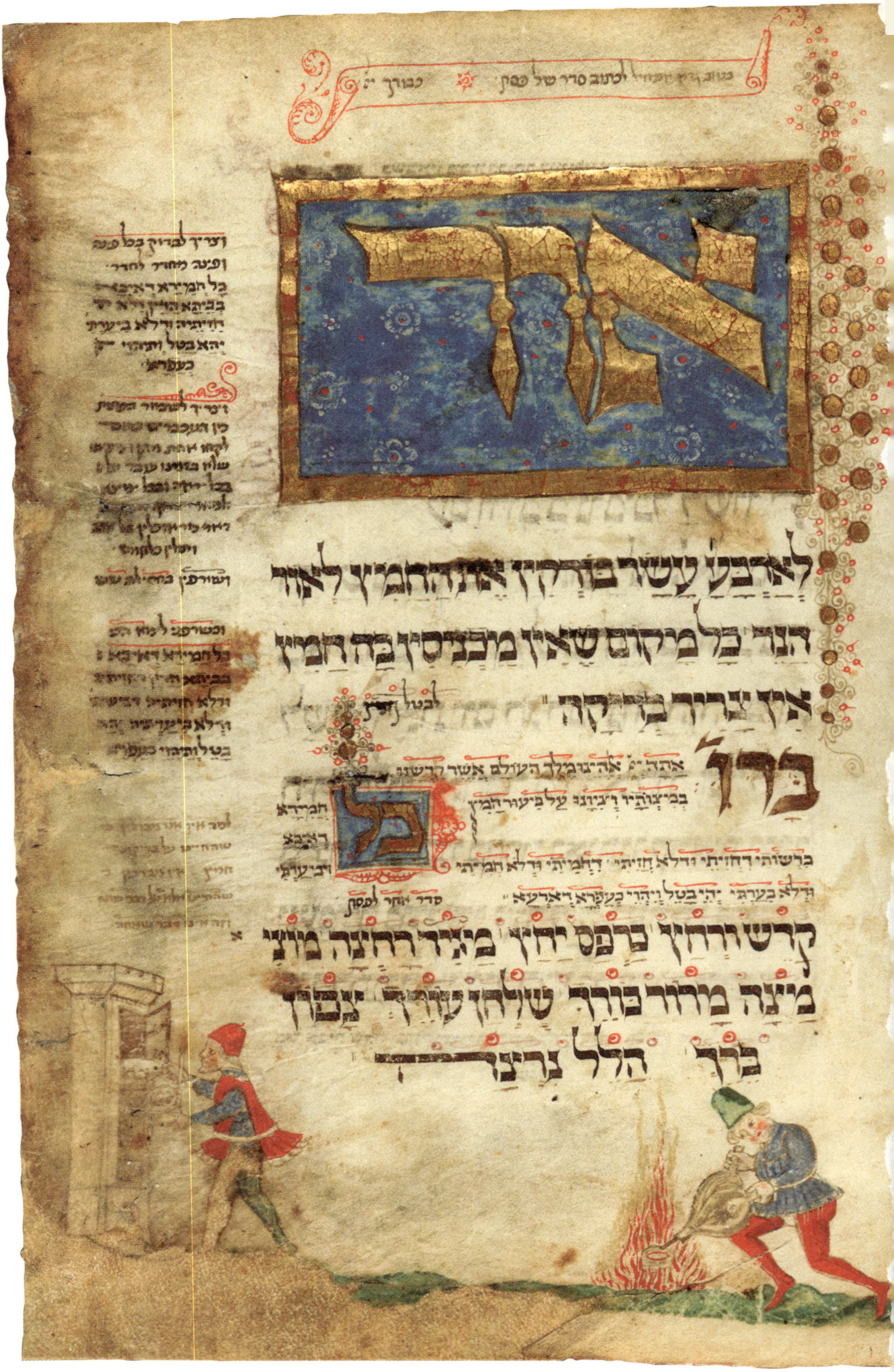

אור

לארבעה עשר בודקין את החמץ לאור הנר כל מקום שאין מכניסין בו חמץ אין צריך בדיקה

ברוך אתה ה׳ אלהינו מלך העולם אשר קדשנו במצותיו וצונו על ביעור חמץ

כל חמירא דאיכא ברשותי דחזיתי ודלא חזיתי דחמיתי ודלא חמיתי דביערתי ודלא ביערתי יהי בטל ויהוי כעפרא דארעא

סדר אחר לפסח

קדש ורחץ כרפס יחץ מגיד רחצה מוציא מצה מרור כורך שלחן עורך צפון ברך הלל נרצה

FOL. I R

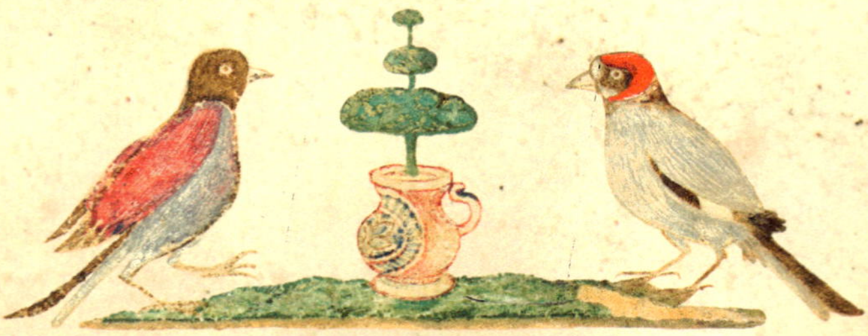